The
Great American
Housewife

The
Great American
Housewife

From Helpmate to Wage Earner, 1776–1986

ANNEGRET S. OGDEN

Contributions in Women's Studies, Number 61

Greenwood Press
Westport, Connecticut • London, England

Library of Congress Cataloging in Publication Data

Ogden, Annegret S.
   The great American housewife.

   (Contributions in women's studies, ISSN 0147–104X ;
no. 61)
   Bibliography: p.
   Includes index.
   1. Housewives—United States—History.   2. Women—
United States—History.   3. Family—United States—
History.   4. Mothers—Employment—United States—
History.   I. Title.   II. Series.
HQ1410.036   1986   305.4′0973   85–9935
ISBN 0–313–24752–8 (lib. bdg. : alk. paper)

Library of Congress Catalog Card Number: 85–9935
ISBN: 0–313–24752–8
ISSN: 0147–104X

First published in 1986

Greenwood Press
A division of Congressional Information Service, Inc.
88 Post Road West
Westport, Connecticut 06881

Printed in the United States of America

∞™

The paper used in this book complies with the
Permanent Paper Standard issued by the National
Information Standards Organization (Z39.48–1984).

10 9 8 7 6 5 4 3 2 1

Copyright Acknowledgments

The author and the publisher are grateful to the following for granting the use of their material:

Excerpts from Frances Trollope's *Domestic Manners of the Americans* (1949), edited by Donald Smalley, courtesy of Alfred A. Knopf, Inc.

Interview with Milo Smith (1980) printed courtesy of Milo Smith.

Every reasonable effort has been made to trace the owners of copyright materials in this book, but in some instances this has proven impossible. The publishers will be glad to receive information leading to more complete acknowledgments in subsequent printings of the book, and in the meantime extend their apologies for any omissions.

Contents

Illustrations

Preface

Ten years ago, when I was still experiencing the shock of my transition from full-time housewife to full-time wage earner, a collection of nineteenth-century American household books landed on my desk at The Bancroft Library. Fascinated, I leafed through the well-used pages and saw there, time and again, my own mother's words: "Catch the dust before it falls." But my mother was born in 1910; furthermore, she does not and never did speak English. All my life her German commandments for good housekeeping echoed in my mind. Now here was proof that my guilty domestic conscience was linked not simply to my German childhood, but to a larger international tradition rooted in a distant past. In 1974, at the height of the women's liberation movement, I decided to trace my roots as a housewife by studying the housewife's role as it was played throughout this country's history.

Since my place of work was a large university library, I had easy access to everything from eighteenth-century advice literature to newly published women's histories. I discovered that for the past 200 years the popular press has portrayed the American home as a white middle-class haven from the industrial world, where children grow up in purity and where husbands rest in peace. And although her attire has changed dramatically over the decades in that same popular press, the homemaker remained the same totally devoted wife and mother we all know so well—if not in reality, then in our guilt-ridden imaginations. Although the true-life letters and diaries written by real women since 1776 go some distance toward contradicting this glossy image of the perfect family in its well-kept house, fathoming the life of the housewife and reconstructing the family home has not been easy. The early housewife was obscured by the fact that most families did not keep old letters and that in any event most housewives worked too hard to write them.[1] With few rebellious exceptions, by and

large they support the well-known stereotype of work never ending and
of women never complaining. Who dares to complain to the folks at home?

Yet if letters and other primary materials were insufficient to describe
the housewife's daily tasks, where was I to turn? I began to suspect that
until recently the housewife's contribution had been denied and ignored
in history works. In his book on the interaction between women's roles in
the family and in society, Carl Degler began to remedy the long neglect
of wives and mothers by the American and family historians, but he still
failed to recognize housewives as primary representatives of the household
labor force.[2] And in their initial effort to liberate women from domestic
drudgery, even feminist historians underestimated the value of housework
and the significance of the housewife. Until recently feminist writers portrayed homemakers either as victims of patriarchal oppression or as per-
petrators of the cult of domesticity. Both perspectives focus on the wife's
economic dependence and her husband's power to control both her private
income and her public status. Although feminists have correctly identified
the political relationship between women's unpaid work in the home and
women's underpaid work in the labor force, they have minimized the
importance of women's caring role in the family. Indeed, my own evaluation of the housewife's role is based on Clair Brown's economic theory
in *Rethinking the Family* (1982), but I feel that the emotional component
of the role also has to be addressed.[3] For me, it is the complexity of the
housewife's experience which makes it so intriguing and so difficult to assess
her past.

In exploring the emotional side of the housewife's life I consulted the
experts in a quite different field: novelists. American literature has vividly
illuminated the domestic lives of its characters, and until recently, in my
opinion, the writers of fiction have described the impact of social change
on private lives more successfully than most academic writers.

Within the last few years, however, a stream of new information has
emerged that is enabling us to attempt a new and broader analysis of
women's work at home. In *Womanhood in America* (1983), Mary F. Ryan
has finally placed the cult of domesticity in historical perspective. And
Dolores Hayden has recognized domestic revolution in depicting the struggle of early feminists to close the gap between private home and public
economy.[4] Recently, too, scholars have measured and analyzed housework
past and present in terms of its national and productive market value.
Suddenly, housework is getting more serious and diverse attention than it
has ever received up to now. Writers are beginning to study the content
as well as the economic value of housework. As their titles suggest, *Never
Done*, by Susan Strasser (1983), and *More Work for Mothers*, by Ruth S.
Cowan (1983), show that advanced household technology has in no way
diminished the amount of housework in modern households. In fact, the
new survey research reveals that female wage earners spend almost as

many hours doing housework as full-time homemakers, even though married women have dramatically increased their wage-earning hours and skills.[5] Married men, on the other hand, have hardly changed their traditional work patterns outside or inside the home. It is clear, then, that an eye to the female side of things reveals changes and shifts that might well have been missed were our research still weighted, as it once was, toward the male's contribution to social and economic change.

My own case was a model for the newly documented shifts in the housewife's role. Although I had added research and writing to my paid job in the library, I still considered myself very much a housewife, since the responsibility for housekeeping remained solely in my hands—or rather in my head. For it seemed that nobody else at home felt guilty about the unwashed dishes or the dirty floors. Even family harmony was my department, because I believed that I could iron out stress and antagonism like wrinkles from our shirts. The strain of my conflicting responsibilities only intensified my desire to know what forces in history had made my attitude so different from my husband's and my children's in conducting our household affairs.

A few years after I had made the typical change from full-time to part-time wage earner, because we could now afford the drop in my income more than in my other commitments, I became involved in a three-year research program on campus devoted to "Women and Their Work: Intersections of the Marketplace and the Household," at the Center for the Study, Education, and Advancement of Women. It was through this project that I began to realize two things. First, my own evolution from helpmate to wage earner matched the course of the domestic revolution of the white middle-class American family over the last two hundred years. And the same home-work conflicts in loyalty that I felt as a result of taking a job had been experienced by generations of women before my time. Second, I learned that my situation was a minor variation on a major theme. For unlike me—I left my career when the children were born and resumed it only when they were old enough to go to school—most female wage earners did not have that option. Their experience was never mentioned in ladies' magazines, except perhaps to elicit pity from the "good housekeepers" who did not "have" to work for pay. We are just starting to understand that the working mother with *no choice* but to perform both roles is perhaps the most misunderstood and neglected laborer in the United States—and, as I write, one whose ranks are growing steadily. In the words of Margaret Wilkerson, director of the research program "Women and Their Work":

The ideal images or stereotypes of women and their impact on women's lives were, in fact, raised throughout the institute as a major problem with many serious ramifications. Public rhetoric, imagery and religion have all been used to create a vision of a family that leads to a variety of manipulations of

women as workers in the household, work-place, community and neighborhood. . . . The division of women's lives and experience into work and the
family is essentially a false separation which obscures the realities of women's
lives.[6]

The separation of work and home life into two distinct areas was part
of the middle-class etiquette and a prerequisite for the American dream.
According to Wilkerson, this false division has obliterated the contributions
of those women who have been involved throughout history in both spheres
simultaneously—women of color, for example, and poor women whose
financial circumstances permitted no such luxury as a home environment
unmarked by the imperatives of work. Excluded from participation in the
mainstream American dream, these women developed more radical alternatives to the cult of domesticity than the most ardent domestic revolu-
tionaries described by Dolores Hayden. Not many sources describe how
these women integrated home and work. Sometimes I was able to glean
a true-to-life picture from the case histories reported by pioneering social
workers. Sometimes I had to rely on reminiscences by older women who
recorded their earlier working lives. But one common denominator clearly
united the experiences of all categories of housewives, from working class
to middle class: a vulnerability to the power of the prevailing stereotype
of society's image of what the housewife should be. In *Changing Images
of the Family* (1979), Barbara Myerhoff and Virginia Tufte discuss the
emotional impact of images, or stereotypes, in conveying critical judgments
about the family.

> Inevitably when images are positive, they become standards against which
> we measure ourselves. They become normative (in the sense of obligatory)
> and operate as models, effecting a great range of action and response—from
> social legislation to our internal evaluation of our own successes and failures
> as family members. . . . Even when we recognize such images as false idols—
> usually selling us something, playing on our sense of inadequacy—they haunt
> us in moments of vulnerability.[7]

In my judgment, the housewife in her combined role as wife, mother,
housekeeper, and frequently wage earner, has been the most vulnerable
target of false idolatry, precisely because her job description has always
been charged with higher expectations than any normal individual could
satisfy on a consistent basis. At any given time—whether in 1776 or 1976–
the housewife has been exposed to public and private criticism for not
doing enough. This has been true for rich ladies as well as working mothers:
both perennially stood accused of neglecting their children for other concerns. As the primary provider of food, comfort, and companionship, the
mother has been worshipped and idolized. But throughout history her
power has been challenged, her place has been restricted by choking sexual
taboos and social etiquette. As the main guardian of family values, she

has borne the blame whenever things have gone wrong with the American way of life. And except in retrospect through the distorting lens of nostalgia, there has never been a time when all was well for her. When American society changed from a rural religious orientation to urban consumerism, the housewife and the house she kept became a status symbol for the husband she married. And mother's work came to be judged by the product she created: the next generation of healthy and wealthy consumers. In the eyes of the family and of society at large, the housewife was held responsible for no less than the quality of American life.

Throughout American culture positive images of the good homemaker have conflicted with negative images of spinsters and working women. Beautiful homes and affluent families in color films and advertisements have been clashing with climbing statistics of urban blight and broken homes. For many years, those in the social sciences and counseling professions saw and wrote of a wide gap between the "normal" majority and the problematic minority—those who could not achieve the domestic American dream. But new research is beginning to document similarities among troubled families across socioeconomic and racial lines. The most notable reassessment has occurred with respect to single-parenthood and minority family systems, both of which had been almost exclusively seen in a negative or pathological light. The new evidence suggests that viable extended and alternative support systems do exist outside the double-parent middle class. Although this book is primarily about what we now call the middle-class housewife in the mainstream of white America, I have frequently contrasted her roles with those outside the mainstream.[8] More than one new book will have to be written to illustrate the experience of those housewives whose family life was rooted in non-white and foreign cultures. Even within the culture of the majority I discovered many variants of "the American housewife," all linked across socioeconomic barriers by the desire to provide their families with the best possible environment for growth, health, and happiness.

Confronted with a vast volume of conventional opinions supporting old theories about the traditional nuclear family and an increasing amount of new documentation on black, immigrant, and female Americans, I came to realize that the Great American Housewife might be but a figment of our national imagination, a legend, even a ghost come to haunt us.

With due respect to demographers and social scientists, I chose in this book to treat the housewife more as an individual than a statistic. I was also drawn in particular toward those women who faced domestic trials with ingenuity and courage—the pioneers who created new systems where old ones failed. It is to them rather than to the ideals of the past that we must look for role models as we are shaping new forms of family life.

My method of dealing with the past has been unorthodox. Traditionally, historians only rarely look at the past with an eye to present dilemmas.

Labor economists have not regarded the home as a genuine work place, and sociologists do not analyze patterns that stretch over two hundred years. Because I was interested in the origins of lasting trends that still influence our personal attitudes today, I searched for traces of family life among scattered sources, looking for information about America's past. I see my method of investigation as a form of "divining," or dowsing for evidence with a historical divining rod. This trickle of information does not bring up a statistically accurate picture of women's work in the American household. Fortunately, during the last decade every topic covered in this book has received attention from other scholars. I offer this book as a personal evaluation of those images which have kept us from transforming traditional into new working patterns at home and in the marketplace. I hope it will not satisfy the reader, but stimulate the appetite for further research and rethinking.

As I look back on my own changing perceptions during the course of my research, I confess to my prejudices, shaped by my upbringing in a middle-class nuclear family and reinforced by my education and my marriage. Although my transition from helpmate to wage earner did not happen without conflicts, I am very much aware of those advantages which enabled me to make choices. I could move between labor for love and labor for pay without interference from anyone except the household ghosts of the past which haunt my home.

I offer my deepest thanks to my husband and our children for keeping my thoughts about the past at all times grounded in our ever-changing present, to Margaret Wilkerson for including me in the research activities at the Center for the Study, Education, and Advancement of Women, and to Suzanne Lipsett for helping me to transform compacted ideas into readable prose.

NOTES

1. I have used both published and unpublished letters and journals to illustrate the changing demands on housewives in different periods, classes, and geographical locations. The selection was based on how much detail the writer provided about household matters and about her attitude toward her work. Although a few individual voices cannot represent a large cross section of the population, I felt that it was important to hear their personal opinions and to compare them with my own.

2. Carl Degler, *At Odds: Women and the Family in America from the Revolution to the Present* (New York: Oxford University Press, 1980) focuses on wife-husband, mother-child relationships from the personal and the social perspective.

3. Clair Vickery Brown, "Home Production for Use in a Market Economy," in Barrie Thorne et al., *Rethinking the Family: Some Feminist Questions* (New York: Longman, 1982).

4. Mary F. Ryan, *Womanhood in America: From Colonial Times to the Present*

(New York: Franklin Watts, 1983, 3d ed.); her dissertation, "American Society and the Cult of Domesticity, 1830–1860" (University of California, Santa Barbara, 1971), provides a detailed study of this much discussed topic. Dolores Hayden, *The Grand Domestic Revolution: A History of Feminist Designs for American Homes, Neighborhoods and Cities* (Cambridge, Mass.: Harvard University Press, 1981).

5. Susan Strasser, *Never Done: A History of American Housework* (New York: Pantheon, 1982); Ruth Schwartz Cowan, *More Work for Mother: The Ironies of Household Technology from the Open Hearth to the Microwave* (New York: Basic Books, 1983), provides excellent bibliography on history of household technology, consumerism, and home productivity.

6. *Women At Work: Conflicting Images of Home and Marketplace, A New Agenda for Research and Action* (Berkeley, Calif.: University of California, Center for the Study, Education, and Advancement of Women, 1984), p. 7.

7. Virginia Tufte and Barbara Meyerhoff, eds., *Changing Images of the Family* (New Haven: Yale University Press, 1979), p. 10.

8. I use the term "middle class" reluctantly in connection with the housewife, because working-class women have middle-class aspirations. The classification is so broad today that it is meaningless, except as a differentiation from the very poor and the very rich.

Introduction

Why read this book? Why look to the past for solutions to crises in our present lives at home and at work? What can we learn from the households of 1776? Nowadays vacuum cleaners and washing machines have replaced brooms and brushes. We buy our meat cut up and refrigerated. We buy wrinkle-free clothes. We limit the size of our families. We send our sick to hospitals and our aging parents to nursing homes. Our children are in school all day, our husbands are away at work, and more likely than not so are we, the housewives. In 1984, the majority of American wives and mothers were wage earners, either full-time or part-time. While 79 percent of American husbands were in the labor force, 54 percent of American wives were in the labor force. Of 48 million married-couple families, 12 million depended only on the husband as a breadwinner. More than half of all mothers (18.7 million) with children under 18 years of age were wage earners. According to Margaret Wilkerson, former director of the Center for Study, Education, and Advancement of Women at the University of California, Berkeley, "the movement of millions of U.S. women into the labor force out of necessity, and hence into dual roles, is one of the most profound developments of this century."[1]

If you play that dual role, consider your own home. If you kept a domestic diary for a week, writing down every chore performed in the house with the name of the person responsible for getting it done, who would be shown to have done most of the work? Chances are, if there is a wife or a mother in the household, regardless of whether she also works for wages, she will score more hours of housework than anybody else.

The standards for cooking and child-raising that influence our household practices today go back to a time when the great majority of married women were full-time homemakers. With this book I show that in our expectation of ourselves we are taking past models and trying to live up to them in a radically different world. We have not changed our ideas of houseworking to meet the changing conditions; we have merely added wage-earning to the job description for homemaking. The 1985 Census listed 19.592 million housewives and 25.322 million employed wives.

Sociologists have found that despite all the amenities that characterize modern life, the full-time housewife spends seven hours a day, seven days a week, on childcare and housework. But increasingly, American women are doing their household chores during those times of the day or night when other people, including their husbands and children, are at leisure. They are shopping during lunch hours, cleaning house on weekends, doing the laundry at night. They do childcare, of course, around the clock, depending on the ages of the children. And when mothers are not actually tending to their children, they are spending a considerable amount of time and money arranging for childcare.

There is hardly a woman's magazine on the stands these days that does not contain an article on the new homemaker, who works for pay outside the home and for love inside it. Most advice sends the two-career housewife to the supermarket and department store for time-saving goods and gadgets. The rest focuses on her guilt feelings, since it is commonly assumed that all housewives suffer pangs of guilt at neglecting hearth and home and family in favor of their job commitments. Why this epidemic of guilt? Where does it come from? Full-time homemakers suffer too, because they have no excuse for not doing a perfect job. This is how one full-time housewife summed up her expectations of competence:

> You run really a tight ship. And by tight ship I mean things are in order, kids have been read to, the kids have been played with. . . . You're serving well-balanced meals and the house is neat, and you're on top of everything, you know. Nothing gets by here.[2]

One survey of newly employed mothers has revealed that when something has to go because they are pressed for time, most women choose to neglect the house rather than the family. Still, they feel guilt at their choice, precisely because a clean home and a well-prepared meal have always been taken for the signs of a properly cared-for family. Although statistics show that wage-earning homemakers cut their hours of housework down, it is apparent that most of them bend over backwards to maintain their inherited domestic standards. Karen Barrett reports in her article "Two-Career Couples" (*Ms.*, June, 1984) that "couples have high environmental standards for the home—waxed floors, ironed pillowcases, home-cooked meals on china so shiny they can see their reflections," which contribute to marital conflict as they try "to have the economic returns and personal satisfaction of two careers, without trading off any of the amenities that Mom used to supply."

We must turn to history to understand why family traditions have failed to shift to accommodate the two-career housewife. Our first trend setters,

those who establishesd our standards for cleanliness and domestic refinement and who are still our models, came from "the very best families."
And they had servants. The models these early American women imitated
had even more household help. These were the British ladies—from whose
milieu, incidentally, came the cookbooks and household guides. Those
women, on the other hand, who had to earn their living outside their own
homes—Black and immigrant women, for example, who took care of other
people's families as well as their own—never had the means to emulate
the affluent trend setters, but learned to work with high household standards just the same.

Historically, then, we do have precedents for homemakers who scrub
their own kitchen floors and then begin their full-time jobs somewhere
else, but these dual-role workers are not our models. Yet today this is the
normal routine for the majority of American women, whether they dropped
out of high school or hold Ph.D.s, whether they are white or Black, whether
they live in poor or rich neighborhoods. But instead they still model themselves either on career women in the past who relied on paid household
help or on full-time homemakers who channeled all their energy into their
own families. Worse, as a society, despite the reality of the statistics, we
still see "working mothers" as poverty-stricken, often tragic figures working
solely to ward off bad times. Through the same nineteenth-century glasses,
we judge the mother who is happy in her outside job as a selfish creature
who works to get away from home.

Men's view of the new money-making housewife is similarly clouded by
inappropriate images from the past. Middle-class husbands today often
treat their wives' jobs as they used to treat their wives' bridge clubs—as
healthy diversions from which the busy homemaker should return to the
kitchen refreshed. Thus, many employed homemakers have difficulty talking about their jobs with their spouses. If they complain, they might hear,
"I told you it would be too much." Conversely, if they show pleasure in
their outside occupation too openly, they might bring out old fears that
they no longer really care for the family. Only women who take on jobs
outside the home from dire necessity escape judgment, since they do not
work for themselves, but to keep up mortgage payments. This reluctance
to accept married women's work outside the home has had serious political
consequences, and it has deprived women of the emotional and active
support they deserve.

When it comes to reshaping family life to incorporate the homemaker's
outside job, it is the wife who makes the adjustments. Married homemakers
frequently stress the fact that they could not successfully perform their
additional outside job without the support of their husbands. Support in
this case usually means permission or occasionally a helping hand in the
kitchen. Surveys indicate that the current rise in the number of employed
homemakers has not been matched by significant increases in the amount

of housework that husbands and children take on. Because our society still considers the male as the primary breadwinner, a wife's support of her husband's job is of course taken for granted.

In reconstructing family life in light of new realities, we must trace the origin of our standards and reevaluate them. Sexual stereotypes seem to flourish in the privacy of our homes. Outmoded concepts about who should do what can haunt us like ghosts. Much has changed since a man could sell his wife's property without her consent, but our attitudes about women's work are still entangled with the lifestyles of the past. Homemaking, like all vital functions, is a continuous process that involves both dramatic and subtle changes. What happens in our private environment easily escapes rational criticism, and even comparison with other people's practices. In spite of what we read, we tend to do things at home on impulse or in imitation of our parents. Just as we link our personal characteristics with certain family traits, we take reassurance in looking to our domestic heritage to reinforce our rigid expectations for ourselves as mothers and homemakers.

Perhaps we will stop blaming ourselves for failing to achieve our goals if we find out that though such expectations were passed on to the succeeding generation, in reality they were never fully met. Only in specific social environments where servants were available could elevated criteria for home and family care be upheld. Others were media hypes from the start, invented to sell goods or ideologies. The well-ordered house and the well-mannered child, for instance, were part of the Victorian ideology in which the home was viewed as the earthly version of heaven and the homemaker as the saint in residence.

The modern housewife's role, then, is like an onion—made up of layer after layer of tasks, responsibilities, and expectations. In order to arrive at a more feasible job description for the modern homemaker, I have peeled off the layers that originated in the past and examined them separately. Once I had traced the homemaker's job back to its source, I could compare it and the value society gave it with the job and its value today. I looked at the tools and skills that were needed in earlier times so I could compare them with the tools and skills we use at home today. I searched through diaries, biographies, and household books spanning two centuries for descriptions of the homemaker's daily life. In this process it became clear that her job remained essentially the same, even while the country shifted from a rural to an urban economy. New concepts and new plumbing came along at regular intervals, but the job description never changed in essence—it only grew longer. Over the years, the job description was stretched to encompass many new responsibilities, but never were any old roles dropped. No wonder it is difficult for today's homemaker to integrate the new role of wage earner. Ghosts from the past continually whisper the old lines from the past, reminding her to leave nothing out.

Each chapter in this book covers one of these major skins, or roles, and its period of origin, starting in 1776. All the roles bound up together still influence our view and expectations of the housewife at home. Tradition-minded homemakers may discover their favorite role model here, while rebellious new housewives may see here the familiar ghosts that haunt their households.

I begin my book with Abigail Adams. Abigail Adams embodies the American ideal. She is the materfamilias of an important clan, an eighteenth-century Rose Kennedy. Novels and soap operas keep her image alive. But more importantly, her growth during her own life from farm housekeeper to MANAGER to official hostess make her an early example of the upwardly mobile HELPMATE who learns new skills for each step in her husband's career.

Next in the 1800s came the LADY, in response to the greater comfort and wealth brought by industrialization to the American home. The daughters of the MANAGER were craving refinement, education, and social activism. The idea that one could be a lady and still do housework was very American and much discussed by the foreign press, and ordinary tasks came to be seen as artistic matters to be brilliantly organized in the hands of a LADY. It was during this period that the ladies' magazines were launched. Then as now, they inspired domestic creativity and fashionable styles to save the homemaker from humdrum housekeeping.

What I call SAINTS and SUFFERERS were offshoots of the LADY. The Victorian lady had higher ambitions than better homes and gardens, and she suffered from the consequences. Quite often she had an above-average education, which was at the root of her discontent. Both physical and mental disorders plagued these saints and sinners, who suffered from guilt feelings for failing to live up to their exalted ideals.

Our domestic culture has always been rich in variations, and these alternatives add a new perspective to the historical panorama I describe in the chapter about the PIONEERS. Immigrants, Western frontier families, racial minorities, rebellious housewives, and single mothers all deviate from the white, middle-class household described as typical.

The SCIENTISTS's role was created in 1900 to free the homemaker from her Victorian ghosts. Now, by channeling her energies into scientific home management, an ambitious woman could use her mind to benefit the home. Following on this tendency were the early home economists' new visions of consumer activism and political awareness. The efficiency principles of the domestic scientists, however, failed to make a laboratory out of the American home. Instead, they gave the American housewives a new worry: germs.

The SCIENTIST was pushed aside by MRS. CONSUMER. Courted and manipulated by the booming food and appliance industries, this version of the homemaker has been given more recognition than any other, because billions of dollars depend on her spending power. But for those housewives who wanted to do more than shop, a new stimulant for the brain was introduced by a small group of intellectual mothers—the scientific approach to motherhood called "child psychology." Mothers in white coats weighed and measured their babies at regular intervals and gathered information on optimum growth and development. In keeping with the consumer society, the child became the product of the mother.

Now the mother turned into SUPERMOTHER—a mother who could not afford to fail. Experts took over the advice-giving and determined that mothers were to blame if children did not turn out well. Moreover, the experts decided that a controlling mother was harmful to a child's health. And by the 1950s, the children were in control of the mother.

This whole pattern of onion-skin images from 1776 to 1986 grows from the solid middle-class concept that the mother's work in the home is supported by the father's labor outside the home. In the past it was taken for granted that the family offered the highest rewards to women. A "good husband" was the key to a woman's success financially as well as emotionally, though even then some husbands turned out to be liabilities rather than assets. Now, however, the rising divorce rate proves that marriage is no longer a secure career. In the last decade a new image—far from ideal—has emerged: the DISPLACED HOMEMAKER. Widowhood and divorce have always moved women outside the economic support system of a well-provided home, but never before in such numbers and never, in white middle-class families, so openly. When Abigail Adams's grown-up daughter and daughter-in-law were left destitute, they simply moved in with her. Today the family welfare system is severely troubled. Still, the family as always, offers the promise of lasting love and companionship. Here growth, continuity, and intimacy can flourish. Here generosity can find its fullest expression, but here violence can crush all hope for peaceful relationships. Children grow up emotionally and economically deprived. Fewer and fewer homes allow the elderly to finish out their years in dignity. Disappointed family members move away from their closest kin to live alone or in alternative support systems. But even here traditional patterns interfere with pioneering ventures. Where are the models for future family life?

Because the American dream family of a money-making father and a money-spending mother is fast turning into another myth, it is time for new images. It is time for us to turn away from the early American household where gender determined women's role as helpmates and to look at the past as a reservoir for fresh beginnings in the spirit of NEW PIONEERS.[3]

NOTES

1. U.S. Department of Labor, *Household Data* (Sept., 1984), pp. 8–18. See also "Families At Work," *Monthly Labor Review*, vol. 106, no. 12 (December 1983);

the data remained valid in 1985; and *Women at Work* (Berkeley, Calif.: University of California, Center for the Study, Education and Advancement of Women, 1984), p. 3.

2. C. S. Piotrkowski, *Work and the Family System: A Naturalistic Study of Working-Class and Lower-Middle-Class Families* (New York: Free Press, 1979), p. 262.

3. The images and main topics described in each chapter are not confined to the period indicated in the chapter heading, but can be followed into present times. I have used this chronological and topical arrangement to organize a wealth of interlocking materials into a sequence of cultural ideologies that have informed our notion of good house- and family-keeping to this day. The last image of the NEW PIONEER is not intended to create another idealization, but rather to recognize the precarious and uncertain state of most domestic arrangements today while acknowledging the courage and ingenuity of individual women and men in providing physical and emotional family care in socially hostile or economically disadvantaged environments.

The
Great American
Housewife

1

The Manager: From Helpmeet to Hostess, 1776–1800

> No man ever prospered in the world without the consent and cooperation of his wife.... I consider it as an indispensable requisite, that every American wife should herself know how to order and regulate her family; how to govern her domestics and train up her children. For this purpose, the all-wise Creator made woman an help-meet for man, and she who fails in these duties does not answer the end of her creation.... I have frequently said to my friends, when they thought me overburdened with care, I would rather have too much [to do] than too little. Life stagnates without action. I could never bear merely to vegetate.
> —Abigail Adams, 1744–1818[1]

The revolution of the American people never conquered the American home, for the American housewife never could declare her independence from it. In 1776, a married woman had no right to the family property, no right over her dowry or private income, and no custody over her children. Legally and practically, she enjoyed as much personal and financial freedom as her husband saw fit to allow her. By his decree she might act as his business agent during his absence or take over the farm after his death. In return, the law required him to provide her food, shelter, and clothing, as he did to his children, servants, and slaves. As his widow she was entitled to one-third of his estate.[2] Without inheritance she was reduced to servitude or penury. War widows, for instance, resorted to begging in the streets, because they received no pension.

Ostensibly the housewife's lot has changed over the course of two centuries, and, as is evidenced dramatically in every facet of American life, is changing still. In terms of financial control and the legal meaning of the marriage contract, however, conditions have remained alarmingly static. In effect, the twentieth-century husband still controls the household's assets and owns his wife's labor in the home. When a woman marries, she automatically enters the occupation of housekeeping full-time or adds housekeeping to her other responsibilities. Legally, her husband is not bound to pay for her labor; only for her support.[3] The extent depends not on her labors nor truly on the amount of his income, but on his regard for her as his wife. In short, now as in the eighteenth century, financial dependency subjects wives to their husbands and gives husbands power over their wives. He may not exert that power openly as men did in the eighteenth century, but the fact that her economic security is tied up with her marriage enters into all aspects of the relationship. Upon marrying, therefore, a woman unwittingly steps back into another century. Rarely does she recognize the implications: she is unaware that she is locked into an eighteenth-century situation while having to live up to twentieth-century expectations.

The wife's role has changed radically in other ways, however, mostly in response to changes in the structure of the household itself. The period from 1776 through 1820 saw a steady evolution among average-income families away from the simple, rural household characterized by endless manual labor and toward a more elaborate, more complex, and more "Europeanized" system. Most dramatically, the housewife's role changed from that of a household manager, who did much of the manual labor required to feed and clothe the family, to that of "lady in residence," who cultivated her growing sensitivity to class distinctions, delegated manual work to servants, and concerned herself with the organizational aspects of her ever more elaborate domestic system.

This same period marked the sinking of roots by American business and manufacturing concerns and the establishing of American cities. The young nation was beginning to provide for itself, and in the process the precursor of today's middle class developed. It was within this group that the changes in the structure of the household manifested themselves most clearly. Poverty never ceased to exist, and, in families with few resources, the bulk of the housework remained squarely on the wives. The fact that their more fortunate sisters were hiring more servants or relying on services outside the home helped them not a whit. As the industrialized nineteenth century eclipsed the agricultural eighteenth, the weight of the housewife's burden became more and more dependent on the amount of money her husband controlled.

The growth of an upwardly mobile group who represented the nineteenth-century "leisure class" resulted in an increasing distinction between lower and higher forms of home life. In the 1980s when we seem to have come full circle by returning to a work- rather than leisure-oriented home it is fitting that we begin with the post–Revolutionary era to trace the roots of the modern American homemaker.

STARTING PLACE: THE POST–REVOLUTIONARY HOUSEHOLD

"Carrying water, performing agricultural tasks with traditional tools, carrying wood and heavy loads, pounding and grinding, cooking with traditional equipment and fuels"[4]—so the International Labor Office characterizes the women of pre-industrial countries in 1976. The passage could well begin to describe housework in 1776. Not mentioned, though, are the myriad nursing, cleaning, child-rearing, teaching, and clothes-making responsibilities that a woman, wife or not, was expected to perform in preindustrial times.

The work of the household went on from early morning until well into the night, regardless of how respectable or well off a family was. European travelers, both ladies and gentlemen, inevitably commented that Americans had an obsession with work and that they turned refined ladies into what they called "upper servants"—housekeepers who rarely sat down with their guests but who rushed from kitchen to storeroom, churning butter, baking bread, and watching over children ceaselessly.[5] These same astonished visitors found that even in affluent homes there appeared to be little demarcation between working and not working—women conversed and sewed at the same time and socialized while they served their guests—but, even more shocking, the distinctions between mistress and servants and between parents and children were similarly blurred. It was clearly a country in which nobody, with the exception of slaves, seemed to know his or her place.

In contrast, a much more segregated social class system prevailed across the Atlantic. Housewives occupied either the leisure or the working class, each of which had a distinct order of responsibilities and code of behavior. To these European travelers of the established upper class the hardworking American housewife appeared to be playing every conceivable role at once.

In addition to commenting archly on the hodgepodge nature of the housewife's role, European visitors were also sure to note the distinct lack of formal entertainments in the New World. Americans seemed simply incapable of availing themselves of such civilized sources of pleasure as balls and receptions, late-night card games, or even theaters and clubs. Left to himself, the American man in this primitive wilderness relied on his wife for companionship. The fact that a wife who died was quickly replaced only confirmed her importance, wrote Sir Richard Phillips, as an "indispensable resource for domestic affairs."

As we shall see, the woman who could manage the phenomenally demanding eighteenth-century household could attain a secure and even commanding position in her own family. But what about the community at large? The notion that her work visibly counted as productive, gainful labor, winning her respect and a sense of participation in society, was part of the popular legend about the Great American Housewife's distant past. In a letter to the editor of an eighteenth-century magazine, a pseudonymous Nitidia revealed the truth: even in those early days, a homemaker earned ridicule rather than admiration for her labors. This Nitidia had been stung by a gentleman's account in *The American Museum* of how during annual whitewashing rituals husbands were cast out of their homes, together with the furniture, so that the walls could be cleaned with lime. Here American women exercised their rights, he had said, "for smearings and scratchings, washings and dashings." Nitidia let fly a heated reply:

> The cares and comforts of a family rest primarily on our shoulders—hence it is, that there are but few female authors; and the men, knowing how necessary our attentions are to their happiness, take every opportunity of discouraging literary accomplishments in the fair sex. You hear it echoed from every quarter—"My wife cannot make verses, it is true; but she makes an excellent pudding. . . . She can't unravel the intricacies of political economy, and federal government: but she can knit charming stockings." And this they call praising a wife. . . . It is the attention and assiduity of the women, that prevent the men from degenerating into swine. How important, then are the services we render! and yet for these very services we are made the object of ridicule and fun:—base ingratitude! nauseous creatures! . . .
>
> I had a great deal more to say—but I am called away—we are just preparing to white wash. . . . The buckets are paraded—the brushes are ready—my husband has gone off—so much the better—when one is about a thorough cleaning, the first dirty thing to be removed is one's husband—I am called for again—Adieu. Yours, Nitidia. Philadelphia, April *1787.*[6]

Thus the chores were harder in the past, but the satisfaction she derived and the respect (or contempt) she earned from society remained remarkably similar. Rebellious wives then did not object to their family cares and responsibilities, but to their lack of recognition for these as contributions to the early republic. Educated women such as the anonymous "Nitidia" and "Constantia" (Judith Sargent Murray) did not call for social reform outside the family, but for a home ruled by feminine intelligence and moral responsibility which would furnish the nation with quality citizens. Unlike their bluestocking models in England who engaged in political battles for women's rights, the daughters of Columbia believed that the elevation of the home would guarantee the elevation of the housewife to equal citizenship. As Linda Kerber and Nancy Cott have shown in their analyses of post–Revolutionary womanhood, the foundation for the separate sphere of feminine influence was already solidly in place at the end of the eighteenth century.[7]   Today we are caught in the conflict between making better homes and better salaries. As career women we move with the 1980s, but as family women we cling to the 1880s. At that time all females in all social classes—be they wives, daughters, sisters, spinster or widowed aunts, nieces, or cousins—were cared for by the heads of households, and all were expected to function as housewives and mothers or as surrogate housewives and mothers. As a result, when new outlets for our energy compete with our household duties nowadays, we find ourselves unable to delegate these duties to others, and instead we add new assignments to our old responsibilities. This is what generations of housewives have done before us.

The Great American Housewife was and is to this day endowed with boundless energy and flexibility. But can she really live simultaneously in the pre-industrial world and in the modern world?

If we still adhere to the eighteenth-century family concept, we must remember that in those days not only a woman's personal satisfaction but also her livelihood and her social standing derived from the family. The home environment was what today might be called a "total experience." Within it, no distinction did exist between work and leisure, solitary and social activities, and private and family ambitions. The authority of the husband was rarely questioned. Therefore girls tended to hesitate before committing themselves to his care. Experienced widows like Mary Noyes made sure they selected wisely. Although she did not opt for a pre-nuptial property agreement, she drew up her own list of requirements in a document entitled "Portrait of a Good Husband," stating that he should be willing to "gratify her reasonable inclinations," that he should not hold the money key too tightly, nor keep his library locked, nor reprimand her in public, and that he should set an example "worthy of imitation" to herself and her children. Her list includes his role as a stepfather, master of servants, and public benefactor—a clear indication that she was looking for more than a private relationship.[8]

The letters and diaries written by eighteenth-century women reveal that most women shared a surprising uniformity in the events of their lives.[9] Certain fundamental conditions were common to all—legal and financial dependence on men, poor health, and high birth and mortality rates—and these conditions kept women of whatever age and marital status tightly tied to the family. Most women, including wives, had practically no choice in selecting their home environments—this was the prerogative of the head-of-household. Moreover, they had only limited control over the home's quality, because how they lived depended on where they lived and on how much help they could afford.

To some of us today these past conditions sound disturbingly familiar. Indeed, radical feminists have challenged our own family system for its archaic patriarchal patterns. But critics of the anti-family ideology point to the all-time popularity of the family which offers children and adults experiences and resources that are not available elsewhere.[10] It is perhaps enlightening to examine the life of one eighteenth-century family woman and compare her situation with our own today. Then as now the very same crisis that brought one woman to the brink of despair inspired another to venture forth as a pioneer. As we shall see in later chapters, many women were not suited to the housewife's job, and many American mothers wept over their daughters' cradles, knowing too well the responsibilities and sorrows that awaited them. But a women who gained and kept control of her household, and who took pride in her husband's career and some measure of credit for his success, could view herself as living out a career of her own, and could take satisfaction in her work.

Such a woman was Abigail Adams. To her and her highly detailed, lifelong correspondence we are indebted for much of what direct knowledge we have of the practical details of the late eighteenth-century home. She also provided an early testimony on behalf of that typical American phenomenon: the housewife who learned to play many roles at once.

ABIGAIL ADAMS: AN EIGHTEENTH-CENTURY HOUSEWIFE

Abigail Adams, born Abigail Smith, was wife of the second president of the United States and mother of the sixth. In the course of her 54–year marriage, she established and managed altogether 16 households, the first pastoral and simple, the later ones ever more refined and expressive of the European influence. Taken together, this string of households roughly mirrored the changes that took place in the American household generally during her lifetime.

Throughout her adult life Abigail kept up detailed correspondences: with her husband, when he served as a diplomat in France early in their marriage; with her sisters and nieces, when Abigail herself lived in Paris and France as the wife of a diplomat; and with a wide circle of friends and family within the United States. These letters have been preserved, and from them we can reconstruct the patterns of Abigail's various domestic systems, even down to noting laundry techniques and changing fashions in the fare served to guests.

Abigail Adams's letters, first published in 1848 by her grandson Francis Adams, furnished a vivid if idealistic portrait of an American housewife-manager. Already by mid-nineteenth century, Abigail's and her New England contemporaries' brand of housekeeping stood for the good old times when women did everything themselves, creatively, efficiently and productively.

In recording the changes in her life, Abigail documented the multiple roles she played as a wife and helpmeet; mother, nurse, and teacher; manager and hostess; and family matriarch. Above all, at a time when wives were treated as chattels, she enforced the belief that the woman who supported her husband's career from the home could rightfully assume responsibility for his success. Thus, to marry well meant more than a good match financially (John Adams was never wealthy and Francis Adams claims that her frugality kept his father from old-age penury). It meant that an investment worthy of the woman's time and energy had been made, because the wife gained respect and prestige as the partner of a worthy man. In some ways, then, a woman such as Abigail Adams served generations of women as a justification for the important roles they played within the home.

To historians, Abigail Adams is the outspoken wife of the second president who preferred her role as a New England housewife and matriarch to that of First Lady. To feminists she is an early advocate of women's rights. Her famous "Remember the Ladies" letter, written to husband John Adams from Braintree, Massachusetts on March 31, 1776, has been quoted and anthologized extensively in women's histories.[11]

But as a housewife, Abigail Adams is the embodiment of a lasting ideal, the opposite of the image of the overworked domestic drudge. In fact, as the driving force at the center of activity in the home, the helpmeet of a successful husband, and the matriarch of an extended, prominent family, she became the prime example for those who created the Victorian cult of domesticity, which would become the foundation of our own middle-class ideology. Both as a myth and as a prototype Abigail Adams offers an important clue to our heritage as housewives.

We are justified here in using her portrait as a prototype, for in reality she lived a substantial part of her life within the modest home of a colonial housewife. Born in 1744, she was 41 years old when she left Massachusetts to join her husband in Europe as a diplomat's wife and official lady. By then, like many women of her time, she had managed the family farm for ten years and brought up four children by herself during her husband's absence. Though she had no formal education herself, she had managed to teach her children the equivalent of an elementary school curriculum. She had nursed them and all her household through epidemics and fevers. She had bartered, saved, and haggled with tradespeople and hired hands. She had cooked and cleaned, woven and sewn, always with a minimum of help from servants. In short, she had lived within the boundaries of a colonial housewife's life for a long time before entering the aristocratic world in England and France, and, upon her return to America, the rather haphazard social scene of the nation's first capitals, New York, Philadelphia, and finally Washington.

As we know from Abigail's letters, most eighteenth-century housewives were occupied with the family, the stock, the farm, and the dairy for 12 hours a day. Moreover, women worked essentially without support from outside systems such as the schools, hospitals, and shopping centers we now take for granted. They did not labor in isolation, however. Nowadays, with isolation a serious social problem, the picture of the all-supportive, all-caring, ever-nurturing extended family is invoked as a lost ideal. But the extended family is not lost in the distant past, nor was it ever idyllic.

Then as now it was a necessary but labor-intensive system that enabled people in crises to draw on resources beyond the nuclear family[12] for financial aid, child- and eldercare, nursing, housing, job hunting, counseling, and companionship. Then as now a complicated network of kinship stretched across individual households. Extra family members not only consumed as much energy as they saved, but, in homes where food was scant and when opportunities to go to school or learn a job were lacking, they became liabilities rather than assets. And then as now ever-absent husbands were common. Often, children who were counted on as future contributors to the labor pool remained at home only as long as they had to before disappearing to forge for themselves. Always short of cash and help, women had to be self-supporting in financial as well as emotional crises. Thus, they were characteristically frugal with their time and energy, and with their emotional as well as material resources. Daughters remembered their eighteenth-century mothers not only for their strength and resourcefulness, but also for their tight lips and tight fists. Abigail Adams's children were no exception. Their childhood fell during the hard, lean years of the Revolution.

Mother and Teacher

When John Adams married Abigail Smith, in 1764, he not only connected himself favorably with the influential Quincy family, but he also provided himself with a capable partner who would carry an increasingly heavy load of the farm and business responsibilities during his prolonged absences from home. In 1774, after ten years of marriage and the birth of four children, Adams wrote the following description of their complementary roles as he saw them:

> I shall arouse myself ere long I believe, and exert an Industry, a frugality, a hard labour, that will serve my family, if I cannot serve my country. . . . If I cannot serve my children by the law, I will serve them by Agriculture, by Trade, by some way or other. . . . I must intreat you, my dear Partner in all Joys and Sorrows, Prosperity and Adversity of my life, to take part with me in the Struggle. I pray God for your Health—intreat you to rouse your whole Attention to the Family, the stock, the Farm, the Dairy. Let every Article of Expence which can possibly be spared be retrench'd. Keep the Hands attentive to their Business, and let the most prudent Measures of every kind be adopted and pursued with Alacrity and Spirit.[13]

Later, when the children were older, John gave a great deal of thought to the course of their education as directed by Abigail. In one of many letters on this subject, he exhorted her to "train them to Virtue, habituate them to industry, activity, and Spirit . . . fire them with Ambition to be useful." He concluded: "It is time, my dear, for you to begin to teach them French. Every Decency, Grace, and Honesty should be inculcated upon them."[14] To take up John's charge, Abigail first had to study French herself. She learned the language with the children from books and from tutors when they happened to be available. The range and extent of the children's education were entirely the private affair of the Adamses, as was the case with most parents at the time. A public school existed for a while in Braintree and the Adams children went to it, but most of their early schooling was administered by Abigail and the private tutors she engaged.

For her own education Abigail wrote, "I never was sent to any school. . . . Female education, in the best of families, went no further than writing and arithmetic; in some few and rare instances, music and dancing."[15] Her mother and grandmother had been her teachers, which perhaps explains why she remained so close to them. For her only daughter's schooling she could think of no better place than the home of her learned friend, the historian Mercy Otis Warren. Warren had written a three-volume history of the American Revolution and two plays, but she had only gained access to "higher" education by participating in her brother's home lessons. When Abigail needed advice on politics, literary taste, or pedagogical matters, she turned to Mrs. Warren. The two women commiserated over the custom of leaving such an important matter as teaching "to our uninstructed sex."

Today professionals have almost eclipsed the mother in educating the young. The many hours women devoted to teaching each day have been taken over by schools. They, not the mother, now decide what the children should learn. An eighteenth-century mother such as Abigail Adams set her own standards, or as she saw it, she imposed God's will upon the young mind. To that generation of parents character mattered more than a great deal of academic learning.

Character-building started early. The eighteenth-century mother swaddled her babies to make their bodies grow straight and shaped their characters with similar firmness. In the colonial period, Americans had treated their children as immature, morally endangered adults requiring constant discipline to ward off self-indulgence. Although gentler methods than the whip were now in vogue—John Wesley's mother recommended withdrawing affection and food and shaming the child with silent reproach—John and Abigail Adams subscribed to the general attitude that a child must be molded to fit both the father's and God's expectations, which presumably were identical. Instead of fostering children's individual potential, parents directed their attention to eradicating any trace of weakness. In keeping with such a program, John Locke advised cold-water baths and walks in the rain to steel the male child for life's harpships, but he was against physical punishment.[16]

In the long view, the most important goal of childhood education in the eighteenth century was, pure and simple, insuring the child's future usefulness to society. Abigail stated as much in a letter to her eleven-year-old son John Quincy, who had accompanied his father to Europe in 1778:

> Improve your understanding by acquiring useful knowledge and virtue, such as will render you an ornament to society, an honor to your country, and a blessing to your parents. . . . I would much rather you should have found your grave in the ocean you have crossed, or that any untimely death crop you in your infant years, than see you an immoral, profligate, or graceless child. . . .[17]

The future president did his part, but his brother Charles never measured up to family expectations. The younger Charles too joined his father and brother in Europe. John Adams found schools, tutors, and useful contacts for his adolescent sons, thus performing his duty as a socially prominent father. While at age fourteen John Quincy went on to Russia as secretary apprentice of ambassador Francis Dana, the affectionate Charles never conquered his homesickness and was allowed to return to America after two years abroad. Such a concession to a son's emotions was unusual for an eighteenth-century father, and later was interpreted as parental weakness by the family. In fact, Charles died at age thirty of alcoholism. At his deathbed Abigail's grief did not diminish her disappointment as she expressed it to her sister: "At New York I found my poor unhappy son, for so I must still call him, laid upon a Bed of sickness, destitute of a home. The kindness of a friend afforded him an assylum. A distressing cough, an affection of the liver and a dropsy will soon terminate a Life, which might have been made valuable to himself and others."[18]

Abigail did not blame herself for her son's failure. The fashion of attributing a child's adult development to his mother's early influence came later in the century when clergy educators started to cite Washington's and Napoleon's mothers as examples for good and bad mothering. After all the pain Charles had caused Abigail she could only pray "that he might find mercy from his maker" and look after his wife and child.

In the Adamses' time, parental responsibility did not end when the children were grown. And, in turn, children and their spouses cared for aging parents. The family in fact provided financial security for all its members as best it could, and acted as training ground for future generations. As materfamilias, Abigail continued to mother her grown-up children and her grandchildren. After Charles's death his young family came to live with John and Abigail. Daughter Nabby stayed with her parents for prolonged and frequent visits, partly because she had made an unhappy marriage. In this time of the extended family, marriage was a family, not a private, affair. John Adams had opposed an early "unsuitable" attachment, and Abigail may have felt responsible for the ill-fated union they had favored. Nabby's four children stayed with their grandparents almost as often as John Quincy's two did with theirs when he and his wife lived abroad. A niece Louisa lived permanently in the Adams household. The Adamses' home, wherever it was currently ensconced, always resembled a boarding house, with children, grandchildren, nephews, and nieces constantly moving in and out.

The eighteenth-century family functioned as a social network. Parents sent adolescents on prolonged visits to the homes of prestigious relatives to expose them to proper behavior, potential marriage partners, and possible employment. A rise in the status of one member gave the rest of the family a better chance to succeed.

Employers hired their kinfolk rather than strangers, thereby helping to support poorer relatives. Farmers increased their acreage with the next generation in mind. Merchants and craftsmen trained sons and nephews as agents and successors. Even servants and slaves passed from one family branch to another, forming the underbrush for the family tree.

The materfamilias, thus, never lost her central role in family affairs and had limitless opportunities to perform her nursing and teaching functions. Though a woman with a large family might tremble at the responsibility and dread the endless work, perhaps she took comfort in the secure knowledge that she would never be discarded as obsolete and useless, as are many of our elderly today.

In countries and cultures where full-time employment of mothers is customary, grandmothers and aunts take over the child-rearing responsibilities. As financial security improves for older women in tandem with anti-family values, these ties may weaken. Even in Black families in America employed mothers now rely more on paid sitters for regular childcare than on grandmothers. But in this case the mother hiring and the surrogate mother hired both occupy a central place in the extended family. According to Harriette Pipes McAdoo, the supportive social network offers a high level of satisfaction to Black family life but is essential to mothers who raise their children alone.[19]

The Nurse

The housewife's role as a nurse was as central as her role as a teacher and made equal demands on her time and ingenuity. Today, home nursing is rare, but in the eighteenth and nineteenth centuries, when good health was far more precarious than it is now, the responsibility for preserving it among family members and servants rested almost entirely with the mother at home.

The sad duty of escorting life out of this world was called upon even more often than the task of bringing life into it.[20] The death of children in infancy seemed as inevitable as dangerous or unwanted pregnancies. Abigail Adams never resigned herself to either fate. She mourned for many months the death of a two-year-old daughter, and feared each approaching birth, particularly her sixth and last (a stillborn baby). The phrase "I hope she is not again in the increasing way" appears many times in Abigail's and other women's letters, along with reports of influenza attacks and epidemics that often decimated whole families.

A large household was rarely without a patient. The few hospitals in existence offered a grim alternative to home care, and only the destitute and homeless resorted to these public dumping grounds of human misery. In this era when doctors could do little more than watch nature take its course, the housewife in a stricken home often went from bed to bed until she herself succumbed to the contagious disease. In 1775, the Adams house was swept by an epidemic of dysentery. First a farmhand, Isaac, was seized and stayed in bed with groans for a week. Next, Abigail herself became sick. She recovered only to nurse the two servant girls, one of whom died. Abigail's youngest boy Thomas caught the disease and gave it to her mother, who also died. Exhausted and despairing, Abigail wrote of her trials to John: "It is allotted me to go from the sick and almost dying bed of one of the best of our parents, to my own habitation, where I behold again the same scene, only varied by remoter connexion. . . ."[21]

For Abigail nursing was almost a lifetime career. Fifteen years later, when she was no longer a young mother, she still found herself nursing children and servants while she set up her new residence in Philadelphia as the vice-president's lady:

> I was so weak as to be able to travel only twenty miles a day, but I gained strength. . . . My furniture arrived the day before me. We got in on fryday. On the Monday following Luisa [her niece] was taken sick. I gave her a puke & set her up again, but on the thursday following Polly Tailor [the maid] was taken sick with a violent Plurisy fever, confined to her bed, bled 3 times, puked & blistered, and tho it is a month. . . . But this is not the worst of all my troubles. Thomas [Adams, the youngest son] has been 18 days totally deprived of the use of his Limbs by the acute Rhumatism, attended with great inflammation and fever . . . having been 9 times Bled, puked and many other applications, he is yet unable to help himself. . . . I have not left his Chamber excepting at nights and meal times for the whole time. . . . In the midst of all this, the Gentlemen and Ladies solicitous to manifest their respect were visiting us every day from 12 to 3 oclock in the midst of Rooms heeped up with Boxes, trunks, cases &c.[22]

The Adamses' rising social status only complicated the situation in Abigail's household, since more help and more visitors meant more potential patients, and the family boardinghouse turned frequently into a hospital.

The nursing aspects of housekeeping did not diminish as the nineteenth century approached. Rather, as we shall see, health problems increased as the American population grew denser.[23] Every cookbook of the period contained recipes for poultices and emetics. This fact alone indicates the extent to which nursing was integrated into the housewife's regular routine. Clearly the quality of the education and nursing that individuals received and the level of the family's welfare generally depended on the skill and stamina of the homemaker and on the network of assistance available to her. Such a family which drew on individual members of varied talents and means might be thought of as a service cooperative. In this context, the housewife had to be not only cook, housekeeper, nurse, and teacher, but also manager of the various levels of activity. Her standards of excellence and her aptitude for training and coordinating the work of others ultimately determined the quality of family life.

THE HOME: LIVING SPACE AND WORKPLACE

As a setting for a service cooperative, the eighteenth-century home had to be practical and efficient to allow for maximum use of space and energy. The colonial cottages that housed the average farming family had no frills. Each room and each piece of furniture clearly served one practical purpose, and sometimes two for greater convenience. In the frontier and in undeveloped rural areas, this type of home survived well into the nineteenth century. But, in urban areas, more Americans began to move away from the simplicity of cottage life as time went by. Housing itself grew more complex: affluent families added dining rooms, parlors, and extra bedrooms. They required furniture designed for comfort and to show off their tastes and fashions. Such refinements demanded more care; thus, more servants were hired to do the dusting and cleaning. The home itself came to consume the energy that the eighteenth-century service cooperative required for other matters—indeed, for survival alone.

During their marriage, John Adams's career involved Abigail in 16 moves. Each successive home reflected in its way the typical setting for a particular class of Americans, and each was a step further removed from the rural service cooperative. Nevertheless, "home" for both was always their first home, the farm at Braintree, Massachusetts, to which they finally retired. This first house was a typical colonial cottage on nine acres of land. It lay next door to the senior Adamses' homestead, where John's widowed mother lived with his brother's family and her second husband. Downstairs, a parlor, a study for John, and two bedchambers centered around the kitchen, which served as the general heating and meeting place. Adjoining the kitchen was a lean-to for dining and storage. A small garret room at the top of the narrow staircase served as sleeping quarters for the two housemaids. Over the years, as the Adamses' holdings increased and the family grew, more rooms were added to the original cottage.

In later years, Abigail recalled with nostalgia her first years of domestic simplicity in Braintree. John rode the law circuit then and poured his earnings into her lap. When he returned home, he would mend the fence and prune the trees or go with her to inspect the stock—two horses, three cows with two yearlings, and 20 sheep. Alternating between farm and office was not unusual for the eighteenth-century man. In fact, this pattern of working seemed both desirable and necessary. In a low-cash society such as theirs, doctors, lawyers, and clergymen all depended on producing farms for supplementing their meager salaries and ensuring the long-term financial security of their families. The house on such a farm was designed to be simple and utilitarian. It was built on the scale of the farm itself, and, as with the Adamses' house, when the farm grew, the house was expanded.

The typical eighteenth-century American home accommodated large families in a minimum of space. Every room might contain one or two beds, and could thus serve both as sleeping and living quarters. Furnishings were sparse, since before American manufacturers could supply their own market, everything that could not be produced at home had to be imported and was, thus, a luxury that only the rich could afford. The British goods embargo made imports even more dear. To make ends meet and pay off debts, Abigail used pieces of china and other scarce items—for example, the house brushes and cheese cloth that John sent home from Amsterdam, when he was there—as barter items.

As a child, Benjamin Franklin shared a single cup with his brothers and sister, and even spoons were sometimes passed from mouth to mouth in that period. Wills itemized each frying pan and soup kettle, pillowcase and bedstead, and designated the inheritor. In these early years of the nation, nothing was taken for granted and the housewife's attitude toward ordinary household items resembled that of a collector. Later in the nineteenth century, when silver, glass, and china became accessible to families with a moderate income, housewives tended to crowd their mantelpieces with knicknacks and whatnot to prove their taste and refinement.

But even in the spare eighteenth century, American hospitality never suffered from the lack of conveniences. Travelers of small means were content to share a bed as well as a meal with the members of a family who needed extra income, and those who provided the lodging welcomed the chance to hear news from distant parts. Even owners of large estates opened their doors to suitably introduced strangers, offering room and board.

The Kitchen: A Space for Living and Food Production

More than any other part of the house, the kitchen is the symbol for our domestic evolution, not only as the focus of technological advancement, but also as the backdrop for family living. In the eighteenth century, the kitchen was the scene of many kinds of work, not just food preparation.

Washing, dying, and salting tubs, the spinning wheel, and the loom were all found in the kitchen.

The American fondness for the kitchen probably goes back to the days when this room was not only the busiest but also the warmest spot in the house. At the turn of the century, upper-class families moved away from the kitchen, but modern democracy has brought them back. Now families and guests meet and eat at custom-designed teakwood kitchen counters.

In the eighteenth century and for rural Americans also in the nineteenth century, the blazing open fireplace in the kitchen was indeed a source of sustenance and comfort, but it generated endless work in the form of soot and ashes. All kitchen implements hung from the wall or stood on legs to make sweeping constantly necessary, an easier task. Besides pokers, tongs, shovels and skewers, roasting ovens, and racks, a large iron crane swung out from the fireplace to hold the large kettle that supplied the hot water for washing and rinsing. Cold water was carried in from the cistern or well, or sometimes entered via a pipe and drained into a stone sink that usually emptied directly into a sewer outside.

Cooking at the fireplace was no easy job. The cook was constantly facing the heat, and kitchens were invariably poorly ventilated. Skillets, toasters, gridirons, and waffle irons were wielded by means of long handles. The cook learned to use different kinds of wood to produce the right temperature and flavor. She could buy charcoal, but matches had not yet been invented. Thus, it was desirable to keep the fire burning, making it stronger when it was in use and letting it burn to embers between meals.

Because boiling and stewing saved fuel and demanded little attention, these cooking methods were the most common. However they did not produce the tastiest results. But visitors from Europe were quick to point out that the American cuisine made up in quantity what it lacked in quality. Recipes from the period give the impression that everything alive was fit to be eaten and that all parts of a beast were used. Oysters were standard New England fare. Throughout the several states, pheasant, woodcock, heron, mallard, plover, pigeon, and swan were all considered edible fowl.

The ambitious American housewife was guided in her more sophisticated and more time-consuming cookery by a Mrs. Glasse, an Englishwoman. Her *Art of Cookery* (1755) boasted of being written by "a Lady" and had many American editions. The first American cookbook did not come out until 1798.

Mrs. Glasse started her recipes with advice on how to treat meat in bulk: "Draw your pig very clean at the vent, then take out the guts, liver and lights, cut off his feet and truss him, prick up his belly, spit him, lay him down to the fire, care not to scorch him, when the skin begins to rise up in blisters, pull off the skin, hair and all."

A calf's head was to be washed and picked clean. Then "[you] take out the brains, and with a sharp penknife carefully take out the bones and the tongue, but be careful you don't break the meat, then take out the two eyes. . . . "[24] Once prepared, the head was stuffed with brains, oysters, eggs, and truffles.

A task even more demanding than cooking was the storing and preserving of perishable foods. Iceboxes were far in the future, though some farms had ice houses in which winter ice was kept as long as possible. All cookbooks provided recipes for pickling, salting, and smoking meats. In one, the housewife was told to cut her piece of beef into smaller pieces, examine it closely for flies, sprinkle the fat with salt, and remove the bones, replacing them also with salt. This procedure was expected to keep the meat fresh for a week.

Flies settled on every dish that was not immediately covered or put away, and food began decomposing in the summer almost as soon as it was prepared. A "powder tub" for salting meat in brine was found in every pantry. Large country houses had their own smokehouse; in smaller homes, the chimney was used for smoking meat.

Poultry was preserved by being kept alive. The housewife killed her chicken early in the morning, plucked it while it was still warm, and drew it and washed it before she trussed it for the spit. Hogs were killed twice a year. At Braintree, Abigail deplored the price of butcher meat, an indication that butchers existed even in small towns and that the housewife bought fresh meat if she could afford it. The American diet was meat oriented; few housewives found time for planting greens. Thus scurvy was a common disease. Cities such as Philadelphia had farm produce markets, and the wives and daughters of even the more prominent families would personally go there to make their selections at dawn.

When in England as a diplomat's wife, Abigail sent seeds from the impressive English gardens home to the farm in Braintree for flowers and vegetables. She had provisions from the farm shipped to her regularly when she lived in New York and Philadelphia. These included fruit from the orchard, cornmeal, grain, bacon, ham, molasses, and cheese. A frugal and rather plain cook, Abigail remained proud of her skills as a dairywoman all her life. She insisted that only the butter she prepared herself "would keep." In 1801, she wrote to her son-in-law from the remodeled Braintree house, to which she and John had retired: "Tell her [daughter Abigail] I have commenced my operations of dairywoman, and she might see me, at five o'clock in the morning, skimming my milk." The so-called Adams Mansion now contained a cider house for John, a new dairy for Abigail, and a large vegetable garden suitable for a large family.

Meals: From Eating to Dining

American colonists had been content with one meal a day, but by the end of the eighteenth century, the day would begin with breakfast of porridge, griddle cakes, and a cup of tea, and another meal would be served in the early afternoon. Only those with time to spare and a wealth of food indulged in the European institutions of afternoon teas and late suppers.

At Braintree, the main meal was served, in accordance with general custom, at 3:00 P.M. In the early years, when she was still a frugal New England cook, Abigail offered cornmeal pudding, molasses, and butter at the start of each family meal to curb the appetite. Next, she might serve veal with bacon, neck of mutton, and vegetables.

As more rooms were added to the Adamses' successive homes, more meals and more elaborate menus were required of Abigail's kitchen. Her private table never reflected the elaborate menus and dining arrangements of European gentlefolk. As official hostess she reluctantly employed the obligatory staff needed to dine senators and cabinet members.

After all, eating was the major recreation of the eighteenth century. Even for simple folk the New World offered heretofore unknown agricultural resources. The quality of food and even more the style in which it was prepared and served distinguished a lady's home from a farm cottage. Generally two courses were expected at every dinner table. Depending on the means of the cook and on the occasion, each course included a variety of meat, venison, fish and fowl accompanied by condiments. Since food spoiled easily, the same dishes appeared from one day to the next, reheated, hashed or baked in pies. A festive meal required a large bill of fare, and each dish had to fit a prescribed position on the table. The repast would be crowned by an ornamental food display, such as a piglet or a calf's head, called a "grand conceit." Successful hostesses devoted considerable time to ornamentation and were familiar with the rituals of carving, which varied subtly with different birds and beasts.

The American hostess in the late 1700s was a country cousin to her sophisticated, high-style counterparts in France and England. The European banquet table offered up gourmet food elegantly prepared and arranged to tempt the aristocratic palate. But, just as importantly, it also served as a setting for the highly refined art of conversation. This form of communication, considered by observers of society to be the most civilized of all pursuits, was guided by a multitude of rules regarding precedence and etiquette and was as carefully orchestrated as a minuet. Publicly, Americans abhorred the aristocratic excesses of Louis XVI and George III. Yet, for lack of better models, French recipes and dining habits, along with French fashions in clothes, though modified to Republican scale, did find their way into the halls of those Revolutionary ladies and gentlemen who could afford them. Over the years, these European tastes were to filter down from the few highly privileged households into the homes of the increasing number of affluent families in a rapidly industrializing America.

In 1784, when Abigail traveled to Paris, where John served as ambassador to the French court, she was duly impressed with the lavish dinners she attended and even allowed herself to envy the grace and ease with which a famous hostess such as Madame de Staël conducted her conversations. The brilliant mind of this grande dame of letters was one thing, but when it came to matters of housekeeping, Abigail stayed true to her New England values: "The dessert was served on richest china, with knives, forks, and spoons of gold," she wrote to her sister in Braintree, adding with a typical note of sarcasm, "You dine upon plate in every noble house . . . although I cannot say that you may see your face in it."[25]

On this trip Abigail began to acquire the fashionable clothes and cosmopolitan manners that eventually translated into a transformation of her general domestic style. She also obtained dining chairs for her future official duties in Philadelphia. Till then, like everyone else in Braintree, she had used pewter and wooden dishes, together with the Dutch crockery that John had sent from Amsterdam. Now she took the first steps toward bringing the European influence home.

Housecleaning Styles: From Cleaning to Polishing

The New England housewife who criticized the lack of polish on Madame de Staël's golden spoons soon learned that elegance did not necessarily mean cleanliness and that greater complexity in housekeeping did not mean greater convenience.

At a time when the paving of roads was unheard of and even cobbled streets existed only in the largest cities, the steady round of dirt and mop added to the drudgery in every home. Cleanliness was taken far less for granted than godliness by most people.

Thus, when Abigail sailed to France, she herself had to see to it that her quarters measured up to her twenty years of housecleaning experience. About her ocean voyage with daughter Nabby and two servants in tow, she wrote home: "I found it necessary to make a bustle among the waiters, and demand a cleaner abode. And as I found I might reign mistress on board without any offense, I soon exerted my authority with scrapers, mops, brushes, infusions of vinegar, &c."[26]

Scrapers, mops, brushes, vinegar, and homemade soap were the tools of the eighteenth-century cleaning woman. The other part was physical strength. Her style of applying the latter varied with national background. English women scrubbed on hands and knees, Scottish women stepped on wet rags with naked feet, and Dutch women flooded the entire room, then wiped it dry with a mop. Walls would be whitewashed with lime every spring.

As Abigail soon found at her rented villa in Paris, not only the style of dining, but also that of housecleaning was more sophisticated and time-consuming in sophisticated France. Her farm cottage in Braintree, which she now called a "wren's nest," had had the typical painted floor boards and wall panels of that period. These would be washed and wiped and periodically repainted when traces of soot became too ingrained into the wood. Polished floors must have been a great luxury and unknown to Abigail. The floors of tile and parquet did impress her as much as the method in which they acquired their luster. The French charwomen scoffed at Abigail's mop and pail and proceeded to scrub the tiles with a brush. For the parquet floor a special *frotteur* had to be hired whose job it was to rub on melted wax with a hard brush. Next he would set his foot on the wax and, as Abigail reported, "with arms akimbo, stripped to his shirt, [would go] driving around your room."

Clothing: From Homespun to Haute Couture

Here in Paris, Abigail also noted, with equal surprise, that even the servants sent out their laundry, and that their mistresses paid the bill. The fashions and status-conscious lifestyle in Paris required a reliance on experts and outside services unheard of even in Boston. Instead of being involved in the production aspects of homemaking, as were housewives in rural America, the sophisticated Parisian housekeeper of an elegant residence devoted herself exclusively to the acquisition and maintenance of goods and services. For Abigail's homespun standards, the quality of both seemed inferior. For one thing, she had to have her American maid wash her muslins by hand, fearing that the commercial laundry would beat them to shreds.

Then as now fine fabrics required special care. Before the advent of washing machines, beating dirty garments with feet, clubs, or arms was the universal washing technique. Together with wringing, the job proved an awesome test of sheer womanpower and made laundering the most despised form of woman's work. In America as well as Europe, only the poorest and most ignorant women took in washing for others or were hired for the day by those who could afford it.

In American towns, public washhouses stood near rivers and lakes. Here sheets and bulky garments could be rinsed and then dried on the ground or on hemp clotheslines. But most households kept a laundry kettle in the backyard. Keeping clothes clean in those days of wells and cisterns was no small achievement, for even the soap had to be made at home. To produce a barrel of soap jelly, a household had to collect six bushels of ashes and 24 pounds of grease. A good deal of luck and a tolerant nose were also necessary to the process. The laundry cycle—involving soaking, washing, rinsing, starching, drying, and smoothing—was further complicated by the nature of eighteenth-century textiles and fashions. Ladies wore dresses embellished with ruffles and enameled buttons, lace and gauze. Fashion required tightly laced bodices which had silk- or brocade-covered stays and might be elaborately embroidered. Skirts billowed over silk or satin quilted petticoats and hoops. There were as yet no drawers. Later, low-cut diaphanous muslins became the style. Unpaved roads and muddy tracks notwithstanding, such dresses were worn with dainty slippers made of silk or calamanco—a sturdier fabric of glazed wool, preferred by Abigail.

The complete clothes washing process, then, could easily stretch over an entire week. And this unrelenting string of tasks had to be followed by ironing, an undertaking that required careful monitoring. Flatirons, in a variety of shapes to match the needs of particular garments, had to be filled with coal or heated next to the fire and then cleaned of coal dust or ashes before being applied to clothes. Petticoats, ribbons, kerchiefs, shawls, aprons, and gowns were always pressed. For eighteenth-century style convenience, aprons, kerchiefs, and chemises of cotton or linen could be detached and washed separately.

Faced with the gargantuan labor laundering entailed, most families usually washed clothes but once a month, and less frequently in winter. Again, affluent housewives could store enough clothes to last over longer periods and could hire more help for the ominous event. But for average families, personal cleanliness was an ongoing struggle. Not surprisingly, simple shifts of homespun cotton or linen and crude leather shoes distinguished the ordinary woman who could neither afford the materials nor the upkeep of a lady's wardrobe.

Even more basic than laundering methods to the housewife's necessary store of knowledge, however, were the skills associated with textile production and clothes-making. In 1776, Abigail proudly announced to John that his homespun suit was waiting for him, adding,

> I think it my duty to attend with frugality and economy to our own private affairs, and if I cannot add to our little Substance yet see that it is not diminished. I should enjoy but little comfort in a state of Idleness, and uselessness. Here I can serve my partner, my family and myself, and injoy [sic] the Satisfaction of your serving your Country.[27]

When in response John inquired as to whether she had tried making saltpeter (for gunpowder), she answered, slightly peeved, that she might try it after soapmaking, but found it as much as she could do "to manufacture cloathing for my family which would else be naked."

Making and caring for clothing and bedding were the most consuming tasks of the pre-industrial American housewife. All the females of a household performed them, but the actual amount of work done in the home—from the planting of flax and the shearing of wool to the final sewing of a homespun suit—depended on the manual and financial resources of the individual family. By the end of the eighteenth century, carding and dyeing

Newest Fashions for May 1828.

Morning and Walking Dresses.

Evening Dress.

W Alais Sc.

1. Early–nineteenth-century fashion plate. Elaborate fashions not only preoccupied the ladies, but provided work and income for seamstresses, milliners, laundresses, and ladies' maids. Reproduced through the courtesy of The Bancroft Library, University of California, Berkeley CA 94720.

was done at the local mill and weaving and spinning could be done from ready-made skeins. In affluent homes, itinerant weavers were employed for several days or weeks, spinning up to six skeins of yarn in a day. Muslins and silks were imported.

An eighteenth-century British encyclopedia found it noteworthy that linen and woolen clothes were manufactured in George Washington's household—the British already had a well-developed textile industry. But even without the support of a large plantation, the patriotic housewife returned to the spinning wheel to contribute her share after America declared its independence and effectively renounced the use of British textiles. And even in homes affluent enough to afford what outside services existed, especially in later years, women practiced the weaving and spinning arts out of pride—much as many women today sew their own clothes.

In looking back over her life, Abigail deplored the fact that she had not taught her daughter to spin and weave (refined young girls did only ornamental needlework). She praised her granddaughter—once more a farmeress—for returning to the spinning wheel. In words that could have been Abigail's, Benjamin Franklin's sister, Jane Mecom, wrote to her daughter in 1778, "Keep yourself constantly employed, which would contribute greatly to a composed mind. . . . You cannot only do plain work, but make bonnets, caps, cloaks and anything [for barter]."[28] Not only did Abigail subscribe to the prevalent belief that manual work was rewarding, but she supported all skills that preserved the self-sufficiency of the home. From experience she knew that commercially manufactured goods were subject to inflation and that the work of specialists rarely warranted the cost. First from Boston, then from abroad, John supplied her with pins, needles, and other sewing materials, and even calamanco cloth for homemade shoes. She did not employ a seamstress until her visit to Paris transformed her from "farmeress" to hostess, and the "mantua-maker" (dressmaker) ceremoniously measured her and young Nabby for courtly gowns. These, of course, could only be produced in a professional haute-couture establishment.

HOUSEHOLD HELP

The woman who spins, sews, and bakes with her own hands has always been the good woman in America. And as a corollary to this rule, homemakers from Abigail Adams to the heroine of Sue Kaufman's *Diary of a Mad Housewife* (1967) have gotten into trouble for delegating their work to others.

Moral dictums aside, however, extra helping hands in the form of servants to carry the water and empty the slop, light the fires, and chop the food were as necessary to the eighteenth-century household as electricity is to that of our own time. Unlike electricity, though, servants added to family life all the problems and the rewards inherent in human interaction.

The question of who was qualified to join the young Adamses in their first home warranted many premarital discussions. Their choices were basically limited to those servants available through each of their parents' families, just as their first home was part of the Adamses' homestead. John's mother lent them her slave girl Judah for the first winter. Judah went back and forth between the two houses; eventually, after she gained her freedom at old Mrs. Adams's death, she and her husband took care of the Braintree farm. John Briesler had been indentured to Abigail's grandfather Quincy and served the Adams household in many capacities together with his wife Esther whom he had courted when they both went to Europe with Abigail. Servants such as Judah, Briesler and Esther were not strictly maids or "hands" but played the roles of household assistants, parental substitutes, secretaries, confidantes, and daily companions, for Abigail regarded them more as family members than as retainers. After nursing a young servant through many weeks of a fatal illness, Abigail expressed her caring concern in a letter to John:

> The death of Patty came very near me, having lived for four years with me under my care. I hope it will make me more continually mindful and watchful of all those who are still committed to my charge. 'Tis a great trust. I daily feel more and more the weight and importance of it, and of my own inability.[29]

Not all housewives responded equally to their charges, particularly if other pressures intervened as in the case of Mary Silliman. Widowed and in debt, she found herself unable to take care of her "great family," which included several slaves. Ordinarily New England families like hers would have freed the slaves, but Mrs. Silliman sold two of them, partly to settle her debts, partly because she considered them troublemakers. The rest were gradually freed, but even then she remained responsible for those who could not find employment.[30]

Traces of mutually caring relationships still exist today where mothers rely increasingly on childcare substitutes which range from family and friends to hired surrogates. But it is indicative of our consumer society that substitutes for mother and housewife belong to our least organized and lowest paid workers. What is more important, they feel little appreciated by their employers.[31] This trend became already visible in the Adams household.

As the Adams family grew, so did Abigail's difficulties in dealing with servants. Few seemed to have warranted the time and energy she invested in their training and supervision. But the larger the household grew the more help was needed. When Nabby, the first of the four children, was born, the original two servants became four. Two law clerks almost always boarded with the family, as did visiting relatives and a series of refugees from Boston (some of them unwanted). Increasingly, Abigail delegated routine tasks to others and assumed the managerial responsibilities of a farmeress along with those of a single parent that she shouldered during John's years abroad.

The move to France in 1784 forced Abigail to break with the agrarian, extended-family pattern. Apologetically she reported to her sister that she had to pay a specialized staff of seven, including a coachman and a gardener, to support their aristocratic lifestyle in the city of Marie Antoinette. She discovered that the housewife with "faculty" relinquished her managerial duties to a professional maitre d'hotel, whose sole business was "to purchase articles in the family, and oversee, that nobody cheats but himself." Her own duties pertained now only to the social functions of a hostess. Even the girl Esther, whom she had brought with the family from Braintree, acquired the special skills of a lady's maid. The French servant at the villa in Paris refused to touch a broom with hands that knew how to dress and coif a lady of fashion. Five years later upon her return to America Abigail—who now lived as the first vice-president's lady in the then capital, New York—wrote to her sister, "My constant family is 18, ten of which make my own family." The servants included "a pretty good housekeeper, a tolerable footman, a midling cook, an indifferent stewart and a vixen of a housemaid" who could not keep up with the ironing, because she was always sick or in a bad temper. Abigail did not want to hire anybody from New York, because "The chief of the servants here who are good for any thing are Negroes who are slaves," she wrote. "The white ones are all foreigners & chiefly vagabonds . . . it is next to impossible here to get a servant from the highest to the lowest grade that does not drink, male or female."[32] She also found that cooks in the "better" society she now inhabited refused to do anything but cook, whereas in Braintree at that time it was still possible to find "all-purpose" helpers. She now experienced sleepless nights, since she was worried or "vexed" over servants. Her difficulties strengthened her original conviction that hired strangers and the social obligations that required their presence interfered with the care of her family.

The hiring and supervising of servants and a daily round of official entertaining replaced her earlier functions as "working" housewife and mother of small children. Her children were grown, the farm in Braintree was administered by relatives, and servants did the cooking and cleaning. But her uneasiness with a lifestyle that required more and more space and people and money to maintain it never subsided.

THE HOSTESS

In managing the vice-president's and then in 1797 the president's home, Abigail lived up to her part in their marital partnership. She and John could not keep up George Washington's aristocratic style with levees, drawing-room receptions, and grand dinners, suited to the 10,000–acre estate and the 500 slaves which his wife's dowry had brought to the President. They never owned slaves and they had no private income to speak of from their estate. The public style of the first American presidents was a creation of their own and much criticized—Washington's for being too aristocratic and Adams's for being too plain. This was the age of Louis XVI and George III. The leaders of the young Republic were not to behave like royalty, but they only had royalty as models for heads of state.

Although she had learned her role in France and England, Abigail never turned into a famous hostess, and she never lived in the aristocratic fashion, not even in the sense of the old Virginia families. More interested in politics than in politicians' wives, she never enjoyed the regular routines of calling on society matrons and receiving them for tea. In Philadelphia, where the capital had been moved from New York, the new First Lady's schedule for 1797 reveals no time for leisure as well as some anxiety about her official duties:

> I keep up my old habit of rising at an early hour. If I did not I should have little command of my time. At 5 I rise. From that time till 8 I have a few leisure hours [for writing letters]. At 8 I breakfast, after which until eleven I attend to my family arrangements. At that hour I dress for the day. From 12 until two I receive company, sometimes until 3. We dine at that hour unless on company days which is Tuesdays & Thursdays. After dinner I usually ride (drive) out until seven [for social calling]. I begin to feel a little more at home, and less anxiety about the ceremonious part of my duty, tho by not having a drawing room (i.e., reception for the ladies) for the summer I am obliged every day, to devote two hours for the purpose of seeing company. Tomorrow we are to dine the Secretaries of State &c. with the whole Senate (32 senators, five cabinet members).[33]

The last and most unmanageable of her official residences was the White House. Newly built in 1800, this great castle, according to Abigail, was unsuitable for family living. Thirteen fires had to burn all the time to keep out the damp air, and 30 servants were required to keep the household running, though the Adamses could barely afford eight. More concerned with housekeeping than with entertaining, Abigail dried her laundry in the unfinished audience room because, as she wrote to her daughter Nabby, there was neither a yard, nor a fence "or other convenience." The fact that her mother-in-law's illness prevented Abigail from attending John's inauguration indicates that the role of first lady came second to that of materfamilias. Indeed, she was happy to leave the White House to John's successor, Jefferson, in 1801 and return home to Braintree.

In contrast to today's fashion of retreating to a smaller home, the Adamses' retirement home, which was also a working farm, was large enough to accommodate their extended-family clan. In their years away in the political capitals of the world, John and Abigail had relied on members of their family to assume the responsibility for their home in keeping with the idea of a family-run service cooperative. John's older brother had managed the land, and Abigail's sister supervised the remodeling of the old homestead. Larger windows, additional rooms, more fireplaces, and a portico reflected Abigail's new taste for French elegance and classical decor, appropriate for an ex-president. But, more importantly, these additions made it clear that Abigail intended to continue her active role both as hostess and as materfamilias.

The younger generation found it difficult to live up to Abigail's seemingly boundless stamina and her capacity to meet every situation with self-discipline. Her daughter and daughters-in-law tended to be intimidated by her strong personality and yearned for a more intimate, private atmosphere. Nevertheless, since individuals depended on their kin for services more than emotional support, formal rather than intimate behavior governed family relationships, and Abigail's style prevailed.

Abigail's strong-willed domination of the extended family represented the fullest expression of satisfaction open to a housewife. To attain it, a woman did not need to have progressed, as Abigail had, from simpler roots to an exceptional social rank. In fact, it might be argued that Abigail Adams's example did not reflect the pattern of an average housewife's life. True, she lived during an extraordinary period in history, she married an extraordinary man, and she herself was endowed with exceptional wit, energy, and self-reliance. Nevertheless, her career as housewife evolved around her husband's career; in that sense she resembled most wives of her time, since they were expected to perform certain duties in accordance with their husbands' rank and social status. In both the eighteenth and nineteenth centuries a lady's public image reflected her husband's station. His status was the chief quality defining her social identity. Even in her most intimate letters to her family, for example, Abigail refers to John Adams as the President.

Appropriately enough, Abigail Adams, the "compleat" eighteenth-century housewife, set up her retirement household precisely at the turn of the century. The young women in Abigail's shadow became the housewives of the new age. It was sentiment rather than utilitarianism that would appeal to the nineteenth-century housewife. In cultivating this proclivity she found herself more and more isolated in the "feminine" sphere—the drawing room and the nursery. Lady-housewives of the new century were content to turn from useful employment to ornamental domesticity when their husbands could afford it. But a sudden change of fortune—a bad marriage or a move to the frontier—put a woman with these aspirations right back into the eighteenth-century farm cottage, where she had to work hard manually to attain cleanliness, let alone respectability. Thus, whether she shone as a manager or a hostess, the American housewife was always just a step away from dust and drudgery. In any event the ideal of the complete housewife remained with her.

NOTES

1. Charles Francis Adams, *Letters of Mrs. Adams, the Wife of John Adams* (Boston: Wilkins, Carter, 1848), 4th ed., p. 402.

2. Divorce was possible, but difficult to obtain. Most cases involved women who had been deserted and needed access to their husbands' property. For more information see Linda K. Kerber, *Women of the Republic: Intellect and Ideology in Revolutionary America* (Chapel Hill: University of North Carolina Press, 1980), pp. 157–184. Mary Beth Norton, *Liberty's Daughters: The Revolutionary Experience of American Women, 1750–1800* (Boston: Little, Brown, 1980), p. 48, gives a survey of women's legal restrictions and financial dependency.

3. Jane Roberts Chapman and Margaret Gates, eds., *Women into Wives: The Legal and Economic Impact of Marriage*, Sage Yearbooks in Women's Policy Studies (Beverly Hills, Calif.: Sage Publications, 1977), vol. 2, p. 101.

4. *Woman, Workers and Society: International Perspectives* (Geneva: International Labour Office, 1976), p. 178.

5. Sir Richard Phillips, *A General View of the Manners, Customs, and Curiosities of Nations* . . . (Philadelphia: Johnson and Warner, 1813), vol. 2, pp. 207–209.

6. Francis Hopkinson, "On Annual White-Washings: copy of a letter from a Gentleman in America, to his Friend in Europe," *American Museum*, vol. 1, no. 1, (1787), pp. 48–53; "Remarks on the Preceding Letter . . . Addressed to the Editor of, and extracted from the *Columbian Magazine*," ibid., pp. 53–55.

7. Nancy F. Cott, *The Bonds of Womanhood: "Woman's Sphere" in New England, 1780–1835* (New Haven, Conn.: Yale University Press, 1977), p. 22; Linda K. Kerber and Jane De Hart Mathews, *Women's America: Refocusing the Past* (New York: Oxford University Press, 1983), pp. 90–92. Both works contribute to the understanding of this chapter.

8. Joy and Richard Buel, *The Way of Duty: A Woman and Her Family in Revolutionary America* (New York: W. W. Norton, 1984), pp. 80–81; a particularly good account of marriage, courtship, and legal proceedings.

9. The above-mentioned work is based on the journal and letters of Mary Fish (1736–1818) and her descendants from three marriages. Claudia L. Bushman, *"A Good Poor Man's Wife"* (Hanover, N.H.: University Press of New England, 1981), offers another document of eighteenth-century life in the first section about the Browne family, ancestors of Harriet Hanson Robinson, whose own diary pertains to the nineteenth century. See also Norton, *Liberty's Daughters*, pp. 8–9.

10. For a summary of the criticism of the family as an ideological construct see Michele Barrett and Mary McIntosh, *The Anti-Social Family* (London: N[ew] L[eft] B[ooks], 1982), pp. 20–40, and for the feminist point of view, Thorne et al., *Rethinking the Family: Some Feminist Questions*, pp. 231–235.

11.

Remember the Ladies, and be more generous and favorable to them than your ancestors. Do not put such unlimited power into the hands of the Husbands, Remember all Men would be tyrants if they could. If perticular [sic] care and attention is not paid to the Ladies we are determined to form a Rebellion, and will not hold ourselves bound by any Laws in which we have no voice, or those customs which treat us only as vassals of your Sex. Regard us then as Beings placed by providence under your protection and in immitation of the Supreme Being make use of that power only for our happiness.

(L. H. Butterfield, ed., *Adams Family Correspondence* (Cambridge, Mass.: Harvard University Press, 1963), vol. 1, pp. 369–370).

12. The eighteenth-century family with its social network of mutual obligations has been called an extended family, although some scholars limit the term to households where other relatives besides parents and children live under one roof. The term "nuclear" family applies to the two-parent household. For an explanation of changing norms and definitions of the American family see Tufte et al., *Changing Images of the Family*, pp. 1–5, 29–55.

13. Butterfield, *Adams Family Correspondence*, vol. 1, p. 119.

14. Ibid., p. 145.

15. C. F. Adams, *Letters of Mrs. Adams*, p. xxix.

16. Carl Degler, *At Odds: Women and the Family in America from the Revolution to the Present*, pp. 86–95, shows that the idea of molding the child to fit the social order lasted at least until the mid-nineteenth century.

17. Butterfield, *Adams Family Correspondence*, vol. 3, p. 37.

18. Stewart Mitchell, ed., *New Letters of Abigail Adams* (Boston: Houghton Mifflin, 1947), p. 255.

19. For a summary of the extended family system in today's Black family see Harriette Piper McAdoo, "Black Mothers and the Extended Family Support Network," in La France Rodgers-Rose, ed., *The Black Woman* (Beverly Hills: Sage Publications, 1980).

20. Catherine M. Scholten, " 'On the Importance of the Obstetrick Art': Changing Customs of Childbirth in America, 1760–1825", in Kerber et al., *Women's America*, pp. 51–65. Midwives with various degrees of experience helped with childbirth at home. Formal training in obstetrics was introduced to American medical students at the very end of the eighteenth century. Until mid-nineteenth century few women availed themselves of trained physicians to assist them in labor. Childbirth is treated more fully in Chapter IV.

21. C. F. Adams, *Letters of Mrs. Adams*, p. xxxvi.

22. S. Mitchell, *New Letters of Abigail Adams*, pp. 65–66.

23. For further discussion of nursing functions at home see Chapter III.

24. Hannah Glasse, *The Art of Cookery . . . by a Lady*, 5th ed. (London: Printed and Sold at Mrs. Ashburn's China-Shop, 1755), p. 3.

25. C. F. Adams, *Letters of Mrs. Adams*, p. 249.

26. Written July 1784. Ibid., p. 158.

27. Butterfield, *Adams Family Correspondence*, vol. 2, p. 4.

28. C. Van Doren, ed., *The Letters of Benjamin Franklin and Jane Mecom* (Princeton, N.J.: Princeton University Press, 1950), p. 181; American Philosophical Society, *Memoirs*, vol. 27.

29. Butterfield, *Adams Family Correspondence*, vol. 1, p. 310.

30. Buel and Buel, *The Way of Duty*, pp. 207–211.

31. Bonnie Thornton Dill, " 'The Means to Put My Children Through': Child-

Rearing Goals and Strategies Among Black Female Domestic Servants," in Rodgers-Rose, *The Black Woman*, pp. 118–122.

32. S. Mitchell, *New Letters of Abigail Adams*, p. 48; see also pp. 34–36:

I have a pretty good Housekeeper, a tolerable footman, a midling cook, an indifferent stewart and a vixen of a House maid. . . . Her constitution has been ruined by former hardships, and she is very often laid up. She has not method or regularity with her business. All her business here is to make 4 or 5 beds, & clean round Rooms which are almost covered with carpets. All the Brass is cleaned by the footman. She helps wash & Iron, but I have been obliged to hire when I have wanted more cleaning than that done in a day.

33. Ibid., p. 91.

2

The Lady, 1800–1860

Whenever ladies of refinement, as a general custom, patronise domestic pursuits, then these employments will be deemed lady-like. It may be urged, however, that it is impossible for a woman who cooks, washes, and sweeps, to appear in the dress, or acquire the habits and manners, of a lady; that the drudgery of the kitchen is dirty work, and that no one can appear delicate and refined, while engaged in it.... If she has no habits of order and system; if she is remiss and careless in person and dress;—then all this may be true.... It is because such work has generally been done by vulgar people, and in a vulgar way, that we have such associations; and when ladies manage such things, as ladies should, then such associations will be removed.

—Catherine Beecher,
A Treatise on Domestic Economy, 1842[1]

The multipurpose housewife who functioned as laborer and manager, cook and companion, mother and governess, hostess and housekeeper—the model for generations of American wives to come—was not a lady in the European tradition. The term *lady* itself is rooted in Europe's feudal past, when knights in shining armor protected the weaker sex and poor peasants obeyed, honored, and slaved for their lords and masters. Though clearly inferior to her lord, the lady stood far above the common woman, and shared with her male partner the comforting certainty that she was superior to the masses and entitled to make use of them as laborers. As strongly, she felt the responsibility of her rank in the form of noblesse oblige: she was beholden to act generously and charitably toward the poor, the helpless, and particularly those individuals who faithfully served her and her family. For centuries the British lady was linked to the aristocracy by blood—or by the blood of her husband—confident that her lot in life lay in running a graceful home for the purpose of breeding new aristocrats.

Charity work to fulfill the responsibility of noblesse oblige blended har-
moniously with that main purpose, because her status freed her from ordinary household obligations. Noble ladies engaged in social, and sometimes
intellectual, pursuits. Common working women labored with their own
hands in farm and cottage industries or were servants in wealthy homes.

Some women could gain status by the proven method of marrying a
gentleman. Low birth had often been compensated for in this way. On the
other hand, in marrying a common man a high-born daughter lost her place
in high society: his low rank, by virtue of their marriage, became her own.
Thus noble birth did not alter the fact that a woman's status was firmly
linked to her husband's wealth—a condition, as noted by Natalie Sokoloff,
that still holds true today. Her analysis of women's home and market work,
Between Money and Love (1980)[2] answers vital questions about status and
gender in today's society. We still adhere to the concept of women's upward
mobility through marriage as distinguished from men's through occupational improvement. But according to Sokoloff, "women are no more likely
to move into a higher social stratum through marriage than men are able
to do through their occupational attainment." While condemning marriage
for profit, nineteenth-century guidance literature abounded with cautionary
tales about unfortunate brides who had wasted their lives on an unworthy
man. Written to deter daughters from choosing husbands against parental
advice, they confirmed the economic reality of married life. Choosing Mr.
Right meant loving an industrious and energetic man, not a drone or
spendthrift who, as *The Young Lady's Counsellor* (1852) explains, "will
sink in seas of difficulty, and drag you down to cavernous depths of sorrow."[3]

Like the endless debate over "The Woman Question" which filled the
pages of Victorian magazines, marital advice books and novels addressed
the growing gap between emotional and economic needs, between feudal
and egalitarian ideals. Could women function independently from men?
Did they have equal rights to be educated, to own property and pursue a
career? Such issues radically undermined the feudal character of marriage.
Queen Victoria herself believed in woman's God-given inferiority to man
which destined her to suffer physically and mentally even when she was
fortunate in linking her life to a worthy man. As a wife she submitted to
her husband's will as her subjects submitted to her authority as Queen.
She was their protector, Albert was hers. Our present struggle in adjusting
married life to equal job opportunities for husband and wife goes back to
the post-Revolutionary period, when Americans blended upper-class life
styles with lower-class work habits. As we have seen through Abigail Adams's eyes: the European aristocracy cultivated a sophisticated life of leisure, orchestrated by rules of etiquette and honor. Work had no honorable
place in this society, unless it was unpaid.

In America in the 1800s, a new breed of man entered the race for status
and power: the rich tradesman, who could buy his rank rather than in-

heriting it. Even in England, trade began to nudge the established gentry from the front-row seats they had occupied for centuries. Self-made men of low breeding could buy estates, and their wives could learn the gentle arts of entertaining and raising educated children. Perfect manners were no longer exclusively the trait of the aristocracy; they could be acquired, like family jewels, along with the perfect home. But in making their advance through the social ranks, the knights of trade did not kill off the landed gentry. Rather, they infiltrated their circles and their families. As the century progressed, the aristocracy allowed the nouveau riche entry, realizing that it needed their money and know-how if it were to survive the Industrial Revolution. Fortunately for the old guard, the newcomers defended the old values, and with a vengeance.

In America, too, some men grew prosperous enough to support the lifestyle of the old European aristocrats. Though their work excluded them from the ranks of certified gentlemen, who were unencumbered by the need to earn a living, their wives could live by high society's rules, refining their behavior and cultivating "good taste." Thus, a woman in possession of the code of correct behavior could redeem a family from low beginnings or common origins. In this compromise between the lower-class necessity to work and the upper-class style for living at home the middle-class couple formed a kind of partnership, where the man provided the money and the woman converted it into visible assets. He built his bank in New York; she furnished a castle in Newport. Their sons expanded their private empires and their daughters married dukes. In the eyes of the American people, that such advances were possible only proved the worth of the democratic ideal. If an immigrant fur trapper such as John Jacob Astor or a Dutch produce peddler such as Cornelius Vanderbilt could forge kingdoms by working hard, so could every man, and such kingdoms could hold sway with the oldest families. The self-made man became the heroic knight of old—and the man-made lady became the heroine.[4]

Previously, in keeping with the legacy of Puritan restraint, the rich had kept their extravagances hidden from the public eye. But, in 1835, James Gordon Bennett permanently altered the newspaper world by inventing the society page for his *New York Herald*. Suddenly, the pomp and glitter, the weddings and balls, of New York's wealthy class were thrust into the purview of the dazzled masses. Menus and evening gowns, travel itineraries, and family events of the trend setters became national news. These tidbits inspired many an ambitious woman to assume the social leadership of her underdeveloped little township. Moreover, the rising influence of newspapers and magazines opened a window into the parlors of the moneyed elite—as television does today—and planted the standards of these overconsuming, society-loving families in the minds of ordinary people all over the country.

The Astors and Vanderbilts served to endorse the ideal of the lady. If

Astor and Vanderbilt could do it, so perhaps could everywoman's husband. And if Mrs. A and Mrs. V could furnish their homes to reflect the new work-based nobility, why couldn't everywoman herself? True, the concepts of helpmeet and working partner did not disappear from the idea of housewife in the ordinary household, but these ideas were often transformed by new ambitions rooted in industry and trade.

Very often in the new upwardly mobile American family, women modeled themselves after the British lady without the wherewithal for hiring servants to do the more mundane housework. Wives of professional men— lawyers, doctors, and accountants, for instance—were especially burdened, since their husbands earned little money for their services in the nineteenth century but were still traditionally considered a part of the ambitious, upward-striving society. Thus, the nineteenth-century American woman's dilemma remained essentially unchanged from that of the post-Revolutionary housewife. In the old days, a woman aspired to entertain in the fashionable European mode while running a complex extended family on a demanding working farm. In the nineteenth century, the problem lay in maintaining the new upper-class standards while still doing the work necessary for running the home and raising the children.

STYLES OF "THE LADY"

Though Europeanizing influences found their way into the most provincial corners of the country, the housewife as lady took on different styles in different regions and different classes. Among the most astute observers of the various manifestations of the American lady were writers Frances Trollope and Harriet Martineau from England. British women in general were relentless though fascinated critics of their American sisters. Perhaps they were afraid of being beaten at their own game and identified each flaw with a mixture of contempt and relief. But perhaps too they could see more clearly abroad a danger that threatened their own security at home: as the technocrats and bureaucrats gained power over the old aristocrats, the clear "superiority" of the latter—and of the latter's ladies— was shaken. If *everyone* could become a lord or a lady simply by emulating the real thing, what was the distinction of the title, after all? British ladies with feminist notions, on the other hand, hoped to find more equality in a democratic country and were disappointed when they did not.

This was the case for Harriet Martineau and Frances Trollope. Though they were not aristocratic ladies themselves, these British writers had been born into a culture in which everyone was expected to understand class distinctions and to learn a complex system of social privilege. These observers seemed to see down the generations into our own time when they wrote of the expectations nineteenth-century American society had for its women.

Trollope and Martineau both observed that a double standard applied to men and women in all areas of American life. And both expressed concern about the growing isolation of the typical American housewife, whose chances for engaging in intellectual, artistic, or socially useful activities were decreasing in direct proportion with the increase in her leisure hours. It is useful to rely on the clear vision of these British observers, however caustic their sarcasm might be at times, in distinguishing among the various kinds of American lady-housewives in the urban North and in the plantation South, among the newly rich and the newly educated, and among the society-conscious and the socially conscious.

The Southern Lady

In the stereotype that has filtered down to us, the Southern plantation lady gracefully matures from a capricious belle to a pious matron, presiding over elegant gatherings in a home styled after the English country house and gently governing her household. Throughout her lifetime, her main function is to sweeten the lives of a chivalrous husband and numerous children, whose bodily functions are conveniently attended to by adoring mammies.

Harriet Martineau's description of a plantation mistress, in her book *Retrospect of Western Travel* (1844), boldly contradicts the legendary image. In the following passage, Martineau invites the reader to imagine her- or himself calling on a plantation lady and being led by a servant into a parlor to await her:

> Your hostess [explains Martineau] is now engaged in a back room, or out in the piazza behind the house, cutting out clothes for her slaves.... You sit down to the piano, or to read; and one slave or another enters every half hour to ask what is o'clock. Your hostess comes in, at length; and you sit down.... She gratifies your curiosity about her "people," telling you how soon they burn out their shoes at the toes, and wear out their winter woollens, and tear up their summer cottons.... She has not been seated many minutes when she is called away, and returns saying ... that they will not take medicine unless she gives it to them; [and how careless of each other,] so that she has been obliged to stand by and see Diana put clean linen upon her infant. Unless she keeps her eye constantly on Diana "the infant may as likely as not, be dropped into the fire or out of the window."[5]

Although slave labor supposedly relieved ladies of all household drudgery, the plantation mistress struggled with workers who were purposely kept in a state of absolute dependence. All supplies, even sugar and bread, were kept under lock and key and had to be constantly locked and unlocked for distribution by the mistress or her delegate. Since slaves had no access to resources of their own, she also had complete responsibility for the moral and physical welfare of a large number of "her" people as well as for the upkeep of a complex physical plant. A plantation household of, say, 12 immediate family members, 27 domestics, two tutors, and two or three permanent house guests or impoverished relatives required 5,200 pounds of flour, 27,000 pounds of pork, 20 beeves, 550 bushels of wheat, and 150 gallons of brandy a year.[6] And, because the kitchen was separated from the main house, the preparation, transportation, and serving of food had to be carefully choreographed. Thus, every meal was a hazardous and complicated production.

In writing about the plantation lady, it was Harriet Martineau's purpose to inform her British readers of the indignities of slavery and its effect on Southern domesticity. Thus, she set out deliberately to expose the double-standard mentality behind the leisurely scenes of gracious living she observed. She noted that the physical obstacles in running a plantation household required great strength and stamina but that the Southern ideal demanded the concealment of such strength under a fragile, ladylike appearance.

If the Southern-belle stereotype underplayed the duties of a plantation mistress, the childlike image of the house slave and the "Mammy" stereotype of the nurturing earth mother have diminished the contribution of the Black working woman who labored in the fields during the day and cooked and cleaned in her cabin at night, who developed skills such as midwifery and nursing that enabled her to support her family in freedom. Recent research such as the documents collected by Dorothy Sterling in *We Are Your Sisters* (1984) has illuminated the great variety of work and family life experienced by female slaves. Only five percent of them had such specialized and privileged positions as a former lady's maid: "Cook? No, ma'm. I never cooked until after I was married, and I never washed, never so much as a rag. All I washed was the babies and maybe my mistress's feet. I was a lady's maid."[7] One is reminded here of Abigail Adams's Parisian expert who never had to touch a broom.

Another ex-slave remembered weaving cotton for all the winter clothes, and still another was apprenticed by her mistress to assist the doctor as a midwife: "I stayed wid dat doctor, Dr. McGill his name was, for 5 years. I got to be good. Got so he'd sit down an' I'd do all the work. When I come home, I made a lot of money for old miss."[8] The money a slave made was of course not her own, just as the money her mistress made belonged to her husband.

The slave who satisfied his or her mistress had little hope of being freed, for even if the lady could bring herself to part with a good servant, she had no legal right to do so. In fact, the Southern mistress's legal rights were equal to the slave's on some fundamental counts: neither could own property or represent him- or herself in court. Still, few Southern ladies dared to compare their own bondage with slavery. One who did was the outspoken Mary Chesnut, a distinguished lady of the Confederacy. She recorded in her diary that as she watched a beautiful slave being auctioned on the block she suddenly realized that *all* women were "sold in marriage from queen downward." Commenting on a certain senator's reason for avoiding matrimony because he did not wish to "reduce a woman to slavery," she added "there is no slave after all like a wife."[9]

Significantly, Southern homes were known to run smoothly without mistresses. Widowers and bachelors lived comfortably under the care of a black steward or housekeeper. Except as mother of legal heirs, the Southern lady could always be replaced by black surrogates. But even if she proved herself capable of managing the entire estate during her husband's absence—as, for instance, many did during the Civil War—the plantation mistress rarely enjoyed the executive power of an Abigail Adams. Southern gentlemen did not feel comfortable with helpmeets; they wished to be in complete control. Therefore, wives preserved their legendary mystique by cultivating the illusion that they needed masculine guidance and protection. This mystique very often masked a profound confusion and frustration regarding a woman's self-worth and her role in her own household.

The institution of slavery had some even more subtle repercussions for the Southern lady within her own home. She was invariably brought up strictly and morally, but she was expected to run her household as if unconscious of the separate code of ethics—often notably the opposite of strict and moral—that governed her husband's relations with his slaves. Writes Mary Chesnut, "There are certain subjects pure-minded ladies never touch upon, even in their thoughts." Elsewhere, she was more specific:

> Note the glaring inconsistencies of life. . . . Bad books are not allowed house room, except in the library under lock and key, the key in the Master's pocket; but bad women, if they are not white, or serve in a menial capacity, may swarm the house unmolested; the ostrich game is thought a Christian act.[10]

Thus, a woman learned early to deny the meaning of what she saw in her own home and to suppress her thoughts, just as she learned as a girl to accept her mother's morality instead of her father's. If the Southern matron could not really be "as nearly as possible holy in thought, word and deed," she gave at least a very good appearance of being so. If she could see, she pretended blindness, silently agreeing to play the "ostrich game."

White Southern gentlemen and ladies, although they generally shared the space under one roof day and night, were in fact segregated from each other by misunderstanding and myth. Young men were kept separate from young girls from puberty onward. They learned physical closeness from their black nurses, whom they "knew" to be inferior to themselves. Their relationships with white women were based on a romantic reverence for the lady-mother. According to one white Southern woman's reminiscences, Southern men seemed to "regard her as some costly statue set in a niche to be admired and never taken down."[11] Again, such deference reflected a double standard that distinguished flesh-and-blood women of lowly rank from untouchable—unreal and thus untouchable—paragons.

This exalted notion of virginal womanhood had its roots in a chivalrous tradition that made no provision for real-life wives as partners and companions. Instead of learning to respect each individual woman on her own merits, gentlemen were encouraged to make an elaborate display of their solicitude for *all* ladies. The women, in turn, could allow themselves to believe that they were constantly being waited upon, but the knowledge that the opposite was true—that they were subservient to their husbands—must have haunted them at times.

Locked in a maze of contradictions, not unlike the slave, the Southern lady accomplished spectacular feats of self-deception and role playing. To this day she is the model for ladies playing the ostrich game and for ladies who like to be admired as lovely statues alone. But our society is finally beginning to acknowledge that the stereotype of this overfeminized, sexually repressed creature was not forged by prudish women too romantic and silly to wish for self-fulfillment. Rather, we see now that the image was the creation of a culture that applied the feudal ideals of the past to a slave-based economy. Sir Walter Scott's romantic novels were Southern bestsellers. Here the medieval setting allowed lords and ladies to play their chivalrous games, but the Civil War jolted Southern society out of its fantasy. Even before the plantation culture was challenged on moral grounds and the economy became obsolete, it was the woman—household manager, wife and mother—who bore the brunt of the conflicting social codes.

On the bottom of the social ladder there seems to have been more room for sexual equality than on the top. In startling contrast to the Southern Lady on her precarious pedestal stood the free Black woman of the South. Suzanne Lebsock's revealing demographic description of nineteenth-century Petersburg suggests that the most autonomous women of that era may have been Black. The fact that this autonomy was due to extreme racism and poverty makes this peculiar phenomenon even more significant for the antebellum South as well as for the future development of a work-oriented woman culture. Free Blacks made up a third of the town's free population. Together with the slaves they even outnumbered the whites. Black women headed more households than white women and constituted almost half of the free workers. Ironically it was possible for a Black woman to own her mate, although she could not marry him. Occasionally a cautious woman waited several years before emancipating her slave. One Martha Scott stipulated in her deed of emancipation that her estranged mate had to leave the state, because he had threatened to burn her house. Yet a Black

2. Anonymous lady, Civil War period. Reproduced through the courtesy of The Bancroft Library, University of California, Berkeley CA 94720.

3. Mother and daughter, Civil War period. Bancroft Library daguerreotype. Reproduced through the courtesy of The Bancroft Library, University of California, Berkeley CA 94720.

woman's liberation from male dominance and her comparatively high rate of employment was but a symptom of oppression. As Lepsock points out:

> What we can see are two features of free black life that look positive through the lens of feminist hindsight. First, among those free blacks who did manage to acquire property, a high proportion were women. And second, for free black women it was not unusual to refrain from marriage, thereby retaining their legal autonomy.[12]

The Eastern Lady

Since the beginning of civilization, the aristocratic lady lived within a social network of amazing complexity. Her prestige—in fact, her very identity—derived from daily interaction with men and women who served and entertained her and whom she in turn served and entertained. The "best-society" that thrived in the eastern urban centers of the United States in the early 1800s functioned as such a network for the ladies within it. Its demands and obligations, prescribed by an age-old etiquette, defined the status of these women and filled their daily schedules with meetings, entertainments, and reciprocal social calls that were imitated by the middle class.

Not unlike modern critics of domesticity, the socially active British ladies deplored the restrictive conditions of the American middle-class home. Generalizing from her experiences as a visitor, Frances Trollope, in *Domestic Manners of Americans* (1832), refers condescendingly to "the lamentable insignificance of the American women." As an example, she portrays a Philadelphia lady who leads the typical life of respectability without influence. The figure she describes is a mere shadow of the active managerial wife in Abigail Adams's mode of 40 years earlier. Sadly, she is also the gloomy precursor of the suburban wife of the 1950s and 1960s.

> Let me be permitted to describe the day of a Philadelphia lady of the first class [writes Trollope], the wife of a senator and a lawyer in the highest repute and practice. She has a very handsome house, with white marble steps and doorposts, and a delicate silver knocker and door-handle; she has very handsome drawingrooms, very handsomely furnished . . . she is always very handsomely dressed; and moreover, she is very handsome herself . . . and her first hour is spent in the scrupulously nice arrangement of her dress; she descends to her parlour neat, still, and silent; her breakfast is brought in by her free black footman; she eats her fried ham and her salt fish, and drinks her coffee in silence, while her husband reads one newspaper, and puts another under his elbow; and then, perhaps, she washes the cups and saucers. Her carriage is ordered at eleven; till that hour she is employed at the pastry room, her snow-white apron protecting her mouse-colored silk. Twenty min-

utes before her carriage should appear, she retires to her chamber, as she calls it, shakes, and folds up her still snow-white apron, smooths her rich dress, and with nice care, sets on her elegant bonnet, and all the handsome et cetera; then walks down stairs, just at the moment that her free black coachman announces to her free black footman that the carriage waits. She steps into it, and gives the word, "Drive to the Dorcas Society. . . . " This lasts till three, when the carriage again appears, and the lady and her basket return home; she mounts to her chamber, carefully sets aside her bonnet and its appurtenances, puts on her scalloped black silk apron, walks into the kitchen to see that all is right, then into the parlour, where, having cast a careful glance over the table prepared for dinner, she sits down, work in hand, to await her spouse. He comes, shakes hands with her, spits, and dines. The conversation is not much, and ten minutes suffices for the dinner; fruit and toddy, the newspaper and work-bag succeed. In the evening the gentle-man, being a savant, goes to the Wister Society, and afterwards plays a snug rubber at the neighbor's. The lady receives at tea a young missionary and three members of the Dorcas Society—and so ends her day."[13]

A key difference between the eastern urban lady as described here and a wife Abigail Adams might have approved of was that the latter shared fully in the life of her husband even when he was away, while the city lady's orbit rarely crossed that of her mate. In fact, the husband in such a household as Trollope refers to entered and left his wife's world at his convenience while totally excluding her from his own. This distinction should ring a bell for the modern reader. In fact, almost all the details in Trollope's account might be found in a description of many a modern wife of a successful business or professional man.

Rather than servants, of course, the modern version of the lady has appliances to ease her work and give her more time. Rather than a strict system of etiquette constraining her behavior, she has to contend with the isolation and the lack of social opportunities characteristic of "bedroom communities." Instead of carriage rides, she takes frequent trips to the dentist, to shopping centers, to various recreational centers, ferrying herself and her children back and forth throughout the day—with the added dis-advantage of having to do her own driving. The Dorcas Society, of course, continues to thrive in one form or another, and often its present form is as pointless as that of the Victorian version, as implied by Trollope. But then as now women's supposedly insignificant voluntary contribution led to substantial social changes. The Dorcas Society was but one of many benevolent groups which originated at the beginning of the nineteenth century in answer to increasing urban poverty.[14] The enthusiasm with which American women took up organized charity reflected not merely the tra-ditional attitude of "lady bountiful," but a mixture of religious fervor and true commitment to social justice. The following letter by a minister's wife shows the attitude of Christian wife, charitable lady, and political activist that characterized religious women throughout the nineteenth century:

Philadelphia, February 28, 1819

Dear Friend:

It has been said by our enemies among the whites that it is doing us harm to set us free. We cannot, say they, maintain ourselves decently and respectably. Some of them must manage for us. To prove which, they bid us look around and see the many poor distressed objects of our color with which this city abounds, where we have every encouragement to do well for ourselves, overlooking the manner in which most of us have been brought up. Very many, in great families where they live on the best, dress in the finest and most fashionable clothing. Of course they carry these customs into their own families. They work hard, therefore they have money to spend, and must enjoy it in the way they have seen others do. And they are apt, too, to think they have a right to do so, as they have *worked* for it.

When I was first married I found myself precisely in this way. We had our parties and tea-drinkings, we must have the best wine and the best cake; our friends had it and we must give them the same they gave us, or be considered mean. But when it pleased the Lord to open my eyes, these things became a burden to me. I thought I would assist the poor if I had the means some people had, but I have no more than I want myself, how can *I* help the poor? Then it occurred to me that Christ lived a self-denying life, and I began to think how I might deny myself, take up the cross and follow him, when dress presented itself to my view. Now a pair of morocco shoes cost one dollar and 50 cts.; a pair of leather will do just as well, and I shall have 50 cts. for the poor. A fine muslin dress costs five dollars. I can buy a very good calico one for three, and have two dollars to spare. I reasoned in this manner till my dress was reduced to the standard which you see. I wore a plain straw bonnet with a white ribbon. The ribbon often soiled and required to be changed. I thought if I wore a plain silk one the strings will last as long as the bonnet, and here will be something saved.

These things were very trifling in themselves, but oh! the peace of mind and the liberty I gained by it more than doubly compensated me for the mortification I at first endured in seeing others who could not afford it so well, better dressed than myself. I could now go to meeting let the weather be as it would, I was not afraid of spoiling my shoes or any part of my dress. I no longer felt disturbed as to whether my appearance was better than my neighbor or not, and I always had something for the poor.

Now, dear friend, if you please, read this in one of your meetings and beg them to try my plan for one year, and I think they cannot fail to be much benefited by it.

> I remain your friend with much regard,
> Grace Douglass[15]

Grace Douglass was the wife of Robert Douglass, founder of the First African Presbyterian Church. A product of Black upward mobility, she was the granddaughter of a slave and the daughter of a prosperous baker who had started his business in George Washington's army. Educated in Philadelphia's public school for Black children, she also learned the millinery trade and operated her own store. This was not unusual for daughters from well-to-do Black homes. Although ladies of the Black middle-class were financially more independent than many of their white counterparts, they nevertheless adhered to the customary deference to father and husband. Like white educated women they formed literary societies in New York and Philadelphia for the elite and participated in the antislavery movement. The first Female Anti-Slavery Society was founded on February 22, 1822 in Salem, Massachusetts for "mutual improvement, and to promote the welfare of our color."[16] But higher social prestige for Black women was closely connected with the higher status of their husbands—the doctors, lawyers, and skilled craftsmen who dominated the political Black leadership in Boston, Philadelphia, and New York. Black newspapers of the period printed the typical "Counsel for Ladies" and "Duties of Wives" articles that appeared in the white press urging women to look after their households and husbands:

> Employ yourself in household affairs. Wait till your husband confides in you, and do not give your advice until he asks. Always appear flattered by the little he does for you. Never wound his vanity, not even in the most trifling instance. A wife may have more sense than her husband but she should never seem to know it.[17]

For the Black lady, the rules of white etiquette may already have intruded into the economic reality of her combined role of wife and wage earner. And as she became more involved in the civil rights struggle she was forced to choose between her own advancement and that of her race, between feminist allegiances with white women and family obligations toward Black men, between being a common laborer or a fine lady. Probably she seldom had the opportunity to make a conscious choice, but by force of circumstance learned to play every part when and where it mattered most. Therefore she would never find herself as isolated and useless as the housebound Victorian wife epitomized in this dreary portrait of a boardinghouse lady.

The Boardinghouse Lady

Traveling Englishwomen often stayed in boardinghouses, and there they encountered a breed of American wife almost unsung except in their accounts of their journeys. This was the boardinghouse wife, the woman who spent months on end waiting for her husband to return from a new job or a business trip. After the turn of the century, boardinghouses catered to enterprising young men in search of new opportunities and to families in search of housing in America's burgeoning cities. For unescorted ladies, they provided a more reputable family ambience than the raucous new hotels.

The married boardinghouse ladies lived as paying guests with no household responsibilities. The foreign observers who described these women considered them appallingly indolent and incompetent. It wasn't that Harriet Martineau and Marian Finch, a compatriot, objected to a life without household chores. Quite the contrary, they believed that women should have better things to do than housework. But they considered it shocking that in America the only outlets for a married woman free to do what she liked were gossiping, shopping, and fancy needlework. The fact is, American society did not endorse any pursuits for married women that did not promote the welfare of their immediate or extended families except charity or community work.

With no households to run or children to raise, these women were truly at a loss for something better to do. According to Marian Finch, even serious reading and study were considered "aimless and useless" pursuits for women.[18] Since white ladies were not allowed to actively assist their husbands in their careers or to follow their own professions, what possible reason could they have to read or study? Paid employment was considered suitable only for working-class women, and even then only those white married women worked who desparately needed the money.

The single, young textile workers who flocked to mill towns such as Waltham and Lowell in the 1830s also lived in boardinghouses. Run by married women with children who themselves worked part-time in the mills, these homes were strictly supervised to assure both respectability and good work habits. Among these girls, idleness was unheard of. The girls worked a 12–hour day and then went to evening lessons or Bible study. They also formed "improvement circles," where they wrote stories and poetry. In contrast to the boardinghouse ladies, the textile workers were an enterprising group in these early years. They wanted to work in the mills to escape the drudgery of farm life and to improve their chances for a good marriage. However, marriage was and remained the only opportunity every girl had to achieve the goal of all working girls—living like a lady.

Harriet Jane Hanson supported her three children by running a company boardinghouse. Her own childhood was typical for a poverty-stricken working-class family of the eighteenth century where children were farmed out to relatives or indentured to service. When she was widowed, she refused to let her children suffer a similar fate. Cooking, cleaning, and shopping for 45 boarders meant endless household labor with never enough cash to break even. The young children had to help out with housekeeping as well as breadwinning. Yet her daughter Harriet Hanson Robinson belonged to that first generation of mill girls who became self-made ladies in keeping with Catherine Beecher's democratic ideal.[19]

THE LADIES' MAGAZINES

The most influential vehicles for promoting the good life of ladies were the ladies' magazines. These immensely popular periodicals attempted the difficult task of explaining to the nineteenth-century woman how she could improve herself without offending the social codes of the day.

Ladies' magazines had their origins in what were called "family week-lies," periodicals such as *The Saturday Evening Post*. In the 1820s, when it became clear that women and men were beginning to have separate interests, publishers began to address directly what they discerned to be a new and distinct market. They operated on the premise that if women had separate concerns, a particular kind of brain, and functions in life altogether different from those of men, then they needed their own culture. In one sense, then, the forerunners of today's ladies' or "behavior" magazines, such as *Redbook* and *McCall's*, were a response to the new feminine ideals that were surfacing as the urban, middle-income family took precedence over the rural, colonial household of the previous century.

The ladies' magazines did more than passively reflect ongoing social changes, however. They actively reinforced and perpetuated the new ideals of womanhood. From a business angle alone, gearing their presses toward the ladies made good sense. The volume of magazine subscriptions sold depended on keeping readers in that special class, described in detail by magazines themselves, and making the most of their sexual apartheid. Women read more voraciously than men by that time, presumably because they had more time, and ladies, of course, had more time than working women.

Clothing, of course, was a chief topic in the ladies' magazines. The changing fashions of the day take on a symbolic significance as one riffles through their yellowing pages. By 1830, heavy petticoats had obscured the natural outlines that had shocked the fashion world of 1800. Analogously, the female mind had begun to lose the courage and initiative it showed earlier. True, more education for girls remained a topic of concern, but fashion and social convention, presumed to be the chief interests of married women, dominated.

Specific costumes were prescribed for staying at home and for going out; for mourning, riding, traveling, and entertaining; for spring, summer, fall, and winter; for early morning, midmorning, afternoon, and evening.

By the 1850s, the clothes the American lady was permitted to wear afforded her about as much freedom to move as bound feet allowed the Chinese lady. Thus, she was imprisoned mentally by the rigid dictates of etiquette and physically by whalebone, laces, and crinolines and the pound after pound of heavy cloth that made up the fashions of the day. Living up to the ideal of the "perfect lady," constantly reinvented and described by the magazines, was a major occupation of upwardly mobile Victorian women, and, indeed, with sewing, embroidering, and crocheting women had their work cut out for them just trying to stay in fashion.

But fashion news and sewing instructions were only one aspect of the ladies' magazines. Under the guise of enhancing the self-image of women, these immensely popular periodicals subtly manipulated the minds of their readers by deluging them with romantic fiction and myth-making articles. These pieces promoted with evangelical fervor such beliefs as, men think but women feel, and men's strength and virtue lay in their brains but women's lie in their beauty and morality. Above all, the magazines advanced the views that women who please their men are good, women who don't please their men are failures, and that success for women lies first in hitching their wagons to the right horse and then in being "studious in the happiness of others."

These messages were *always* implicit, though at times the explicit message seemed to contradict them. It was the implicit material that carried the clout. Thus, a Victorian writer might actually advocate education and a wider scope of action for women while simultaneously pointing a disapproving finger at the misguided heroine who allowed her own selfish interests to distract her from making her husband and children happy. In this way, Victorian journalists injected such a strong measure of guilt into the bloodstream of the American housewife that the effects are still being felt. Every issue of every ladies' journal featured a story of an ignorant or careless young wife who had to learn to please a kindly, critical husband. If she did not learn her lesson—and she usually did not—she faced the terrible certainty of losing her husband through alcoholism or depravity and demoralizing or ruining her whole family.

More popular still was the young and beautiful, but spoiled, young heroine, "*the daughter of one of our merchant princes*, the owner of that beautiful and aristocratic mansion. *A proud, supercilious beauty* she is; the idol of doting parents, *whose foolish over-indulgence* from her earliest childhood, has rendered her now, in her eighteenth year, a selfish, imperious being, *who cares for naught save the gratification of her own desires, unmindful whose convenience, or even happiness, was overthrown in the accomplishment of her purposes*,"[20] her purpose being to turn into a lady with noblesse oblige and into a loving wife and mother.

In keeping with the idea that women's sphere of interest was totally distinct from men's was the belief, also reinforced by the magazines, that women's power remained totally distinct from men's power. To have any effect at all in the world, women had to make use of the gift that God had bestowed on them alone: physical weakness and grace. The magazines explained that by exercising her moral strength a woman could turn her weakness to advantages. Since it was her very inferiority that assured her security—by confirming men's superiority, which obligated them to look out for the lesser beings in their charge—this weakness had to be cultivated:

"In proportion as men are themselves superior, they are accessible to this appeal," explains the *Ladies' Vase: or Polite Manual for Young Ladies*, 1843. A really sensible woman feels her dependence; she does what she can, but she is conscious of inferiority and therefore grateful for support; she knows that she is the weaker vessel, and that, as such, she should receive honor.[21] In fact, conveying this inferiority by means of language, facial expressions, clothing styles, posture, and all other means of self-expression was high art form. It was to the refinement of this art that the ladies' magazines were devoted while still postulating the active materfamilias ideal.

"Weakness is strength" was not the only contradiction in the messages woven throughout the women's journals. Another contradiction had to do with the relationship of the "lady" concept and the democratic ideals on which the nation had been founded. One function of the ladies' magazines was to translate the undemocratic, feudal notions of nobility and noblesse oblige for the average American consumer. Thus, hardware-store owners became noble lords, and their wives were portrayed as mistress-protectresses, generously extending the mantle of charity to cooks, parlor maids, washerwomen, and the motley flock of trade and service people with whom they were forced to deal. Further, every American home had the potential to be made into a castle by a clever decorator. With the table properly set and the food properly served, every dinner could take on the glow of a noble occasion. Though these magazines kept ladies cloistered in a private world of wishful thinking and domestic bliss, one must remember that society at that time still permitted husbands to beat their wives and to squander their earnings, that mill girls worked for a dollar a week, that the sewing machine had not yet been invented, and that even fine homes lacked fresh running water and bathrooms. Like the fashion plates in *Godey's Lady's Book*, framed and hung on cottage walls, the word "lady" held the promise of upward mobility—or, better, upward nobility. Not unlike women of today, the American woman of yesteryear was assailed on all sides by conflicting messages: be virtuous; be pure; be desirable; be beautiful; be mother, wife, helpmeet; be trend setter and fashion plate; be thrifty, be judicious, be gracious, be charming.

Modern women might be tempted to consider themselves immune to the power of the nineteenth-century ladies' magazines in setting fashions and exacting conformity from their readers. They might even permit themselves to smile condescendingly at the gullibility of their Victorian sisters. But though the crinoline and whalebone have disappeared, the power of the images that shine up from the pages of modern women's glossies remains unabated. The modern lady is encouraged to move vigorously to her tennis dress and jogging suit, but never too far from home. And the clothes, the shoes, the lines of the brows, the color of the cheeks and lips—all must be just right, with the difference between ladies in fashion and ordinary women so subtle that even a finely tuned Victorian lady might be hard-pressed to distinguish between them.

In fact, the notion of upper-class nobility in general remains embedded in the modern magazines. True, fashions have changed and the women's and civil rights movements have had an undisputed effect on the lady as defined by mainstream American culture. Thus, on the cover of one trend-setting magazine, *Ladies' Home* appears in much smaller type than *Journal*. The glossy pictures show few baronial manors and only occasional portraits of ladies in great estates. The image of a perfect lady nowadays is a compilation of more subtle details. The women portrayed are almost impossibly well-groomed and conventionally beautiful. Their homes are perfectly co-ordinated and decorated. In fact, the whole world as viewed through the *Ladies' Home Journal* or *Vogue* is a place of wishful thinking in which ugliness is conquered with new slipcovers and new hairstyles, diseases are cured with diets, and drudgery is eliminated with dreams.

The modern American magazine lady is neither extravagantly elegant nor exclusively eccentric. Nevertheless, she belongs to a privileged, protected class. Isolated from all but domestic controversies, she follows the easy directions in the magazines for mending broken cups and broken marriages. And, like her Victorian counterpart, she escapes from anxiety and boredom by reading romantic fiction and glamorous "true stories," in which love and goodness win over greed and self-interest. To this very day, the ladies' magazines hold their readers by appealing to the hidden Victorian in them all—the one who craves beauty, sentiment, comfort, refinement, status, and respectability, in short, the dollhouse existence of the perfect lady and gentleman.

THE EDUCATION OF A LADY

In the early nineteenth century, as now, the ladies' magazines had their critics. But those literary writers who condemned the ladies' magazines for aiming their material at twelve-year-olds ignored the fact that for most girls schooling ended at about age fourteen. Women were treated as if they were charming adolescents who knew very little, and ordinarily this was the case. In keeping with the weakness-is-strength philosophy, females were viewed as needing protection from the knowledge of vulgar words and deeds, from mental strain, and from everything unpleasant and indelicate.

Ignorance in a young lady spoke charmingly for her innocence and reserve and for her virtuous character as long as she displayed beauty and breeding. A girl who could not communicate in correct English—and there were quite a few—was clearly an embarrassment in polite society, but so was a young woman who read too much and talked too well, or worse, who might show off publicly if allowed into lecture halls. Gentlemen pre-

ferred the unfinished woman, who could mature in marriage according to
their tastes. And, in keeping with this preference, women had performed
their domestic duties from the beginning of time without going to school.
In the eighteenth century, neither fathers nor educators, who were almost
exclusively clergymen, thought that ordinary women—or in fact anyone
but "true" gentlemen—needed to be educated. The pursuit of learning
was still a leisure activity and the world of learned men was a private club,
given to civilized conversation in the humanities and self-styled experimentation in the sciences.

Sex was not the only constraint on educational opportunity, however.
The time-honored system of segregating the rich from the poor, the white
from the Black, and the men from the women had flourished in early
America, especially in Virginia, where English aristocrats had established
the first private schools for boys. Only poor children went to coeducational
charity schools, and then only to acquire basic skills that would keep them
from poverty, crime, or other activities that might interfere with the public
good.

However in the post-Revolutionary era democratic idealists began ar-
guing for the right of the common man to an education, and in this context
the question of schooling the future wives of common men arose. While
the young lady of a rich family studied at home or went to a boarding
school to learn those skills necessary to perform the role of a gentleman's
wife, the middle-class girl benefitted from the continued growth of the
public education system during the nineteenth century. From the outset,
however, her right to any kind of education—public or private—above the
rudimentary level became a controversial subject. Tax-financed public education, available to all men and women, had to be justified with a practical
purpose. The purpose of education generally agreed upon was the one that
had served the Adamses generations before: making people useful to society.

For men education for utility meant job training. The demand for special
information increased as the nation moved toward industrialization, and
the curriculum designed to meet this need ultimately resulted in a new
white aristocracy, the professional class of our own day. As reflected by
the wives of this new, male-dominated elite, education of women often
meant making school at the higher level subordinate to marriage and motherhood. Many a college-educated wife has interrupted or diverted her
preparation for professional competence to comply with the demands of
husband and children. Thus, in spite of our success in developing a public-
education system to which girls and women have free access, the unfinished
woman still prevails, even in our best society. The question that nineteenth-
century parents asked so anxiously—How much education is right for our
daughters if they want to raise a family?—still elicits controversial answers.

One seeking information on what was considered an appropriate plan
for educating a girl at the beginning of the nineteenth century might read

"A Father's Inquiries Relative to the Education of Daughters," from the *New England Quarterly Magazine* (1802). This article explicitly identifies what men at the turn of the century thought women needed to know. The first requirements named are preparation for domestic duties. Music is recommended to the talented whose parents can afford the expense of instruction. Drawing and painting are allowed to be good occupations for leisure time and have the added advantage of contributing to the decor of the home. Furthermore, a young lady finding herself in straitened circumstances might use such skills to make her living. Novel reading is considered an acceptable activity as long as the daughter does not exceed the quota of one novel in six months and reads each one two or three times in order to understand the moral lessons implied. First among the recommended authors is Samuel Richardson, the most widely read novelist of the time, followed by Goldsmith, specifically, *The Vicar of Wakefield*. By the time she is 18, the daughter should have read Shakespeare, Pope, Milton, and Gisborne's *Duties of the Female Sex*, as well as suitable female biographies and the most important sermons of the past and present clergy.[22]

Considering that just a few years before this article appeared the Bible had been the only book considered fit for female consumption, this reading list reflected a new confidence in women's intellectual prowess. In spite of dangerous evidence that too much learning for females contributed to difficulties in conception and even to infertility, liberal educators gradually convinced the more progressive nineteenth-century parents that ladies actually needed a "great depth of judgment" that could only be attained through education, and if properly directed could prevent ladies from becoming domestic slaves or learned slatterns—"two extremes . . . disgusting to a man of sensibility."[23]

By the mid-nineteenth century, much progress had been made. Women began the century by overcoming the illiteracy hitherto characteristic of their sex, and eventually they gained access to the elysian fields of higher learning in the form of the ladies' academies cropping up across the nation. But though the gains were indisputable, the motivation behind them was still questionable. Learning for learning's sake was hardly the theme of the trend toward greater educational opportunities for future housewives.

The difficulty with the motivations shaping women's education was clearly demonstrated in the work of Emma Hart Willard (1787–1870), who founded the first women's preparatory school and was one of the earliest pioneers for women's colleges. Willard developed a magic formula for convincing even the most reticent reactionaries that women ought to be allowed to go to college. Higher education, she argued, met the purpose served by American education in general, that of producing right-minded citizens who would be useful to society. "The character of children," she argued, "will be formed by their mothers and it is through the mothers that the government can control the character of its future citizen."[24] Thus, if ladies weren't worth educating in themselves, surely they could do with some instruction as mothers participating in the solemn duty of shaping the nation's future. This argument held great sway with both parents and educators, and as the century progressed education became a certificate of respectability for the middle-class girl, with even more desirability than a dowry.

Obviously, people convinced of the need for educating women on these terms would have a fairly strict idea of what ought to be taught to the future mothers of America. With the exception of a few academies (the famous Franklin Academy of Philadelphia and the Abbot Academy of Andover, Massachusetts), ladies' academies shaped the moral character rather than the intellect and prepared students for responsible gentility rather than for academic excellence. After all, women didn't have to know *facts* to raise respectable future citizens. The curricula of the first women's academies, then, were characterized by the traditional women's subjects: morality and religion, morally uplifting literature, and the domestic and ornamental arts. Such ladies' academies meticulously avoided competing with their masculine counterparts and provided no professional training whatsoever except teaching, which was considered useful for future mothers or for women who had no hopes of marrying. Clearly, the nation never stopped fearing that, given half a chance, women would abandon housewifery to pursue other interests, maybe to follow the example of Elizabeth Carter, a British author who at the age of 23 devoted herself to celibacy, snuff, and Greek.

With its concern for turning young ladies into good wives and mothers, the women's education movement in America began to smack strongly of the finishing school, modeled after the British institution of the upper classes. But as the economy of the nation shifted during the first decades of the nineteenth century, Americans began to take a rather critical look at their own aspirations to emulate the European aristocracy. In 1829, when the economy teetered on the brink of a depression, Lydia Maria Child (1802–1880), a housewife and well-known abolitionist writer, published a criticism of women's education that gained wide currency. The critique appeared in her book *The American Frugal Housewife* (1829), which by 1850 had run for 32 editions. Although basically a cookbook, it was free with its editorial comments and blamed foolish housewives for indulging in the wasteful habits of the wealthy, who in turn copied the caprices of European aristocrats. Such foolishness, Child argued, resulted from the misguided education of young ladies, who acquired "the elements of a thousand sciences, without being thoroughly acquainted with any." Generally a supporter of feminist causes, she advocated "the formation of quiet, domestic habits" and the return to old-time home management.[25]

The *American Magazine* of 1841 followed suit with this advice:

Be a woman ever so wealthy, in this country, she must know how to cook her food, to wash and iron her clothes and those of her family, to nurse her children and teach her daughters to do the same. The daughter early in life becomes a wife and mother; retires from the world, to her own peculiar empire—her home. The son, if not thoroughly educated for his calling, at first, is compelled by circumstances, by the world, all around him—by rivals in business—by his own shame and emulation, to educate himself. Indeed, he is always learning something useful for him to know. It is not so with the daughter, who must learn early in life or never.[26]

Thus, by the 1840s, the trend toward higher education for women shifted. A new pressure was set for women to look to their homes and act sensibly in keeping with the old values—those associated with cleaning, cooking, laundering, and serving and with making their people happy and healthy in the tradition of the "compleat" housewife.

The Educated Lady

Not surprisingly, educated young ladies often married educated gentlemen who, however, earned little money despite their learning. These were the clergymen, the professors, and the lawyers who appreciated a well-read wife but could not keep her in the style offered by rich businessmen. In such households, the full responsibility for running the home devolved onto the women. Household matters, like childbirth, remained an exclusively female concern. Educated lady-housewives did the accounts, planned the menus, nursed their families. With or without housekeepers, they managed a myriad of tasks with no help and little sympathy from their educated husbands. Not until these tasks were completed did the more enterprising of them go off to prepare a lecture or work on a book. Like their less-educated sisters, the wives of ordinary working men, these ladies turned to teaching or writing in order to supplement the meager income of their husbands.[27] Or, as in the case of Sarah Hale (1788–1879), the editor of *Godey's Lady's Book*, they undertook a career because they had to support their children alone.

Sarah, like many of her contemporaries, had never gone to school, but learned enough Latin and mathematics from her older brother at Dartmouth to open a grade school to support herself until she married. She continued her education during her nine-year marriage to lawyer David Hale, who taught her French, botany, mineralogy, and geology. When she found herself widowed and responsible for five children under eight, she wrote the obligatory novel—teaching offered not enough income for family breadwinners. Upon request by a publisher she founded in 1828 the first women's magazine and later became the editor of *Godey's Lady's Book*, the most widely read ladies' magazine of the nineteenth century until it was overshadowed by the *Ladies' Home Journal*. That Sarah Hale could advocate the education of women and the participation of women in the medical and teaching professions while simultaneously endorsing woman's total involvement in a domestic career seems inconsistent only from the modern perspective.

Sarah had been happily married and wished the same for her readers, but both before and after her marriage she had experienced poverty. Basing her ideas on her own experience, she wanted more than an accidental education for women, one which would open respectable, well-paid jobs to them. Elizabeth Blackwell, America's first woman physician who had been forced to go to Europe to study medicine, became Sarah Hale's cause célèbre. And by 1841, Hale was able to boast that her magazine was edited soley by women.

Still, like many a magazine editor before and after her, Sarah yielded to the demands of her time and gave the readers of *Godey's Lady's Book* what they wanted most: encouragement for wives in distress, household tips, fashion plates, and fashion news from Queen Victoria's tea parties, plus an endless flow of sentimental stories, poems, and engravings that warmed the heart and offered the household woman an hour's escape from housekeeping.

For better or worse, Sarah Hale shaped the behavior of three generations of women. In the words of Helen Woodward, former advertising executive for *Woman's Home Companion* and *McCall's, Godey's Lady's Book* "became the mother of all the giant women's magazines which have changed and are still changing the lives of our people.[28]

Imitation Lady

To the dismay of frugal daughters of the American Revolution, the wives of the newly rich devoted themselves not to charity and family, but to the trappings of the British "lady." Society columns filled the papers with news about grocers' wives who had returned from Europe to exhibit their Parisian gowns at the local ball. Footmen in livery opened the doors to republican men and women who had changed their names from Fitz to Wellington, from Coon to Calhoun, and from Coker to Byron.[29]

Foreign travel established a lady's prestige. The more she traveled, the closer she could get to the roots of her newly acquired culture. But foreign birth was another matter. Of the 23 million Americans living in 1850, three million were foreign born, and fully half of these were refugees from the Irish potato famine. Along with free Blacks and Southern slaves, these immigrants were the servants for those emulating the old feudal way of life. With luck, ingenuity, and a fair complexion, a small percentage of these poor people managed to jump over the gap, contributing to a con-

tinuous shuffle from rags to riches. For the majority, however, the jump
was possible only in the American dream.

The unfortunate housewife in the average family who was attempting to
live out her upper-class fantasies inevitably made some bloopers. In 1852,
*The American Ladies' and Gentlemen's Manual of Elegance, Fashion, and
True Politeness*,[30] which in its British form had already gone through 22
editions, took a pragmatic approach to the difficulties of learning proper
behavior. The manual discouraged the American reader from emulating
the manners of established European society. Instead, the handbook suggested that a commonsense approach, rather than strict adherence to the
old rules, might be more appropriate in elevating the masses in the New
World. Thus, American wives were instructed to face the possibility that
their husbands might want to spit, new ideals or no new ideals, and that
therefore the women ought to consider incorporating decorative spittoons
into the household decor. The women were strictly warned not to indulge
themselves, since chewing and snuffing were offensive habits in polite society. The author of the handbook also saw fit to warn readers against
using the tablecloth to dab the lips instead of the napkin, eating in a noisy
manner, dropping food, or putting large pieces in the mouth with a knife.
Ladies were instructed not to eat with their gloves on, not to pick their
teeth at the table, not to gargle their water, and not to scold other people's
servants.

As styles of behavior became more refined, the physical house grew
more complex and more heavily laden with social significance. With guests
"calling" upon the lady on formal and informal occasions, her domestic
decor became more important. The art of acquiring and displaying possessions began to distinguish the lady from the housekeeper, who merely
took care of them, and from the social climber, who spent her husband's
fortune on ostentatious furniture. An enduring example of the last was
Mrs. Potiphar, created by the satiric pen of George William Curtis. Her
hardworking captain of industry would have preferred the simple life, but
Mrs. Potiphar had turned her home into a warehouse. "My drawing-rooms
strongly resemble the ware house of an ideal cabinet-maker," complains
Mr. Potiphar.

> Every whim of table—every caprice of chair and sofa, is satisfied in those
> rooms. . . . There are lofty chairs, like the thrones of archbishops in Gothic
> cathedrals, standing by the side of the elaborately gilded frames of mirrors.
> Marble statues of Venus and Apollo support my mantels, upon which 'or
> molu' Louis Quatorze clocks ring the hours. . . . They are there, because my
> house was large and I was large and I was able to buy them.[31]

It was this first tide of consumerism that prompted Catherine Beecher
and Harriet Beecher Stowe to write their manifesto on behalf of the real

American lady, "a woman of education, cultivation, and refinement...
who without any material additions or changes, would be recognized as a
lady."[32]

THE LADY WHO DOES HER OWN HOUSEWORK

With *A Treatise on Domestic Economy* (1842) Catherine Beecher took
a revolutionary stand on household affairs, inspiring housewives of humble
origin and modest means to turn away from aristocratic standards and to
rely on their own values in creating a democratic American home. As the
oldest daughter of Lyman Beecher's brood of eight, she had learned to
take care of a large household with a minimum of outside help. Her mother,
"a compleat housewife" and helpmeet of the eighteenth-century mold, had
"carded and spun the cotton, hired it wove, cut and sewed it to fit the
parlor" and painted it later with oil paints that she prepared from a recipe
in her encyclopedia. If Americans had come to think that the woman who
cooks and washes and sweeps is not a lady and "that the drudgery of
the kitchen is dirty," wrote Catherine, they felt this way because such
work was generally done "by vulgar people, and in a vulgar way." But if
ladies would do the housework in the ladylike—that is, intelligent and
creative—style, the vulgar associations would disappear from the kitchen
scenario.[33]

Harriet Hanson Robinson, who prided herself on being "a good poor
man's wife," was precisely the type of cultivated woman Catherine Beecher
had in mind when she wrote her *Treatise*. The Beecher idea that a lady
could do her own housework reassured Mrs. Robinson about her slow
progress from mill girl to middle-class respectability. Besides her mother's
helping hand and her own ingenuity, her resources were sparse. Self-ed-
ucated and married to a struggling newspaper editor, she had all the ambition of keeping a fine home on a limited bugdet. Even when she could
finally afford a servant, she had little patience with the various Bridgets
she engaged who "seemed to have all the faults, and none of the virtues
of help."[34] Like many fastidious housewives then and over the next generations, she found it difficult to train the young girls who showed little
aptitude and less enthusiasm for the demanding work at $1.00 a week. One
Julia, an Irish girl, actually went on strike, demanding twice the amount,
and was dismissed. William Robinson only earned $30.00 a week himself.
Disgusted with the daughters of Erin, Mrs. Robinson turned to the Black
minister's wife, who ran an agency for colored servants, but none was
available. Finally Mrs. Robinson agreed with the Beecher theory that it
was nobler to do the housework yourself rather than hire somebody else
to do it. An article entitled "The Lady Who Does Her Own Work" had
appeared in *The Atlantic Monthly* (June, 1864) under the name of Harriet
Beecher Stowe, who repeated her sister Catherine's message. Mrs. Rob-

inson had read it as part of a series entitled "The House and Home Papers" that was later incorporated in *The American Woman's Home* (1869).[35]

Harriet Robinson was so impressed by the advice that mothers should train their own daughters in housekeeping skills that for 25 cents a week she immediately hired her own two girls to help wash the dishes and set the table. Her diary clearly shows her own grasp of accomplishment at what she was doing. Her contribution mattered. Her entries about washing windows, dusting, mending, carpeting, and the annual spring cleaning read like a case study for Catherine Beecher's *Treatise*.

This book, later enlarged as *The American Woman's Home* (1869) with Harriet Beecher Stowe as co-author, represented a prophetic glance into the future. It predicted quite accurately a time when even ladies would have to do all the housework themselves. But it also predicted that manual labor in America would eventually be respected as noble work and that drudgery would disappear from housework altogether. These notions turned out to be wishful thinking. Like many subsequent books on this subject, *A Treatise on Domestic Economy* tried to reconcile the housewife to her menial role by promising her better working conditions and more recognition for her contributions. In her effort to upgrade housework Catherine Beecher was successful, since, at least for the standards of her own time, she gave housework back the luster of craftsmanship that it had lost since Abigail Adams's time. In its intentional effort to control the physical environment of the private family, the book marked the arrival of home economics as a field of study.

Previously, cookbooks had seldom bothered with exact measurements, and household advice consisted of random hints on moral behavior and etiquette. Even Lydia Child's *Frugal Housewife*, published in 1829, lacked Catherine Beecher's methodical how-to approach and wide scope, characteristics that used to be found in male-oriented encyclopedias alone. The author offered specific information about slop pails, tin tubs, laundry, dishwashing procedures, carpet cleaning, and bedmaking. From her own experience in taking over the housekeeping for her widowed father and eight younger siblings at the age of 16, she clearly understood the dirty realities of a house that had no running water or modern plumbing.

As chief instigator of the movement to train female teachers for the Western frontier, she wrote the book both for the pioneering woman who had to fall back on the skills of colonial times, and for the artistically or socially inclined lady. In fact, the author addressed the cultural differences inherent in the American readership. Further, she recognized and acknowledged the complex interrelationships among home and family care, wife- and motherhood, physical and emotional welfare, and private and public action. This recognition, as with many aspects of both Beecher sisters' thinking, evoked the spirit of Abigail Adams, who indeed had belonged to their own mother's generation. It also reflected that genera-

4. Illustrated page from Catherine Beecher, *The American Woman's Home*
(Boston: H. A. Brown, 1869).

tion's striving for public recognition of the housewife. Like these post-Revolutionary ladies, Catherine Beecher focused on the domestic realm, but as the first writer ever to assess housework in terms of time and energy conservation, hers was a radical rather than a reactionary view. She remembered, after all, that her mother had died of consumption—which in the case of many women was another term for exhaustion—after the birth of her ninth child. Catherine's expression of interest in the housewife's health was the first practical step toward establishing standards of health and hygiene nationwide.

Nevertheless, much of the Beecher sisters' thinking was rooted in the eighteenth century, when hard labor, performed cooperatively but with clear role distinctions, was necessary for survival. From the modern political perspective, their ideals were diametrically opposed to those of the women's rights movement, which began at this crucial time. Yet initially both camps set out to affirm women's right to education and to an active role in society at large. One side—represented by the Beechers—clung to a mystical faith in woman's spiritual superiorty and the belief in a natural division of labor between the sexes. The other—whose standard bearer was Elizabeth Cady Stanton—propounded the equal distribution of rights and responsibilities and the deliverance of women from male oppression. As today, both sides evolved their positions from their personal experiences as daughters, wives, and mothers. As today, the conflict between public recognition and private responsibility, between economic reward and personal satisfaction, between working for wages and working for love took its toll on women's health and happiness.[36] For the Victorian period these conflicts created new images of the American housewife: *saints and sufferers*.

NOTES

1. Catherine Beecher, *A Treatise on Domestic Economy* (Harper, 1842), p. 62. It defended American ladies against British critics such as Martineau and Trollope and was reprinted almost every year for two decades.

2. Natalie J. Sokoloff, *Between Money and Love: The Dialectics of Women's Home and Market Work* (Praeger, 1980), pp. 6–7.

3. Daniel Wise, *The Young Lady's Counsellor; or, Outlines and Illustrations of the Sphere, the Duties and the Dangers of Young Women* (New York: Lane & Scott, 1852), p. 243.

4. The family as promoter of consumer-oriented upward mobility is the basis of the Marxist-feminist theory. For a summary see Rayana Rapp, "Family and Class in Contemporary America: Notes toward an Understanding of Ideology," in Thorne et al., *Rethinking the Family*, pp. 168–187. Rapp sees social class as a process "by which different social relations to the means of production are inherited and reproduced under capitalism." Mary P. Ryan's history *Womanhood in America* traces the connection between industrial capitalism and the development of a "women's sphere" within the privileged private household from the nineteenth century

to the present. For a critique of Marxist feminism see Michele Barrett, *Women's Oppression Today: Problems in Marxist Feminist Analysis* (London: N[ew] L[eft] B[ooks], 1980), chapter 6.

5. Harriet Martineau, *Retrospect of Western Travel* (London, 1844), in K. M. Jones, *The Plantation South* (Indianapolis, 1957), pp. 112–118. For a comparison with a slave's point of view see Dorothy Sterling, *We Are Your Sisters: Black Women in the Nineteenth Century* (New York: W. W. Norton, 1984), pp. 6–12.

6. Reference to Nomini plantation in Ch. Spruill, *Women in the Southern Colonies* (Chapel Hill: Univ. of North Carolina Press, 1969), p. 66.

7. Sterling, *We Are Your Sisters*, p. 15.

8. Ibid.

9. Mary Boykin Chesnut, *A Diary from Dixie*, ed. Isabella Martin and Myrta Lockett Avary (Gloucester, Mass.: P. Smith, 1961), pp. 13, 51.

10. Ibid., p. 46.

11. L. M. Burwell, *A Girl's Life in Virginia before the War* (New York: F. A. Stokes, 1896), in Jones, *The Plantation South*, pp. 60–61.

12. Suzanne Lebsock, *The Free Women of Petersburg* (New York: W. W. Norton, 1984), p. 103.

13. Frances Trollope, *Domestic Manners of the Americans*, ed. Donald Smalley (New York: Knopf, 1949), pp. 281–282.

14. Chapter III deals further with reformers and religion, Chapter IV with charity and social work. See also Nancy F. Cott, *The Bonds of Womanhood*, chapter 4, pp. 135–136, for a list of literary and charitable societies of this period. Nancy Hewitt, *Women's Activism and Social Change, Rochester, N.Y., 1822–1872* (Cornell University Press, 1984), shows that women activists did a lot of housework.

15. William T. Catto, *A Semi-Centenary Discourse, delivered in The First African Presbyterian Church, Philadelphia, On the Fourth Sabbath of May, 1857: With a History of the Church*... (Philadelphia: J. M. Wilson, 1857), pp. 36–37.

16. Sterling, We Are Your Sisters, p. 113.

17. Ibid., p. 220, quote from *Colored Americans* (Sept. 8, 1838). According to Sterling this type of article disappeared in the 1840s.

18. Marianne Finch, *An Englishwoman's Experience in America* (New York: Negro Univ. Press, 1969), p. 80.

19. See pp. 75–76 for more information about Harriet Hanson Robinson.

20. Josephine Pollard, "Emilie Woodward," *The Ladies' Wreath*, vol. 23, no. 3 (January, 1861), p. 61.

21. *Ladies' Vase: or, Polite Manual for Young Ladies, Original and Selected by an American Lady* (Lowell, Mass.: N. L. Dayton, 1843), p. 56.

22. "A Father's Inquiries Relative to the Education of Daughters," *New England Quarterly Magazine*, vol. 3 (February, 1802), pp. 57–58.

23. M. Pennington, "Memoirs of the Life of Mrs. Elizabeth Carter," *Boston Review*, vol. 9 (Sept., 1810), pp. 194–195.

24. Quoted by Isabel Bevier, *Home Economics in Education* (Philadelphia: Lippincott, 1928), p. 79.

25. Lydia Maria Child, *The American Frugal Housewife*, 32d ed. (New York: S. S. & W. Wood, 1850), pp. 92–93.

26. "The Daughter," *American Magazine and Repository of Useful Literature*,

vol. 1 (July-December, 1841), p. 179. For more information on women's education see Cott, *The Bonds of Womanhood*, pp. 101–125.

27. Harriet Beecher Stowe, who is discussed in chapter III, belonged to this category.

28. Helen Woodward, *The Lady Persuaders* (New York: Obolonsky, 1960), p. 14.

29. Thomas C. Grattan, *Civilized America* (London: Bradbury and Evans, 1859), p. 324.

30. Day, Charles William *The American Ladies' and Gentlemen's Manual of Elegance, Fashion, and True Politeness* (Rochester, N.Y.: Wanger, Beardsley, 1852).

31. George William Curtis, *The Potiphar Papers* (New York: Putnam, 1853), pp. 117–118.

32. Catherine E. Beecher and Harriet Beecher Stowe, *The American Woman's Home* (New York: J. B. Ford, 1869), p. 307.

33. Catherine E. Beecher, *A Treatise on Domestic Economy* (1858), p. 62.

34. Bushman, "*A Good Poor Man's Wife*," p. 109.

35. Ibid., pp. 111–115.

36. For a detailed analysis of "The Woman Question" see Elizabeth K. Helsinger, et al., *The Woman Question: Society and Literature in Britain and America, 1837–1883*, 3 vols. (New York: Garland, 1983). Vol. 1: *Defining Voices*, pp. 63–76, includes a discussion of Queen Victoria's point of view. Pivotal for this and the next chapter is Kathryn Sklar, *Catherine Beecher: A Study in American Domesticity* (New Haven, Conn.: Yale University Press, 1973).

3

Saints and Sufferers, 1860–1900

> She comprehends all, she balances and arranges all.... Everybody in her sphere breathes easy, feels free; and the driest twig begins in her sunshine to put out buds and blossoms. So quiet are her operations and movements that none sees that it is she who holds all things in harmony; only alas, when she is gone, how many things suddenly appear disordered, inharmonious, neglected! All these threads have been smilingly held in her weak hand. Alas, if that is no longer there!
> —Harriet Beecher Stowe, 1896[1]

The perfect lady, fashionably frail, was never outmoded in the nineteenth century. But she was criticized for leading an unhealthy, unproductive life that rendered her unfit for the responsibilities of motherhood. Since God had endowed her sex with a delicate body, she was expected to make the most of her natural gift for leading a virtuous, inspirational life. For the sake of her husband and children she was to keep up her limited strength, not waste it on other pursuits, no matter how worthy they might be.

The death of a young wife and mother was the greatest calamity that could befall a nineteenth-century family. In the mid-1860s, when early death from disease was much more likely to occur than it is now, the loss of a mother inspired what amounted to a dead-mother cult. So unbearable was the loss, and so traumatic the family's adjustment to the inevitable replacement of the deceased, that the dead woman, in memory, was converted into a saint.

The idea of wifely sainthood gained ever more credence as housewives found themselves increasingly isolated from the male-operated world. Cloistered behind her velvet curtains, the frail and saintly wife was the nineteenth-century version of the feminine mystique. The family, the press, the experts, the reformers worried about the women of the 1850s and 1860s. Theories about their behavior, their mysterious bodies, their intense emotions, and most importantly their influence on the mental and physical health of children kept writers and advice columnists as busy as a hundred years later in the 1950s and 1960s. Even in mid-nineteenth century, women were acting on the realization that wife- and motherhood represented their last remaining stronghold over men. The more cut off they felt from the outside world and the more they feared to step out of their designated sphere, the more they craved and resented the power of the outside world that lured the husband away from home.

From the moment that American society accepted the cult of domesticity and the Beechers' argument that women inhabit a separate sphere, the veneration and idealization of motherhood followed naturally.

Roxana Beecher, mother of Catherine and Harriet Beecher, whose words open this chapter, died when her children were young. After her death, the Beecher children idealized Roxana's memory almost the point of canonization. As noted in the preceding chapter, Catherine's memory of her mother inspired her, in her treatise on domesticity, to call for a revival of the past when mothers improved the quality of life with ingenuity and skill. For Catherine, the family home was the training ground of future citizens and the family the moral backbone of the country. For Harriet, however, the "compleat housewife" of the earlier novels gradually took on the spiritual, ethereal qualities of the wifely saint, whose home was "the nearest image of heaven."

A brother to Catherine and Harriet, the famous preacher Henry Ward Beecher was only three years old when Roxana died. He grew up to foster a powerful, new mother-oriented theology (as opposed to the father-oriented Calvinism that prevailed until then), where God's love for humankind resembled a mother's love for her children. As Ann Douglas has pointed out in *The Feminization of American Culture* (1977), clergymen and women of the era formed a peculiar alliance as "champions of sensibility." They shared the same ideals about love and self-sacrifice, and these ideals bolstered them against the dehumanizing effects of masculine crudity and industrial greed.[2]

The Beechers were more prolific than most families in creating enduring myths, and they certainly demonstrated American attitudes more dramatically than most other people. Still, their sentiments reflected, as well as contributed to, a general tendency toward dead-mother worship and a new reverence for the saintly mother. These cultural developments both colored family life and affected American literature and religion. Literature in particular was "feminized" by the new focus on homely concerns and domestic tragedy. Soon this trend would be swept away by the waves of masculine realism that began with *Moby Dick* and lasted through *The Naked and the Dead*. But in 1860, it was the death of a young mother, not the noble victory of a man over his enemy, that inspired women and clergymen.

This trend of sentimentality was part of a general change in the quality of America's emotional life. The rational, stiff-upper-lip response to hardship and death considered acceptable in the previous century was giving way to free emotional expression. Instead of stoically accepting God's will, people were beginning to admit to the fear of death and to celebrate the memory of the deceased. Expressing emotion—by crying, laughing, exhibiting affection—came into fashion, even for men, and the effort to maintain decorum at all costs gave way to ritualized displays at funerals, weddings, and other family-oriented events. The home, in turn, became a sanctuary, a sharp contrast with the notions of home as service cooperative or display case. Nevertheless, it is important to note that these three alternative versions of the home coexisted in decades that followed. Like the different images of the wife, these conflicting visions made the job of homemaker increasingly complex and added to women's difficulty in defining the tasks that they were expected to accomplish.

What had appeared as a logical division of labor between husband and wife, with equal rights and opportunities for each, soon grew into a maze of contradictions and subterfuges where extreme ideals fostered deep disappointments and strong feelings of guilt. From our own perspective the Victorian age is wrapped in the mystery of hidden agendas and double meanings. Here the roots of our modern problems sprouted in the fetid soil of crowded cities, industrial blight, and capitalist corruption. In the land of the free, more and more people were oppressed. The solution to the problems of one group created more injustice for another. The idealization of one type of family contributed to the discrimination of another. By the same token the advancement of women within the boundaries of the home inhibited their progress in every undertaking outside the home. As a result they learned to disguise strength as weakness, selfish ambition as selfless sacrifice, and individual growth as family development. Rather than ask whether the family—particularly the male head of the household—oppressed daughters and wives while liberating sons and husbands, we might wonder how women thrived in spite of the odds and whether they were not indeed much stronger and freer than anybody including writers and historians have been allowed to believe. The debate among scholars, such as Degler and Barrett, who argue for marriage and motherhood as sources of power and pleasure, and those who perceive the family as capitalist and sexist means of entrapment can prove either case.[3] But in fairness to women's lasting contribution to the nation's health, education, and welfare one should evaluate their experience in light of the human as well as the political condition.

True, women were oppressed and often they knew why, but so were men. Women suffered from bad health, poverty, discrimination, and marital rifts, but so did men. Women's strength often grew out of political weakness, but does this make them less strong? Victorian women

searched for a separate peace at home, at church, in benevolent societies, and their "feminine" ways often led to humanitarian reforms. They
seldom engaged in open confrontation with their opponents, but were
nevertheless successful in breaking new ground. Some of them were called
saints only by those who knew them personally, while others achieved
historical recognition for their endeavors on behalf of man- and wom-
ankind. Many suffered from the personal and public consequences of what
they attempted to do. Some were not equipped to carry the double load
of family and public responsibility and some never reached the goal set
by their own expectations. The latter was the case with Harriet Beecher
Stowe.

THE SAINTS

Harriet Beecher Stowe

To the great surprise of the intellectual establishment, exclusively male
through the end of the eighteenth century, writing became the most lucrative profession of women. Women writers managed to bring America's
budding popular culture under the female influence. Between 1800 and
1860, at least twenty-four best sellers were written by women. Most were
directed toward other women, and could therefore be ignored by the literary critics of the time. One book, however, became the century's best-
selling novel and in so doing conquered a hitherto all-male territory: the
realm of political propaganda. Harriet Beecher Stowe's *Uncle Tom's Cabin*
(1852) was a superb piece of propaganda literature that heralded the power
of the female's pen. The book moved millions of readers against the in-
humanity of slavery. Further, it expressed the intense emotional involvement of Victorians with good and evil and their fervent belief in social
reform.

Harriet Beecher Stowe was a self-made woman, and her name became
a household word the world over, but ironically her reputation rested on
a book that reinforced the notion that weakness was strength. Its purpose
was to convince its readers that woman's mission in the world was to
exercise her inner, spiritual power over men, and that little Evas were the
guardian angels of the nation.

Harriet Beecher Stowe (1811–1896) is also an example of the female
activist encumbered by the conflict with traditional female responsibilities
of housework and child rearing. In 1850, shortly after the birth of her fifth
child, Harriet wrote the following to a friend:

> I was really glad for an excuse to lie in bed, for I was full tired, I can assure
> you. During this time I have employed my leisure hours in making up my
> engagements with newspaper editors. I have written more than anybody, or

I myself, would have thought. I have taught an hour a day in our school, and I have read two hours every evening to the children. . . . Yet I am constantly pursued and haunted by the idea I don't do anything. Since I began this note I have been called off at least a dozen times; once for the fishman, to buy a codfish; once to see a man who had brought me some barrels of apples; once to see a book-man; then to Mrs. Upham, to see about a drawing I promised to make for her; then to nurse the baby; then into the kitchen to make chowder for dinner; and now I am at it again, for nothing but deadly determination enables me ever to write; it is rowing against wind and tide.[4]

Although *Uncle Tom's Cabin* brought Stowe fame, fortune, and household help, the book might never have been written if her older sister Catherine had not come to her rescue by taking over the housekeeping for a year.

Far from repudiating housework, she sanctified it. In her novels and stories, domestic bliss conquers all hardships and the compleat housewife rises above the frivolity indulged in by society ladies. The typical Stowe heroine is a New England housewife "of faculty" who does everything herself and who provides not only food and clothing but spiritual sustenance as well. Often she is the mother of a less practical but more intellectual or poetical daughter, as in *The Minister's Wooing* (1859). Doubtless it was Harriet's own struggle to be all things to all people—practical and spiritual, self-reliant and feminine, active and submissive, religious and flirtatious— that is reflected in her heroines. Harriet Beecher Stowe succeeded more fully than any other writer of her time at portraying the new multifaceted middle-class woman whose aspirations stretched beyond her domestic reality, but who was bound to her home through love and social conventions. On one hand, the Victorian cult of domesticity endowed the home with all the features of the newly invented creature comforts. For example, in *The American Woman's Home*, Catherine and Harriet furnished their readers with precise drawings of closets, floor plans, kitchen sinks, bathtubs, and toilets. On the other hand, the same cult glorified the Christian home as a refuge from a commercialized, debased outside world. Here, as the Industrial Revolution began to rage without, fragmenting the family and casting individuals onto their own resources, women could domesticate men, the hunger-profit makers, offering them a haven from the industrial urban environment.

Catherine Beecher's commonsense approach to practical matters combined with Harriet's exalted faith in female spirituality gives the modern reader an intriguing view into the Victorian home. Unfortunately, that glorified edifice, "the New Jerusalem of a perfect home," was growing top-heavy with expectations. Like many highly motivated but socially restricted Victorian ladies of that time, both sisters switched from the role of activist to that of suffering saint.[5]

Perhaps, then, it is not surprising that the Beechers and the Stowes were given to self-doubt, chronic depression, and neuralgic pain whenever their ideals clashed with the reality of human frailty. American health spas, which by the 1870s catered not only to fashionable ladies but also to tired housewives and overextended saints, became regular stopovers for feminist lecturers and women doctors who took their own "female complaints" seriously. Catherine Beecher periodically went to Brattleborough, a resort in Vermont, and on one occasion she persuaded Harriet to escape from her five children and go there too. From there Harriet wrote apologetically to her husband, who also suffered from nerves, claiming that she was a poor wife and wishing that he too could take the opportunity to cure his "hypo" with baths, wholesome walks, and moonlight sledding parties. Notwithstanding her concern for him, she stayed at Brattleborough for eleven months. Upon her return she became pregnant again. The baby died of cholera while Dr. Stowe was away in Vermont on a fourteen-month rest cure of his own. The Stowes' seventh and last child was conceived immediately after his return from that retreat.

At least with respect to her housewifely duties and attitudes, Harriet was the prototype of the domestic saint. She felt herself to be constantly under pressure to prove herself a perfect wife and mother, and saw herself as solely responsible for her family and the quality of her family's life and health. The many domestic tragedies she endured she viewed as tests of her faith in a merciful God and of her own qualifications for motherhood. The death of a baby and the accidental drowning of a twenty-one-year-old son, Henry, brought her grief, but her son Fred's alcoholism and eventual disappearance in the West tormented her to the end of her life. In contrast, Abigail Adams had not blamed herself for the wasted life of a son who had the potential to match his brother's success. But Harriet, as a Victorian mother, was haunted with the fear that she had somehow neglected her duties, as proven by Fred's sad fate.

Harriet's depression was undoubtedly offset to some extent by her creative productivity and public recognition. Her daughters, however, did not have these channels of self-expression. Twin daughters, Eliza and Harriet, were able to meet their mother's standards as housekeepers, but they never married and never left home. Did their reticence indicate an insecurity related to their parents' neurasthenic conditions or were they simply unconvinced of the rewards of matrimony? The question remains unanswered, but the story of Georgina, another daughter, is somewhat more clear. Like her brother Fred, Georgina, who of all the children most resembled her mother in talent and ambition, inherited her parents' neurasthenic tendencies. A physician miraculously cured her depression with opium, leaving her a morphine addict. She died of her addiction.

Harriet Beecher Stowe belonged to that circle of successful novelists that Mary Kelley has called "literary domestics." In her study of literary domesticity, *Private Woman, Public Stage* (1984), the author examines the puzzle of these bestselling authors who wrote within and about the home.

Although they drew their characters and domestic scenes with autobiographical accuracy, their plots stretched beyond reality toward the ultimate ideal of selfless devotion between husbands and wives, parents and children—in short, the "New Jerusalem" of Harriet Beecher Stowe. Unlike modern authors of domestic fiction they smoothed from the faces of their heroines all traces of marital tension, reveling in prolonged courtships and family bliss. Yet like Harriet Beecher Stowe they inevitably experienced the anxieties of leading a double life. In Kelley's words:

> Anomalies in a man's world, they found that their ability to appreciate themselves in the public sphere was hampered by their ambiguous regard of themselves in the woman's private sphere. Beset by a lingering convinction that private domestic women were the "humblest" performing the "lowest office," they nevertheless sought "dignity" through "dutiful performance" in the private domestic sphere. Reluctant and fearful to claim more, they condemned any woman for doing less.[6]

Like Stowe, who eventually became the sole support of her family, they earned substantial incomes which they justified in terms of family necessity. By narrowing women's success formula to the family experience, they denied their own contribution to the world outside the home. Moreover, they believed that their writing actually interfered with their housekeeping priorities. They also denied the single woman of the nineteenth century a place in the sun. That an unmarried writer such as Catherine Maria Sedgwick contributed her novels to this conspiracy only adds to the poignancy of the dilemma.[7]

However, not all educated ladies suppressed their yearning for independence. Although some scholars have suggested that the literary domestics were secret subversives who revolutionized the male culture with a feminine subculture of their own, there were other "saints" who confronted the injustice of male domination head on. The similarities between Harriet Beecher Stowe and Elizabeth Cady Stanton make it intriguing to ponder the question why one chose the path inward and the other ventured outward into the political arena.

Elizabeth Cady Stanton

The great suffragist Elizabeth Cady Stanton (1815–1902) was a contemporary of Harriet Beecher Stowe and shared with her a similar background as well as similar early ideals. As youngsters, both women had vied for the attention of strong fathers and both profited from the best education available to girls at that time. Harriet went to her sister Catherine's own boarding school in Connecticut, where she both studied and taught English, Latin, and geography. Elizabeth attended the Troy Female Seminary, founded by Emma Willard. Both married their fathers' students—Calvin Stowe was a professor of theology; Henry Stanton a lawyer—liberal idealists with moderate income who believed in social reforms and women's intellectual equality but who showed little inclination to involve themselves in practical family concerns. Significantly, Elizabeth, like Harriet, suffered intensely from housewife's blues as her family grew along with her more far-reaching ambitions.

Two quotes written several years apart and in very different domestic contexts illustrate a serious shift in Stanton's concerns. The first, written when she had only two children and adequate household help, reflects the ambitious, educated housewife:

> I studied up everything pertaining to housekeeping, and enjoyed it all. Even washing day—that day so many people dread—had its charms for me. . . . I felt the same ambition to excell in all departments of the culinary art that I did at school in the different branches of learning. My love of order and cleanliness was carried throughout, from parlor to kitchen, from the front door to the back. . . . I tried to give an artistic touch to everything—the dress of my children and servants included.[8]

Four children later, after moving to rural Seneca Falls, New York, into a house in need of repair, Stanton sounded very much like Harriet Stowe:

> I set the carpenters, painters, paperhangers, and gardeners at work, built a new kitchen and wood house, and in one month took possession. . . . Mr. Stanton was frequently from home, I had poor servants, and an increasing number of children. To keep a house and grounds in good order, purchase every article for daily use, keep the wardrobes of half a dozen human beings in proper trim, take the children to dentists, shoemakers, and different schools, or find teachers at home, altogether made sufficient work to keep one brain busy, as well as all the hands I could impress into the service. Then, too, the novelty of housekeeping had passed away, and much that was once attractive in domestic life was now irksome.[9]

Both women seemed to bear out the prevailing belief that education spoiled women for a domestic life. It is true that their earlier vision of combining family and personal interests faded with each additional child. However, in both cases the determination to persevere in nondomestic activities was renewed with each child. Both women complained of their lot and called for help. Fortunately, their calls were answered. Elizabeth's associates in feminist causes, Lucretia Mott and Susan B. Anthony, lured her away from the kitchen and nursery. Harriet's sister Catherine took over her housekeeping so that she could write *Uncle Tom's Cabin*. And in both cases, a professional homemaker-substitute eventually arrived to take on the burden of domestic responsibilities: for Elizabeth it was "a noble, self-sacrificing Quaker woman"; for Harriet, "a noble-hearted English girl."

Clearly, the activist lady suffered from the outside pressures to excel as a housewife and the inner drive to fulfill her personal ambitions. She still does today. But Victorians shied away from such terms as personal ambition and self-fulfillment, which have currency today. Rather, they preferred to see their efforts outside the home as expressions of *usefulness* and *unselfishness*. Helping others was the best way for nineteenth-century women to help themselves. In this motivation toward social activities we see the roots of the women's support groups that make up the core of the modern women's movement.[10]

Elizabeth Stanton's desire to help took the form of true radical action. In 1840, on her honeymoon, she attended the World Anti-Slavery Convention in London and endured the humiliation of being barred from the convention proper because she was a woman. At that meeting, she met for the first time women who believed outright in the equality of the sexes. One, Lucretia Mott, personally inspired Elizabeth with a new sense of dignity and self-confidence. To these new relationships, which were based on an explicit shared concern for women's issues, she brought her memory of women she had met or heard of through her father's law practice—women who had been wronged by husbands and employers but who had no recourse to the law. And, of course, she also brought the full weight of her own domestic experience, described in her reminiscences:

> The general discontent I felt with woman's portion as wife, mother, housekeeper, physician and spiritual guide, the chaotic conditions into which everything fell without her constant supervision, and the wearied, anxious look of the majority of women impressed me with a strong feeling that some active measures should be taken to remedy the wrongs of society in general, and of women in particular. . . . I could not see what to do or where to begin—my only thought was a public meeting for protest and discussion.[11]

In 1848, her social conscience fully developed and her empathy for women cemented by social purpose, Elizabeth Cady Stanton found her starting point. She initiated the first Women's Rights Convention at Seneca Falls.

When Elizabeth, with Lucretia Mott, drew up the "Declaration of Rights and Sentiments" for the Convention, she discovered her ability to write. Then at the Convention—where only Lucretia Mott had ever addressed a public audience—she made her debut as a powerful political speaker. It took more than a lifetime to bring all the resolutions to pass, from the Married Women's Property Act, which was amended in 1860 to give women the right to dispose of their premarital property and their postmarital earnings, to the nineteenth Amendment of 1920. To this day the physical obstacles and emotional blocks have not been fully removed from this

5. Nurse with baby. Reproduced through the courtesy of The Bancroft Library, University of California, Berkeley CA 94720.

issue, nor have the educational and professional barriers been lifted everywhere, but for those who wished to continue in Elizabeth Stanton's foot-
steps the path had been laid.

Harriet Hanson Robinson

One of the early followers was Harriet Robinson, the lady who did her
own housework. She started out in Lucy Stone's camp, because she was
more impressed with a genuine housewife who made her own bread and
butter than with Susan B. Anthony—that "poor, forlorn soul, wearing out
for the want of getting married and having babies."[12] But after her local
campaign work was passed over in *The Woman's Journal*—as president of
the Middlesex County Woman Suffrage Association she had organized
three conventions and raised funds managing the restaurant of the suffrage
bazaar—she switched to Stanton and Anthony's National Woman Suffrage
Association. It is interesting that her conversion to the suffrage movement
happened four years after she had read and implemented Harriet Beecher
Stowe's "The House and Home Papers." For Harriet Robinson there was
apparently no difficulty in reconciling the Beecher's domestic principles
with women's rights. Although she did not believe in the religious establishment, the suffrage movement to her was a spiritual awakening, and her
writing on behalf of the cause often turned to religious language. Her book
Massachusetts in the Woman Suffrage Movement (1881) talks about the
sacrifices of devoted souls "who thus early took up the cross when it was
a cross, in this weak, and as it was then often called, ridiculous movement."[13] The support from her fellow campaigners encouraged her to write
more: a play about a female boat captain and then two volumes of recollections about her childhood in Lowell, *Early Factory Labor in New
England* (1883) and *Loom and Spindle, Or Life among the Early Mill Girls,
with a Sketch of "The Lowell Offering" and Some of Its Contributors*
(1898).[14]

In light of her domestic problems with servants, it is significant that in
her recollections she attempted to prove that the early—as distinguished
from the later Irish immigrant—female mill workers were "the grand-
daughters of patriots . . . of good New England blood, and blood tells even
in factory people." Her plea for social acceptability of the working girls
such as herself sounded similar to the Beechers' elevation of housewives:

> They earned their own bread, and often that of others. They eked out their
> scant education by their own efforts, and read such books as were found in
> the circulating libraries of the day. They sought to help one another. They
> were wholly untroubled by conventionalities or thoughts of class distinctions,
> dressing simply, since they had no time to waste on the entanglements of
> dress.[15]

The cult of domesticity now seems diametrically opposed to the Women's Rights Movement. Yet both set out to affirm women's education as well as active participation in society. One side believed in the equal distribution of rights and responsibilities to deliver women from male oppression, while the other clung to an almost mystical faith in woman's spiritual superiority and an existential division of labor between the sexes. The Beechers wanted to go back to Abigail Adams. As children of eighteenth-century parents, they could not realize that the Industrial Revolution would split the American family into individuals who would be cursed or blessed in having to make it on their own.

Elizabeth Cady Stanton on the other hand scoffed: "There is an immense amount of sentimental nonsense talked about the isolated home." At eighty-four years of age, she insisted that "woman's work can never be properly organized in the isolated home. One woman cannot fill all the duties required as housekeeper, cook, laundress, nurse, and educator of her children. Therefore we should oppose all sly moves to chain women in the home."[16]

Saints and Sinners

If modern women follow man's example in quest of sexual freedom, Victorian women hoped to develop his taste for celibacy. In fact and fiction, a husband's abstinence was considered greater proof of his love and devotion than his sexual advances, since physical desire in a man was as common as his need for breakfast, lunch, and dinner.

In keeping with the new saintly ideal of the housewife, Protestant ministers embraced the Virgin Mary as the image of perfect womanhood. Correspondingly the residential architecture of the time affected certain characteristics common to medieval cathedrals. Religious sects experimented with sexual relations, and sexual relations took on religious overtones, with God as one side of a domestic triangle. The work of Harriet Beecher Stowe, as a chief exponent of the new domestic idealism, offers countless examples of the melding, if not confusion, of domestic and sexual experience with religious experience. Consider the following example, from *My Wife and I*:

> My mother, [says the novel's hero] from her deep spiritual nature, was one soul with my father in his life-work [as a clergyman]. With the moral organization of a prophetess, she stood nearer to heaven than he, and looking in, told him what she saw, and he, holding her hand, felt the thrill of celestial electricity. With such women, life has no prose; their eyes see all things in the light of heaven, and flowers of paradise spring up in paths that, to unanointed eyes, seem only paths of toil.[17]

The correspondence between Harriet and Calvin Stowe reveals the typical tug-of-war between saint and sinner, she yearning for a soul mate and he lusting for a bedfellow—"my arms and bosom are hungry, hungry even to starvation." The stereotypical conclusion that Victorian women had no sexual appetites, however, must not be drawn too quickly. Mary Kelley and Lois Banner suggest that the Stowes and the Stantons used abstinence as the main form of birth control. Both couples spent considerable time apart, and both apparently suffered from sexual frustration among other marital problems. Elizabeth Cady Stanton herself admitted in later life that she had been ignorant of contraceptive techniques. More frankly sexual than Harriet Beecher Stowe was, she claimed that she was "able to enjoy the connubial relationship to a high degree."[18] But her enjoyment, like Harriet Beecher Stowe's, was clouded by the fear of unwanted pregnancy.

For both it was a double dilemma since the Victorian ideology sanctified the pleasures of conception with the blessings of sainted motherhood. According to Banner's biography, "the lack of control over her reproductive life increased Cady Stanton's sense of subordination and eventually contributed to her birth control messages in her feminist theory and activism." Harriet Beecher Stowe, on the other hand, resorted to fictional idealization in order to achieve the satisfaction she missed from her real-life marriage. Not that Cady Stanton was free from the saintly cravings, because she too hoped to find in Henry a husband she could "reverence and worship as a God."[19] But Henry Stanton fell short of such high expectations as did Calvin Stowe. The two men had different temperaments. Henry was pragmatic and condescending. In his political autobiography he only mentioned his wife once, when he admitted to "more than the usual matrimonial friction."[20] Calvin was unstable and clinging. Even financially he came to rely totally on Harriet. Both wives were strong willed, yet dependent on their husbands' intellectual and emotional support.

Elizabeth Barrett Browning, a happily married contemporary of Harriet Beecher Stowe and Elizabeth Cady Stanton, was more straightforward in her approach to sex. She gave the Victorian wife a poetic taste of the erotic pleasures possible in the marital union of soul mates:

Embrace that was convulsion; then a kiss
As long and silent as the ecstatic night,
And deep, deep, shuddering breaths, which went beyond
Whatever could be told by word or kiss.[21]

A lady's sexual drive was as carefully concealed in public as her nude body, but she had both even if she pretended not to. Elizabeth Browning's eulogy to orgasm, quoted above, was reprinted in 1866 by Russell Trall in one of the first explicit marriage manuals, *Sexual Physiology*. The famous spa doctor believed that if sexual intercourse was worth doing at all it was worth doing well. Like modern experts on the subject, Trall wished to dispel the blatant ignorance of newlyweds as well as older couples, explicitly stating that sex could be enjoyed as much at sixty as at thirty. But he also believed that conditions had to be right for enjoyment; in the morning, as long as there was no hurry to get up, when the body's magnetic forces are at their highest and the body in its most vigorous condition—or better, at a time especially "appropriated for the purpose." The author's detailed instructions included advice on the rhythm method and on the benefits of sponges or diaphragms. In this, he made it clear that he acted in response to the pleas of thousands of suffering women in the United States.

Behind the Victorian screen of dignified modesty lurked a growing interest on the part of both sexes in explicit sexual conduct and the means of increasing sexual pleasure. To these issues, too, the prolific O. S. Fowler addressed himself. A chapter called "Specific Love-Making Rules and Directions" in his very popular *Creative and Sexual Science* (1870) offered counsel based on case histories of unhappy couples, as do many modern sex manuals. But in contrast to most modern sources (a *McCall's* survey indicates that most wives don't get enough sexual attention), Fowler's advice was largely concerned with curbing the voracious male appetite.[22] A gentleman was instructed to respect a lady's wishes, according her the same courtesies after marriage as before. Like Dr. Cowan,[23] whose advice book Elizabeth Stanton recommended, Fowler condemned all means of artificial contraception and promised that the source of the greatest sexual gratification was the act of procreation that was consciously chosen.

Fowler's definition of sexually attractive women indicated that men loved "emotional, exquisite, spiritual" women. Women, on the other hand loved courage, force, and firmness in men, combined with gallantry and generosity, originality and talent, a masculine physique, sexual vigor, and passion. In short, virginal women loved virile men, sinners loved saints. Victorians thrived on love stories about the conflict between vice and virtue, with the moral victory unfailingly accompanied by a covert sexual thrill.

Neither Elizabeth Stanton nor Dr. Elizabeth Blackwell, who now was an authority on female physiology, denied woman's capacity for sexual pleasure, but both agreed with most feminists of the time that "equal chastity for men and women" would liberate wives and mistresses from sexual exploitation and eliminate the double-standard morality.

In mid-century, a kind of conspiracy developed between the Transcendentalists, or "feminized" idealists, and the educated ladies who hoped to subdue men's animalistic instincts, make them more sensitive, and reduce their reproductive urges. The transcendentalists, who centered around poets Ralph Waldo Emerson and Henry Thoreau and feminist writer Margaret Fuller, believed in the sexual equality of men and women. This notion embraced that of the equal right to sexual pleasure and, to the consternation of mainstream society, free love. However, in contrast to modern advocates of free love, these nineteenth-century liberals believed strongly in self-control. Also they disagreed sharply with contemporary libertines, who freely practiced a double-standard morality, switching between good women at home and bad women in brothels. Thus, the transcendentalists saw the function of birth control as controlling not only conception but also desire, and in this they echoed the more conventional Owen and Knowlton.

Transcendental philosopher John Humphrey, for example, made male self-control a central ideal in Oneida, his utopian commune. Here sexual practices reflected the underlying socialistic philosophy of the community, which distributed the labors of farming, housekeeping, and childcare among the members but within male-female role divisions. Its leader, John Humphrey Noyes, taught his men and women to distinguish between amative and reproductive sexual intercourse. The former amounted to petting among lovers with males refraining from ejaculation; the latter was reserved for rational intercourse among partners carefully selected for genetically perfect mating. Semen at Oneida, like capital, belonged to the entire community. Sexual pleasure, free from possessive greed, was encouraged, but with moderation and a high degree of Christian revivalism. Not surprisingly, the community and its leader met with outraged criticism from their political opponents for licentiousness and free lovemaking.

In contrast to the Transcendentalists the capitalists believed that nothing was free. Instead, this more conservative sector considered sperm to be a commodity, like stock, that had to be transferred carefully to the right party—the lawful wife. Sperm was not to be squandered in coitus interruptus or wasted in masturbation, nor held back unnaturally from circulation. Like a thrifty investor, the perfect capitalist husband spent his "vital force" wisely to insure his own marital happiness and the well-being of future offspring. He believed that by giving in to promiscuity or masturbation, men endangered their future investments either through infection by syphilis or the loss of virility—the pearl of great price that matched female virginity in the Victorian context of purity. Then as now, sexual impotence was a symbol of failure in the world at large. "Normal" men expressed their strength and assertiveness in the old way: with the fruits of their labors and the fruits of their loins. A poet or preacher might get away with keeping a low sexual profile, but a real he-man was expected to perform regularly and without constraint.

If the struggle between female saints and male sinners was already uneven within the walls of their own homes, a public confrontation offered almost no winning chance to the weaker sex. Undaunted, however, more and more housewives took to the streets and the lecture halls, converting sinners to domesticity. Prostitution and alcoholism interfered with the healthy development of the family. Therefore even the most conservative mothers felt compelled to step outside the female sanctuary and face the enemy in the dens of iniquity. For the president of the Woman's Christian Temperance Union public and private morality flowed together in one campaign for "that blessed trinity of movements, Prohibition, Woman's Liberation and Labor's Uplift." Although Carl Degler has suggested that "voting was not a part of domestic reality because it was man's sphere," the following excerpts from Frances E. Willard's "Home Protection" address indicate that some women felt differently.[24]

> It has been said so often . . . that women of the better class will never consent to declare themselves at the polls. But tens of thousands from the most tenderly sheltered homes have gone day after day to the saloons . . . places in which not the worst politician would dare to locate the ballot box of freemen. . . . Nothing worse can ever happen to women at the polls than has been endured by the hour on the part of conservative women of the churches in this land, as they, in scores of towns, have plead [sic] with rough, half-drunken men to vote temperance tickets they have handed them, and which, with vastly more of propriety and fitness, they might have dropped into the box themselves. . . . I spent last May in Ohio, traveling constantly, and seeking on every side to learn the views of the noble women of the Crusade. They put their opinions in words like these: "We believe that as God led us into this work by way of the saloons, He will lead us out by way of the ballot. We have never prayed more earnestly over the one than we will over the other. One was the Wilderness, the other is the Promised Land."[25]

According to Barbara Epstein's analysis in *The Politics of Domesticity* (1981), the temperance movement became one of the strongest vehicles of antagonism toward men for white Protestant women of the middle class.[26]

With equal religious fervor Black women devoted themselves to save the race. Like the white reformers with whom they partly aligned themselves, they wrote and spoke in missionary terms. As Anna Julia Cooper, author of *Voice of the South* (1892), told a group of Black clergymen: "Only the *black woman* can say 'when and where I enter . . . then and there the whole Negro race enters with me.' "[27] Black churches pioneered in social activism with their ministry in the vanguard. In the transition from slavery to freedom Black women not only had to defend themselves against the white accusation of immorality, but also against prejudice in their own communities, where a woman was not welcome to preach like a man. Such was the case with Maria Stewart (1803–1879). After she had exhorted the "sons of Africa" to form temperance societies and spend their money on schools and colleges, she was banned from the Black community of Boston. "What if I am a woman?" she asked in her farewell address. "Is not the God of ancient times the God of these modern days? Did he not raise up Deborah to be a mother and a Judge in Israel? . . . God has tried me as by fire. Well was I aware that if I contended boldly for his cause I must suffer." Although she enjoyed a distinguished teaching career in New York and became matron of the Freedmen's Hospital, she never again spoke in public.[28]

A man out of control was indeed a destructive adversary of women and children who depended utterly on his benevolent protection. Without equal political weapons, women have long struggled to check his power. And the battle is far from over. The home is still not safe from sexual assault. Alcoholism and violence today are driving increasing numbers of women and children into public shelters. And while women now do have the right to vote, they still do not have the right to control their own bodies.

THE SUFFERERS

The Body In Question: Sexual Politics and Birth Control

In a very real sense, the state of women's health was seen as an indicator of the state of the nation, because healthy mothers produced healthy children. And America needed large, healthy families, preferably from native white stock, to provide the manpower for the seemingly unlimited territorial and industrial expansion the nation promised. Therefore, procreation was a matter of public concern. Although sexual intercourse was an equal right for husbands and wives, its consequence—children—had a greater effect on the potential mother, since she risked her life in childbirth and took on the work of child rearing almost singlehandedly.

Thus, the great amount of attention given to women's health in the popular press and the drawing rooms centered around one unmentionable issue of great political and personal importance: birth control. Though the birth-control issue was not identified outright at mid-century, it became the focus of a standoff between women and men. The struggle was not limited to the domestic scene, but involved the nation in a conflict of ideals. A woman's body was both a private and a national commodity. If she took steps to control her fertility she entered into the public domain and came into conflict with laws governed by public interest. If she interfered with her husband's right to her body, she offended him as a man and a potential father. Politically as well as privately, then, delicate health gave her a legitimate excuse for not complying with the demands that were made of her as wife and potential mother.

Thus with respect to the issue of fertility control, women were maneuvered to use their health as a defensive weapon. Information about birth control did not appear in print until economic arguments were advanced in support of population control. In England and Ireland overpopulation had already threatened the economy by the end of the eighteenth century. When Thomas Malthus delivered his famous treatise in 1803 on the necessity for population control to avert hunger and poverty, he innocently believed that the dangers of overpopulation could be averted by a program of late marriages and socially inspired abstinence. It was not Malthus's desire to start a mother's rebellion, and he certainly had no intention of initiating a sexual revolution. And in fact Malthus's ideas did not have much impact in America until surges of immigrants began to enter the country from England and Ireland, and later from other parts of Europe and from Asia. Suddenly Americans developed a self-protective chauvinism, brahmins became worried about the pollution of American stock, and the issue of birth control began to surface. Population control was encouraged among the problem-makers of society, those who lived in squalor and who did not blend in as good servants or factory workers. The folk wisdom, the superstitions, the birth-control techniques that had been passed down from mother to daughter for generations began to find their way into print.

At best, the information on fertility control was limited, though not for lack of interest. Ever since women began committing their thoughts to paper, they documented their anxiety at the idea of having too many children too quickly. Various forms of population control had been practiced since the beginning of civilization—from blockage of the vaginal canal to abortion and infanticide. It was not until the early nineteenth century, however, that the principles of the generative process came to be fully understood. For this reason abortion, which was to inspire heated debates from this time to the present, was in previous centuries considered acceptable during the first weeks of preganancy, even by the clergy, since life was generally believed to begin with the first felt movements of the child. As a rule, abortion was practiced most commonly among working-class women: At this time period ladies ostensibly resorted to variations on the theme of abstinence. Given the extent of the ignorance that still remained concerning reproductive functions, any sort of rhythm method was precarious at best.

Coitus interruptus, a method that had been practiced in the past, but not publicized, was written up as a philosophical experiment by Robert Dale Owen under the title *Moral Philosophy, or a Brief and Plain Treatise on the Population Question* (1831). Owen treated the subject with such delicacy that his practical advice almost escaped the reader, but Charles Knowlton finally described the reproductive functions with a frankness unusual for the period so the layman could understand the mysterious process, perhaps for the first time. Knowlton's *Fruits of Philosophy: or the Private Companion of Young Married People* (1832) recommended coitus interruptus and douching with sperm-killing solutions. Prophylactic skins for men and sponges for women had been used for centuries, though proper Victorian matrons had probably never heard about such tactics.

Judging from the literature and from the tone of the debates it caused, birth control as an issue fell into the male rather than the female domain.

In keeping with the spirit of the time, the initiative to employ birth control was supposed to come from the husband and he selected the techniques as well. Nevertheless women exercised what options they had. Feminists advocated male chastity for the sake of equality, and preachers and teachers promoted it for the sake of morality, but their arguments were met with resistance on the part of the captains of industry and conquerors of real estate and they were ignored by ordinary working men.

Birth control altered the face of America despite all objections. The American birth rate was at its highest in 1800, but declined noticeably following publication of birth-control literature. The middle-class white woman of 1870 had half as many children as her grandmother in 1800, though she still had twice as many children as her own granddaughter, in 1930, would have. The slowdown in the birth rate alarmed the male law-makers. By 1873, the evidence that women in possession of birth-control information had the power to stop procreation became so threatening that the distribution of such information was deemed a punishable offense by federal law.[29]

The voices raised against birth control had much in common with those crying out against abortion today. They intruded into the privacy of the bedroom, particularly at a time when official propaganda from pulpit and press ranked personal sexual pleasure far behind the public duty to repro-duce. Doctors, preachers, lawyers, and even most novelists sympathized with the risks of childbirth and the burdens of motherhood but did little to dispel the ancient male suspicion that every woman tried to withhold from man his due, using her suffering as an excuse for avoiding risks. In the public eye, a woman who refused to give birth was like a man who refused to defend his country.

Typically, "scientific proof" was mixed with moral judgments by the birth-control opponents. Contraceptives were "proved" to be dangerous for married couples as well as for their children. By 1870, the physiology of sexual reproduction was well understood, but the distinction between sperm and fetus was nevertheless deliberately blurred so that the waste of sperm could be viewed as approaching feticide and the use of contraceptives could therefore be called abortion. True abortions, which by mid-century were illegal, were far from unknown in Victorian America; they were widely practiced in spite of a high mortality risk. Newspapers even carried thinly veiled advertisements of abortionists alongside numerous quack medications that promised to prevent or cure "irregularity." In such an-nouncements the title "female physician" often meant abortionist; for that reason Elizabeth Blackwell could not use it. The majority of women who sought out such abortions, many of whom lost their lives, were married mothers of several children who simply wanted no more. In his widely read advice book *The Physical Life of Woman* (1879), Dr. George Napheys advocated birth control to reduce abortions which were practiced by "Mothers of families, respectable Christian matrons, members of church, and walking in better class of society."[30]

As the birth-control controversy raged across the nation, opponents of contraception directed their efforts not at the American woman per se, but at the American lady, the well-born breeder of strong American stock. The immigrants of "lower races," who presumably could not control their animalistic natures and could be counted on to produce the next generation of paupers, were encouraged to practice birth control. At the same time, pressure was put on the "better class" to apply itself to parenthood. In his "Appeal to Anglo-Saxons to Multiply," O. S. Fowler, echoing many late nineteenth-century scientists, advocated genetic control as the salvation of future Americans. Fowler predicted, correctly, that in two generations at most people of foreign origin would outnumber the descendants of the Puritans unless Anglo-American women adopted the prolific breeding patterns of their grandmothers. Selective breeding was explained in terms of animal husbandry; good Puritan stock should be produced like Hereford cattle.

The Victorian lady, however, did not see herself as a breeder. On the contrary, she had special reasons for cultivating the image of a Platonic wife-companion and soul mate, since she remembered her mother as a breeder and a household drudge. Dr. Napheys supported her right to space her children in consideration of her own health and that of her children, a consideration, he argued, which breeders extended even to their stock. In the power struggle between herself and her husband and the nation over her body, the wife moved cautiously, using veto maneuvers or sexual intercourse by invitation only—*her* invitation. As she had earlier pleaded her case for better education with better motherhood, she now insisted that choosing the right moment for conception would improve her chance of bearing a healthier child. Husbands who forced themselves upon their wives risked serious damage to her delicate organs. Separate bedrooms or prolonged travel for either party remained their favorite means of insuring the spacing of births. Naturally, these techniques were practiced only by those people who could afford them. It was through these methods that the Stowes and the Stantons managed to keep their large families from becoming even larger. Whether the wife won her case or whether the birth rate went down because middle-class husbands no longer wanted to support a big family has yet to be proven. In any event, educated women then as now did have fewer children.

However, once a mother managed to limit her family to a select number of wanted children, her problems were only beginning. Inevitably the domestic saint had not only the responsibility to redeem her sinner husband, but also the duty to produce a holy child.

6. According to the late–nineteenth-century advice books, courtship was supposed to last beyond the wedding. Reproduced from Marion Harlan, *House and Home: A Complete Housewife's Guide* (Philadelphia: J. H. Moore, 1889).

The Holy Child

The wanted child, conceived in love and planned for, would be a better child than the accidentally conceived one, not only because it would be better loved and better cared for, but because the perfect child, like any perfect product, simply could not come forth by accident. The planning began with healthy, genetically sound parents who chose the right moment for conception and monitored all prenatal influences.

In this notion again we see reflected a new urge, characteristic of the industrial age, to assume responsibility for the quality of the family and of human life in general rather than fatalistically to trust in God, as the Puritans did. A Victorian child who showed weakness or defects was seen as suffering not from unknown or God-inflicted causes, but from its parents' neglect of duty before, during, or after pregnancy. Infant or early death was now viewed as the result of inherited deficiencies deriving from weak seminal fluides on the father's part and an unresponsive attitude during impregnation on the mother's part. Some doctors believed that strong semen produced boys and weak semen, girls. Dr. Trall's advice on achieving joyful sex included the warning that indulging on a full stomach could result in the birth of a deformed child.

Although child rearing was officially a joint venture, the blame for failure still rested with the mother. Religious advice books had long since admonished mothers to stay at home like generals at their posts, to ward off "the dangers of contamination and the incurable mischiefs of early impressions." Elizabeth Blackwell, childless, recommended a softer attitude but no less vigilance when she insisted that a mother's eye "full of tenderness and respect, must always watch over her children."[31] The gaps in women's education on children, which Catherine Beecher had deplored, were now addressed by Dr. Blackwell in *Counsel to Parents on the Moral Education of Their Children* (1883), and by special monthly publications, such as *Babyhood* and *Motherhood*, which began to flourish in the 1880s. Now young mothers were alerted to the importance of feeding and weighing their babies, registering their progress on charts, and keeping diaries of Baby's early life. The proud parents of Astaroth Victor Haskell, born in 1886, kept an illustrated history of his babyhood with detailed entries about his ancestors, his birth, his first books and adventures up to the age of five.[32]

A child's young mind was as delicate as his body. The nursery not only needed to be kept free from germs, but also from corruption, which could enter by way of vulgar servants and friends, bad novels, coffee, tea, tobacco, and opium. Furthermore, not only for the sake of her own health, but also for that of her daughter's, the sophisticated mother could no longer feign ignorance about her bodily functions. Dr. Blackwell forced herself to acknowledge the existence of "evils to which the child may be exposed,"

"MOTHER AND BABY"

7. The dutiful mother leaves worldly pleasures behind. Reproduced from
Marion Harlan, *House and Home: A Complete Housewife's Guide* (Philadelphia:
J. H. Moore, 1889).

in order to guard actively against them.[33] And in another step in the up
grading of consciousness that would have important consequences for late
generations, the sophisticated mother became acquainted with the to then
unknown stage in child development known as puberty. By defining puberty as a developmental stage of late childhood, the Victorians not only
extended the maturation process, but also gave parents a last chance to
detect and correct signs of a weak character in children otherwise destined
to succumb to bad influences. From conception to adulthood, then, the
perfect child had to be protected against the destructive forces beyond the
nest.

In keeping with the new attention given to sex and the belief that its
quality had a bearing on the mental and physical health of the next generation, "self-pollution" was regarded as the surest sign of secret corruption. Despite their differences, all health manuals univerally agreed that
the consequences of masturbation could range from listlessness and leth-
argy to a softening of the brain and a direct path to a mental ward or a
prison. Observations of inmates in such institutions were used to support
these beliefs. A conscientious mother, therefore, kept her children's hands
busy at work during the day and above the bed covers at night. Domestic
tasks, particularly needlework and moderate outdoor activities, helped to
keep her girls out of trouble. Boys were encouraged to take part in sports,
to develop good study habits, and to take regular cold showers.

Dr. Elizabeth Blackwell and Frances Willard firmly believed that mothers had the power and the responsibility to educate their sons and daughters
to purity. The chastity of men secured the chastity of women, since chaste
men would not resort to either celibacy or fornication, considered equally
despicable, but would gratify their passions safely in marriage. Unmarried
herself, the doctor believed that the permanent union of one man with one
woman was essential to the welfare of the American family and that national morality would be secured "by the cumulative effects of heredity."

In their attempt to define sexual norms, Victorian writers mass-produced
the American dream of the perfect family and started the trend, picked
up by television, of marketing the ideal model for the real thing. Instead
of cameras, high-intensity words glorified specific acceptable qualities in
human beings and damned the unacceptable. The nineteenth-century Dr.
Spocks, and there were many, left no room for error and offered no excuse
to the mother who failed to deliver the perfect product. Such a mother,
according to John C. Abbott, the most widely read authority on child
management in the 1800s, "looks upon her ruined sons, and reproaches
herself with the just reflection, that if she had pursued a different course,
they might have been her joy and blessing . . . and attributes all their guilt
and wretchedness to her bad government."[34]

In the Victorian Americans' zeal to assign responsibility to parents,
however, and in particular to mothers, for the quality of their homes and

OBEDIENCE IS THE FIRST LESSON.
OBEDIENT AND DISOBEDIENT CHILDREN. *Page* 100.

8. Discipline in childhood. Reproduced from Marion Harlan, *House and Home: A Complete Housewife's Guide* (Philadelphia: J. H. Moore, 1889).

health of their children, we can detect the seeds of guilt that characterize the relationships of many parents with their children today. As the nine-teenth century moved toward the twentieth, raising children and keeping house became increasingly complex. A host of experts—most of them still in the guessing stage—advised the family woman how to perform better. The middle-class housewife became the main target for an avalanche of information on new and "scientific" approaches to every task within her private sphere. At this point the avalanche was only gathering momentum. It would grow stronger each decade until the homemaker wound up being pulled like a puppet by experts bent on shaping her own and her family's behavior. Some of the new behavioral standards they advocated improved radically the nation's general health and living conditions, but others merely increased consumption and enforced class and race distinctions. Moreover, the improvements in health and sanitation affected only those people who could afford to live in affluent neighborhoods. In keeping with the pattern of ethnic-group insularity, as more and more divergent groups moved into the already crowded cities, poor health and poor sanitation came to be viewed as synonymous with poor housekeeping and bad mothering. In mid-nineteenth century, when religion still provided the ground rules for bringing up children, the press was just as critical toward rich ladies who ruined their health with tightly laced corsets, late-night dancing, and dining. Then as now bad health claimed its victims mostly among the poor, but due to medical ignorance, no home was safe from infectious diseases. And as in Abigail Adams's day, the mother spent much of her time either as a nurse or as a patient.

Wanted: A Healthy Wife

One indication that a shift was occurring away from the image of the lady and toward that of the domestic saint was the spate of articles that appeared around mid-century bemoaning the poor health of American women. "Our own dear women of America are the most unhealthy women in the world!" cried *Harper's Magazine* in 1856. According to many such articles, ladies lived only half as long as men, since they spent their days idly in overheated drawing rooms and their nights overexcitedly in drafty ballrooms. Under the appropriate title "Wanted: A Healthy Wife,"[35] the *Harper's* article remonstrated with upper-class women for squandering their strength. In the process, the article revealed the traditional bias of the popular as well as the medical press: that women had only themselves to blame for their premature demise. In fact, the claim that American women were failing was untrue. Then, as now, women's mortality rate was lower than men's, except during childbearing years.[36]

Clearly, the call for American women to shape up was a response to the family's need for housekeeprs and nurses in the form of healthy working wives, not fragile butterflies or birds with broken wings who demanded rather than gave tender, loving care. The lives of family members depended on them to a very great degree. Often they alone, consciously or not, stood between the family and the countless diseases to which everyone in the nineteenth century was vulnerable.

The Conditions She Faced

Nowadays, birth and death rarely occur at home. Our medical sophistication has all but removed these fundamental processes from our experience. We have come to rely so heavily on hospitals that even when our sick no longer respond to treatment there we feel incapable of caring for them at home. Throughout the 1800s, however, the home was not only more comfortable, but also safer than hospitals.[37] Housewives applied their own standards of cleanliness long before doctors recognized that dirt was dangerous. Clean floors, clean sheets, and fresh air were almost unheard of in hospitals before 1876. Instead, filth permanently saturated wooden floors and sheets remained on beds that patients shared on crowded days. Most appalling of all—and a fact that had direct significance for housewives, as we shall see—doctors never even considered washing their hands or changing their blood-stained coats until they left the premises at the end of the workday.

But hospitals had no monopoly on filth. The burgeoning cities proved to be the perfect breeding grounds for bacteria and viruses. By the sixties, housewives in the countryside still had a fair chance in their war against dirt and disease, but urban women were losing the battle. Conditions in the urban centers were terrible. According to the first New York Council of Hygiene, in 1863 filth clogged the streets in the form of house-slops, vegetable refuse, decayed fruit, store and shop sweepings, ashes, dead animals, and even human excrement.

When the cities were young, sanitation had been a prerogative of the rich. Families that could afford the service hired scavengers to dispose of their refuse and empty their household privies. But by the 1870s, the problems resulting from increased population density overwhelmed even the rich. Scavenging dogs, pigs, and geese roamed every neighborhood. Sewage drains overflowed regularly and contaminated the fresh water supply, creating a major source of typhus. By the turn of the century, only 1.5 percent of the American population drank filtered water. Further, unsanitary dairies, slaughterhouses, and fat-boiling establishments operating near or even in residential areas increased the health hazards. Against them the housewife had to take elaborate precautions in both kitchen and storeroom.

As usual, the poor suffered most—a mortality rate of 50 to 60 per 1,000 residents was recorded in the teeming tenement districts of New York compared with 10 to 17 per 1,000 for the less crowded areas. But epidemics regularly crossed the poverty line via street vendors and service workers. It was during this period that the infamous "Typhoid Mary," an Irish cook, apparently infected fifty New York families with typhoid fever. This disease along with yellow fever raged in cities. Twelve thousand cases of typhoid fever were reported in New York in 1860, and 4,000 people succumbed to yellow fever in Memphis, Tennessee, in 1878. Cholera decimated the West and malaria plagued the South. Scarlatina, diphtheria, and whooping cough kept the child mortality rate as high as it had been a hundred years before, and these diseases were often fatal for adults as well. Even minor surgery without aseptic precautions could bring death if wounds began to fester. In short, the odds against succumbing to ill health were great indeed.

Consumption, or tuberculosis, was the major killer in the nineteenth century, however. The very poor, the very young, the very old, and mothers weakened from too much childbearing or too much work died most easily of this dreaded disease, as in the case of Roxana Beecher, a woman often "wasted away" after safely delivering a baby—that is, after escaping the ever-present risk of childbed fever. In the census of 1860, 26,046 of the 180,267 women who died were victims of consumption (tuberculosis). There wasn't much anyone could do in the face of this disease. Its psychological impact was equivalent to that of cancer in our own time.

Womb and Tomb: The Housewife as Patient

Women were, of course, subject to all the conditions that threatened the health of everyone in the nineteenth century. But they suffered special ills as well, among them the fatal effects of childbirth.

The 1860 census shows that 4,066 women actually died in childbirth that year. In itself, this figure is perhaps surprisingly low since much was made of the dangers of childbirth, but interpreting the significance of such a number is difficult. Causes of death were not easy to ascertain in this era, especially since too many births and poor postnatal care made new mothers susceptible to consumption and other contagious fatal diseases. Therefore, women's mortality rates were highest during the childbearing years between ages twenty and forty, actually higher than men's mortality rates during this particular age range. Since this period was the most important time of a woman's life—from the standpoint of the family at least, they needed her services most then—the dangers of childbirth were not necessarily exaggerated despite the census figures. Nevertheless, the panic that could grip women who knew little about their own physiology, plus the general preoccupation with death and dying, undoubtedly contributed to the prevailing belief that the womb placed a woman closer to the tomb. Many precautions were taken during confinements. Some of these steps were practical, while others originated in fear and ignorance, from which doctors were by no means exempt.

Consider, for example, the advice of G. H. Napheys, author of *The Physical Life of Woman* (1879). He insisted that the new mother be not only confined to her bed, but "rigidly in the recumbent position for the first few days, not raising her shoulders from the pillow for any purpose,"[38] not even to change her afterbirth gown (it was rolled up during the birth). Her pubic area was to be cleansed every four or five hours without being exposed to the air, rubbed with wine and goose grease, and then bandaged in heavy muslin. Her sanitary napkins were, of course, made not from disposable paper but from old sheets. Oiled silk cloth protected her bed until rubber sheets became available. After delivery, fresh sheets folded at one side of the bed had to be drawn under her while she remained on the bed. Napheys cautioned the new mother to refrain from changing her shirt until after the fourth day, when, again, she was to do so without raising her head from the pillow. She could sit up after a week and get up after two for short periods of the day. After four weeks she was allowed to return to her household duties, though she had to wear her well-fitted bandage for several months. The bandage was supposed to prevent the fallen womb—a dreaded permanent debility that resulted from a weakening of the abdominal muscles. The prolapsed uterus contributed both to the unmentionable pains Victorian women suffered and to the danger in subsequent pregnancies. Pessaries continued to be worn until the recent practice of postnatal exercises all but eliminated this widespread "female complaint." The most dangerous aspect of childbirth was septic poisoning, then called "childbed fever," a condition endemic in lying-in hospitals, awful places where poor and unmarried women unable to afford private home care had their babies. These institutions were on a par with charity hospital wards, and women who were bound by necessity to deliver in them justifiably feared for their lives.

In 1843, the senior Oliver Wendell Holmes alerted American physicians to the bacterial origin of childbed fever. Identification of the organism led to his realization that doctors in the lying-in hospitals spread this virulent disease themselves simply by failing to wash their hands between dissecting corpses and giving pelvic examinations, and then between one examination and another.

The lying-in bed at home, as opposed to the ward, was prepared with clean sheets that had not been contaminated by other patients. And the neighbor's or the midwife's hands had perhaps baked bread before aiding the laboring woman, but they had not dissected a body or touched a diseased person. In Dr. Holmes's day, the maternal mortality rate (the number of birth-related deaths per new mothers in a year) was rarely under 10 percent, but fully 75 percent of all women in lying-in wards died of childbed fever.

Though family physicians were routinely called in to attend births in upper-class households, most clinicians found the normal birth process fairly uninteresting.

Victorian doctors often compared American women to Indian or European peasant women with regard to the birth process, and the American ladies particularly came out woefully weak. The fast deliveries and quick recoveries experienced by women of hardier stock were impossible for the refined and weakened bodies of women who spent their days sitting in drawing rooms. Actually it was from the primitive state of the medical art that women suffered most. Little was known about "female complaints," but Victorian prudishness inhibited learning. Such doctors as Marion Sims, inventor of the speculum, who actually examined the uterus, stood accused of prurient curiosity and even rape. Those who experimented with surgical treatment risked their patients' lives and therefore, like Simpson and his anesthesia experiments, operated mostly on charity cases. These poor women were hardly the most representative subjects, since they had the least chance of survival due to malnutrition and lack of hygiene. Better-off patients, protected from such invasions, perpetuated both their own and their physicians' ignorance.

Faced with such agonizing treatments of the uterus as cauterization with nitrate of silver or hot iron needles or the application of leeches to combat cancerous or infectious inflammation, women resorted to homemade poultices and liniments, keeping their pains to themselves as long as they could. Haunted by fear, they took to their beds at the slightest sign of discomfort, particularly during menstruation, and instructed their daughters to do likewise. It is this fear that prompted Catherine Beecher to lament: "The writer has repeatedly heard mothers say, that they had wept tears of bitterness over their infant daughters, at the thought of the sufferings which they were destined to undergo; while they cherished the decided wish, that these daughters should never marry."[39]

Neurasthenia

Interestingly, while the magazines continued to insist on a totally false premise—that American women were collectively on the brink of expiring—a new disease, or, more accurately, a new manifestation of an age-old one, was gaining ground across the United States. The condition was neurasthenia, for centuries diagnosed in both sexes under the names melancholia or hypochondria ("hypo") and in our own day under depression. Until the mid-1800s, it had afflicted men and women, rich and poor, driving them to drink and to suicide across all class boundaries. The disease had always been viewed as a reaction to stress and anxiety. So far it had never been viewed as restricted to any one type of person or social class. The Victorians, however, changed that.

Depression or neurasthenia was first diagnosed as a male affliction, related to the pressures of brain work involving a high degree of concentration. Workers in the ever more complex urban areas were subject to the stress of competition and risk-taking. These factors along with a notable lack of fresh air and exercise in stuffy city buildings were seen as leading naturally to the neurasthenic condition. Also seen as a significant contributing factor was the loss of virility, believed to be the inevitable result of masturbation, uncontrollable nocturnal emissions, and too much sexual intercourse. In this context, neurasthenia in the 1860s became a metaphor for the decline of urban men and the moral decay of the nation's leadership. Like syphilis, though less disgraceful, it was seen as a social disease, but with the peculiarity of lending a touch of class to its sufferers, since college graduates and rich men's sons appeared to be particularly vulnerable.

Soon, however, ladies came to realize that "a case of nerves" drew attention to their otherwise neglected or unmentionable problems, and neurasthenia became the disease of upper-class women as well as men. By 1870, it was a fashionable affliction, bringing ladies and gents flocking to health spas, where they were treated with water cures, exercise, and a wholesome diet and exposed to clean air, a rarity in the badly ventilated homes of coal-polluted cities. Gradually, neurasthenia became a primarily female, or at least an effeminate, upper-class disorder to which weak characters unable to cope with their duties fell victim. Since that time, the nervous breakdown has kept its associations with the heavily curtained drawing room, and has been viewed by many as the retreat of women who wished to shrug off their responsibilities.

Neurasthenia was made to order for Victorian women, since the new model of the saintly, perfectly competent housewife exacted a level of responsibility that few human beings could meet. Catherine Beecher and Harriet Beecher Stowe were typical sufferers from the disease.

When neurasthenia was seen to be solely a working man's disease, the medical community seemed to consider it an unavoidable risk inherent in the pursuit of a stressful career. But in the late 1800s, doctors treated female neurasathenics as suffering the just deserts of a sadly misdirected life. Ladies were told that their aspirations toward higher education and their nondomestic interests were directly responsible for the nervous debility they suffered and that this condition in turn endangered their naturally weak bodies. Men might have difficulty coping with the complexities of urban life, but women were sure to suffer dire consequences for attempting to do more than their bodies could endure. The underlying message was that women were under an obligation to direct what strength they had to more appropriately female activities.

Misuse of the female brain led to hysteria and depression, claimed experts who saw women dissatisfied with their domestic lot. Charlotte Perkins Gilman demonstrates this attitude. After the birth of a child, Gilman was

gripped by depression and consulted Dr. S. Weir Mitchell, whose reputation rested on his treatment of "nervous" conditions in women. He
admitted her to his Philadelphia sanitorium for his standard cure and left
her with the following prescription for her future health, apparently bent
on extinguishing her spirit as an individual forever: "Live as domestic a
life as possible. Have your child with you all the time. Lie down an hour
after each meal. Have but two hours intellectual life a day. And never
touch pen, brush or pencil as long as you live."[40] Suffice it to say that the
Victorians' tendency to blame women's sexual characteristics for their emotional difficulties did not vanish with the advent of modern psychology.
Clearly, neurasthenia and its repercussions were serious social problems,
much akin to our current struggles with depression and with drug and
alcohol abuse.

In our own Valium-haunted culture, we have good reason to trace to its
root the practice of treating emotional disorders with drugs. Victorian
physicians had no compunction about prescribing alcohol-based tonics and
opium for ladies' "nervous" troubles, and in the process they unwittingly
created a substantial number of alcoholics and opium addicts. Female
alcoholics were able to keep their condition invisible by drinking bitters
and tonics (Lydia Pinkham's Vegetable Compound, 20.6 percent alcohol;
Ayer's Sarsaparilla, 26 percent alcohol). "Nerve fortifiers" and "blood
cleaners," with high but unspecified alcohol contents, were also readily
available. Thus, the genteel alcoholic could support a significant addiction
by drinking a bottle a day of this or that compound.

Opium was readily available from the druggist or by mail order at $2.50
per pound. Physicians freely prescribed it for such female complaints as
depression, neuralgia, nervousness, and restlessness. An effective remedy
for Victorian saints, opium diminished anxiety, reduced sexuality, and
encouraged passivity. Habitual female users outranked men at a ratio of
three to one; housewives outranked all other classes of women, including
prostitutes, at a ratio of nine to one.[41]

From all appearances the domestic saint lived neither a healthy nor a
happy life. Depending on the camp to which they belonged in the battle
of the sexes, writers attributed women's suffering to idleness or overwork,
boredom or overstimulation, dissipation or drudgery, education or ignorance. Husbands blamed wives and wives blamed husbands; doctors blamed
patients and patients blamed doctors. The result was a deluge of advice
literature on women's health in American books and magazines. The trend
has never abated.

To this day we give credence to that perfect human being envisioned by
Harriet Beecher Stowe who "comprehends all" and "holds all things in
harmony." Even those of us who no longer profess a religious faith are
haunted by that Victorian ideal. The "ideology of patience," as Chaya
Piotrkowski has named the modern equivalent for domestic sainthood,

affects the housewife in particular: When things go wrong she blames herself. She is not allowed to feel anger or frustration, nor can she admit to disliking the work that she does on behalf of her loved ones.[42]

The image of the domestic saint followed the housewife from eastern cities to the western frontier, and with the Statue of Liberty it welcomed millions of immigrants to their new home in America. No matter how much the switch from one identity to another taxed the physical and mental strength of the housewife, the domestic saint admonished her to create order and harmony—from miners' cabins to city tenements. Trying to live up to the demands of a less than perfect reality inevitably led to disappointment and frustration. Yet if she could muster the personal resources and strength, ingenuity, and bravery, the housewife could change her passive role and look at her new surroundings with the eyes of a *pioneer*.

NOTES

1. Harriet Beecher Stowe, *Household Papers and Stories* (Boston: Houghton Mifflin, 1896), p. 53.

2. Ann Douglas, *The Feminization of American Culture* (New York: Knopf, 1977; reprint, New York: Avon, Discus Books, 1978), pp. 94–143.

3. Carl Degler, *At Odds*. Chapters 7–11 are particularly valuable for a positive perspective on women's increasing power in the family. See also: Michele Barrett, *Women's Oppression Today*, chapter 6, "Women's Oppression and 'the Family,' " pp. 187–247; Mary P. Ryan, *Womanhood in America* (New York: Franklin Watts, 1983), chapter 3, "Creating Woman's Sphere: Gender in the Making of American Industrial Capitalism: 1820–1865"; and Barbara Berg, *The Remembered Gate: Origins of American Feminism* (New York: Oxford University Press, 1980)—all of which offer a political analysis of Victorian domesticity.

4. Charles E. Stowe, *The Life of Harriet Beecher Stowe, Compiled from Her Letters and Journals by Her Son* (London: S. Low, etc., 1889), p. 128. The entire letter deals with her chores.

5. Barbara Leslie Epstein, *The Politics of Domesticity: Women, Evangelism, and Temperance in Nineteenth-Century America* (Middletown, Conn.: Wesleyan University Press, 1981). Chapters 2–3 interpret religious experience as a cycle of rebellion and submission to accommodate inevitable male dominance.

6. Mary Kelley, *Private Woman, Public Stage: Literary Domesticity in Nineteenth-Century America* (New York: Oxford University Press, 1984), p. xi.

7. Ibid., pp. 241–249. Barbara Berg stresses Sedgwick's discontent with marriage in a quite different interpretation from Kelley's.

8. Theodore Stanton and Harriet Stanton Blatch, *Elizabeth Cady Stanton as Revealed in Her Letters, Diary and Reminiscences* (New York: Harper, 1922), vol. 1, pp. 132–134.

9. Ibid., p. 142.

10. Berg, *The Remembered Gate*, pp. 243–270.

11. Stanton and Blatch, *Elizabeth Cady Stanton*, pp. 144–145.

12. Bushman, "*A Good Poor Man's Wife*," p. 157.

13. Ibid., p. 165.

14. Ibid., pp. 254–255. Harriet Hanson Robinson wrote two plays, *Captain Mary Miller* (Boston: W. H. Baker, 1887) and *The New Pandora* (New York: Putnam's, 1889), as well as several other historical works, but her name is virtually unknown even in her hometown, Malden, Mass.

15. Ibid., p. 186.

16. Theodore Stanton and Harriot Stanton Blatch, ed., *Elizabeth Cady Stanton as Revealed in Her Letters, Diary, and Reminiscenses*, vol. 2 (New York: Harper, 1922), p. 346. She is referring to a proposition by the Knights of Labor to remove women from factories because the factories take them away from the home.

17. Harriet Beecher Stowe, *My Wife and I* (New York: J. B. Ford, 1871), p. 35.

18. Lois W. Banner, "Elizabeth Cady Stanton: Early Marriage and Feminist Rebellion," in Kerber et al., *Women's America*, pp. 190–201, excerpted from Banner's biography *Elizabeth Cady Stanton: A Radical for Women's Rights* (Boston: Little, Brown, 1980).

19. Ibid., p. 196.

20. Ibid., p. 197.

21. Russell Trall, *Sexual Physiology* (New York: Wood & Holbrook, 1866), p. 283. For further information see Degler, *At Odds*, chapter 11, "Women's Sexuality in 19th-Century America," which points to the difference between earlier tolerance of women's sexuality and mid-century restrictions.

22. O. S. Fowler, *Creative and Sexual Science* (Cincinnati, 1870), p. 327. Result of *Redbook* Poll, June, 1975, reported in *Newsweek*, vol. 86 (September 1, 1975): 40 percent of the women complained that they did not have enough sex. By 1985 according to Ann Landers (*Newsweek*, January 28, 1985), women don't get enough loving.

23. John Cowan, *The Science of a New Life* (New York: J. S. Ogilvie, 1869), p. 52.

24. Degler, *At Odds*, pp. 281–282, chapter 12, "Organizing To Control Sexuality" excludes temperance movement in favor of Social Purity movement which was closely related.

25. Anna A. Gordon, *The Beautiful Life of Frances E. Willard* (Chicago: Women's Temperance Association, 1898), pp. 120–121.

26. Barbara Epstein, *The Politics of Domesticity*, chapter 5, pp. 115–146, offers analysis of female versus male power structure in regard to the WCTU's development and to F. E. Willard's political role.

27. Paula Giddings, *When and Where I Enter: The Impact of Black Women on Race and Sex in America* (New York: W. Morrow, 1984), pp. 81–83.

28. Ibid., pp. 49–55; Sterling, *We Are Your Sisters*, pp. 157–159.

29. The Comstock Law of 1873 made birth control information through the mail illegal. Cf. R. G. Walters, *Primers for Prudery: Sexual Advice to Victorian America* (Englewood Cliffs, N.J.: Prentice-Hall, 1974).

30. C. H. Napheys, *The Physical Life of Women: Advice to the Maiden, Wife, and Mother* (Walthamstow, Mass.: F. Mayhew, 1879), p. 99; *Notable American Women* (Cambridge, Mass.: Harvard University Press, 1971), vol. 1, p. 163, about Elizabeth Blackwell. For a detailed study of abortion see Mary K. Zimmermann, *Passage through Abortion* (New York: Praeger, 1977).

31. *The Young Lady's Own Book: A Manual of Intellectual Improvement and*

Moral Deportment (Philadelphia: Uriah Hunt, 1848), pp. 242–243; Elizabeth Blackwell, *Counsel to Parents on the Moral Education of the Children* (New York: Brentano Brothers, 1883), pp. 112.

32. "A History of the Babyhood of Victor Verulam Astaroth Haskell," manuscript scrapbook in Haskell family papers, The Bancroft Library. For more information about the father, socialist lawyer Burnette G. Haskell (1857–1907), and his wife Anna (Fader), see Chapter IV.

33. Blackwell, *Counsel to Parents*, p. 154.

34. John S. C. Abbott, *The Mother at Home; or, The Principles of Maternal Duty* (New York: Harper, 1852), p. 302.

35. "Wanted—A Healthy Wife," *Harper's Monthly Magazine*, vol. 13, no. 73 (1856), pp. 77–81.

36. U.S. Bureau of the Census, *Historical Statistics of the United States, Colonial Times to 1970* (Washington: U.S. Govt. Printing Office, 1975), vol. 1, p. 56. (1860 death rate for Massachusetts only!)

37. Sources for this section: *U.S. Dept. of Commerce, Historical Statistics of the U.S., Colonial Times to 1957* (Washington: U.S. Govt. Printing Office, 1957); W. Martin, *The Standard of Living in 1880* (Chicago: Univ. of Chicago Press, 1942); Council of Hygiene & Public Health of the Citizen's Assoc. of New York, *Report upon the Sanitary Conditions of the City* (New York: Appleton, 1865).

In 1860 there are 55,055 physicians in the United States; in 1900 there will be 119,749, and 226,625 in 1957; in spite of this increase the number of doctors which are available per 100,000 Americans will decline from 175 in 1860 to 157 in 1900 and 132 in 1957. Nurses however, grow in number from zero in 1860 to 430,000 in 1955; hospitals from 149 in 1873 to 6,840 in 1953, with an increase of 1,538,561 beds (Ibid).

38. Napheys, *The Physical Life of Woman*, pp. 141–193.

39. Catherine Beecher, *Treatise on Domestic Economy*, pp. 42–93.

40. Mary A. Hill, *Charlotte Perkins Gilman: The Making of a Radical Feminist 1860–1896* (Philadelphia: Temple Univ. Press, 1980), p. 149.

41. John S. Haller et al., *The Physician and Sexuality in Victorian America* (Urbana, Ill.: Univ. of Illinois Press, 1974), p. 283.

42. Piotrkowski, *Work and the Family System*, pp. 262–264; see also Arlene Skolnic, *The Intimate Environment: Exploring Marriage and the Family* (Boston: Little, Brown, 1983), chapter 4, "Ideal and Reality in Family and Society," pp. 74–95, for a summary of the modern family ideology.

4

The Pioneers, 1870–1915

They beautified the rudest homes, and in all our labors were veritable helpmeets. Whether fighting savages, swimming rivers, crossing trackless wastes by night or day, they were examples of fortitude and devotion worthy of all praise. Taking up cheerfully the all too neglected burdens which refined society and tamed our wilderness, they achieved...immortality of fame....And succeeding generations will bring them votive offerings of gratitude and praise.

—"The Pioneers," an address, 1910

As a child and in my adolescence, living in the heart of New York's Neapolitan ghetto, I never heard an Italian singing. None of the grownups I knew were charming or loving or understanding....Italian immigrants, all the fathers and mothers that I knew, were a grim lot....I did not understand that their lives were a long labor to earn their daily bread and that physical fatigue does not sweeten human natures.

—Mario Puzo, 1971[1]

While heady debates over "the quality of the race" raged on in the parlors of the well-to-do, an unprecedented population upheaval was taking place throughout the nation. A restlessness swept the population at the end of the nineteenth century that until then had been associated only with gypsies, considered shiftless and altogether untrustworthy by less mobile Americans. The boundaries that marked the unsettled territory of the United States were blurred by the new changes. East Coast Americans left the impoverished, overworked soil to seek out better land in the West, spurred on by promises of homestead sites or gold. From the South, Blacks and whites surged into the Northern cities and Western mining towns to escape the post–Civil War depression. Rural Americans flocked to the cities, and city people traveled to the prairies to escape the ever-increasing competitiveness within the labor market. Finally, European immigrants, at the rate of more than 1 million annually *to every state*, swept into the Eastern seaboard in wave after wave, like the Americans on the move, bent on beginning life anew.

It was the latter category that sparked anxiety about "the immigrant problem." Between 1882 and 1914, 12 million "new" immigrants joined the American population. By 1930, 25 million foreign-born people would be counted as Americans. The newcomers were distinguished from the "old" European immigrants, people from Northern Europe. The new immigrants belonged to what the newspapers called, "foreign" races from southern and eastern Europe and Asia—they were Italians, Poles, Russians, Croatians, Hungarians, Greeks, Basques, Portuguese, and Chinese. These groups were considered significantly less acceptable than the English and even the Irish, who had constituted the bulk of the immigrant population since 1840.

The new travelers entered the country and settled near people of their own backgrounds, in labor camps along railroads and mines or in tenement boarding houses. As these ethnic groups grew larger, they competed with members of other, more established communities, for jobs and housing. Thus, far from "melting" into happy conglomerates, of assimilated but colorful cultural groups, Americans at the turn of the century were becoming segregated from each other along every conceivable dividing line: culture, religion, race, color, language, dialect, generation, and, of course, economic class.

Despite the fact that all Americans except American Indians trace their ancestry to a foreign land, so-called native sons and daughters have typically harbored a long-standing prejudice against newcomers. This is perhaps one reason why foreign immigrants and Blacks have often been separated from the pioneer in past descriptions of the phenomena considered heroically American. In most accounts, the traditional image of the Western pioneer—that staunch, stern character, caught shading his blue eyes with a strong sun-browned hand—is so far removed from that of the forlorn immigrant at Castle Gate (the port of entry before Ellis Island was created) that the latter might appear to have strayed in from an alien culture. Yet the pioneer experience of the immigrant family matched that of the frontier family in many respects. Both families left home to settle a new territory; both had to create a new way of life whole from the resources they found there, unable to rely for long on the limited supplies they brought with them. The experience of making the most of what they found at the end of a long, arduous journey, and of constructing a new way of life within a fundamentally hostile environment, links the rural and urban pioneer across the thousands of miles that often separated them.

Whereas the traditional distinction between the urban and rural pioneer is in many ways an artificial one, another distinction, that between the male and female pioneer in both categories, deserves emphasis and examination. Our stereotype of the Western pioneer family is of a husband and wife united against a ruthless environment, together putting down the first tentative roots from which their children's successful future will grow. As for urban immigrants, we are given to picture husband and wife as equally intimidated by the rush of life in the New Country, and equally subject to the inner conflict between new and old values. As we shall see, the rural and the urban pioneer housewife probably had more in common with each other than they did with their husbands. In contrast again to the legendary pioneer couple, migration often had an unsettling effect on marriage, heightening the chance of separation and divorce.

The new life in the West or in America represented escape, adventure, or at least a new start for a husband, but for his wife beginning such a life was often an uprooting, terrifying, and traumatic experience. The lure of gold, or of streets paved with gold, might create a prospector's fever in men looking for greener pastures, but women were apt to focus with anxiety on the health hazards or the lack of comfort involved in the long one-way journey to a new land.

It was fitting that the wives considered these aspects of their journeys, for, wherever they came from, the women were responsible for both the health and comfort of their families, and it was true that the places their husbands viewed as most promising often involved the most difficult living conditions. The similarity, and the irony, that linked the rural and urban pioneer housewife was that each left the environment that she had been trained to deal with and entered one for which she was often wholly unprepared. Thus, the Eastern housewife might have left town or city to set up housekeeping on the rugged, unsettled, lonely frontier, while Southern Black and foreign immigrant women might have traded a rural, tight-knit community life for a chaotic existence in a crowded tenement within an urban ghetto. Men faced the unknown too, of course, and they lived through difficult transitions alongside their wives. But by leading the way rather than following they were cast in the role of initiators—a role that was expected of men in European and Asian cultures.

Temperament, too, divided husbands and wives and linked frontier and immigrant women in an unacknowledged sisterhood. Though the men were able to pool their enthusiasms and keep each other's sights on future possibilities, the women traditionally looked back at what they had left behind, unwilling to relinquish the memories of family, friends, furniture, flower gardens, or the grave of a child.

In turning our attention away from relatively prosperous, middle-class households and focusing on the pioneers of the late nineteenth century, we reenter a subsistence-level economy that evokes the old colonial ways.

The context of this new poverty was different from that in colonial times, however. The society had grown more affluent, and the pioneers suffered from the contrast they made with the rest of the nation.

Even that great majority of Americans who never reached economic stability believed in middle-class ideals of family life with all the trimmings of respectability: a good job for him, a fine home for her, and a better education for their children. Regardless of the color of their skin or the accent of their English, these migrating Americans wanted a better life for themselves and a better future for their children. Those accustomed to hardship and discrimination brought with them a patience and resilience that outlasted their troubles, but younger couples with stronger ambitions tended to break up under the stress of shattered hopes. Wives left husbands and husbands left wives—the women more often initiated divorce proceedings while the men left home, perhaps intending to resume their breadwinning roles when things got better. Wives on the other hand, particularly Blacks and North Europeans, had strong reasons for wanting to terminate the relationship—such as long-term desertion, alcoholism, and physical abuse. As Robert L. Griswold suggests in the title of his book *Family and Divorce in California, 1850–1890: Victorian Illusions and Everyday Realities* (1982), heightened expectation could indeed lead toward a more rewarding life, but it could also contribute to progressive deterioration of family ties under the strain of mutual disillusion. Griswold's work, as well as Elizabeth Pleck's demographic study, *Black Migration and Poverty: Boston 1865–1900* (1979), shows a strong connection between economic and marital stability for Blacks and whites with definite indications that out of the poverty and discomfort of frontier and urban pioneer life emerged a much stronger role for the woman. She not only performed her household duties, but she also worked outside the home for the sake of the family's survival.[2] In this new kind of wife we see the pathbreaker for the modern wage-earning housewife. By studying the women who first began to work in a new environment, we can trace the development of modern prototypes, represented by women we might call today's New Pioneers. Examining the first manifestation of the wage-earning housewife, along with the legacy of the middle- and upper-class lady, which was evolving simultaneously, will help us to identify the origins of the conflicts many women experience today.

THE HOUSEWIFE ON THE WESTERN FRONTIER

The Victorians' exalted notions of the housewife's role, expressed in detail in the work of the Beecher sisters, inspired a stereotype of the pioneer housewife that has survived to this day.[3] The image is of the pioneer wife as the gentle civilizer of the raucous Western frontier. She plays a supporting role to her trail-blazing husband's lead in an aura of picturesque romance, receiving an occasional spotlight in scenes of massacres, epidemics, and natural disasters. The *real* pioneer is painted in masculine colors, and the concept of pioneering is expressed in terms of pure male heroics.

> To be a pioneer is to have a certain state of mind that can best be characterized as full of faith. To be a pioneer is to be at liberty to indulge in constructive contemplation. And to be a pioneer one must have freedom of action; freedom to do. Thus to be a pioneer is to have, to be, and to do.

So begins the introduction to *Pioneer America* by C. W. Drepperd (1949).[4] This description is long on the traditional American masculine ideas—faith, right thinking, and freedom. The full meaning of the word *pioneer* reinforces this notion: The term implies the quality of being first in a given venture, first in time or place. The idea in turn implies that the pioneering individual has the will and the power to effect change. In short, the term implies individualism, a treasured quality of the ideal American male. But for the pioneer housewife, it was the power to endure adverse conditions rather than the power to change them that defined her role. In spite of her myriad duties and her seemingly endless workday, the role she performed was mostly a supportive, if not a passive, one.

As the legend has it, white men went to the frontier to master the wilderness; while women arrived later to bring the men the comforts of home. In reality men and women went to the frontier to farm, to find employment, and to do business. Blacks, Chinese, and later Japanese immigrated for the same reasons.[5] Almost without exception, the white woman pioneer of the nineteenth century was a pioneer *wife*. Single women did arrive in the West with the intention of teaching, nursing, or homesteading, but they soon married. As in colonial days, women were at a premium in the Western territories. They were considered marriageable when they were barely out of puberty, when they were widowed, and even when they were past childbearing age. They may have arrived in the West, like the men, "full of faith," but they had very little time for "constructive contemplation" before they were swept into the role of homemaker. In that role their freedom to act was severely curtailed by their responsibilities to house and children. Clearly, the prescribed function of women in the West was not to open the frontier, but to settle and populate it.

The pioneer housewife, like most of the housewives in our pantheon of images, had little choice in what she was to be or what she was to do with her life. In this respect, the Western pioneer woman's situation did not differ from that of her more settled sisters in the East. Regardless of social class or family resources, the control American housewives had over their environments, their economy, and their bodies was still severely limited. All wives were dependent on their husbands while being simultaneously responsible for their families' welfare.

The most dramatic example of marital dependency was the frontier officer's wife. Until 1878, when the Army discontinued the practice, the wives of enlisted men were treated with economic equality. As company laundresses they appeared on the payroll, entitled to housing and medical care. But an officer could survive in relative comfort without a wife. His clothes were laundered and mended, his bed was made, his meals were served on time. If his wife chose to come along on the campaign trail, she had to surrender her own needs to army regulations and rituals. Officers' wives complained about the same problems as pioneer wives—the threat of epidemics, the loss of children, the constant moving from place to place, the lack of physical comforts and female companionship, but in addition they had far less control over their domestic domain than the farmers' wives in a neighboring community. Although they were officially honored in the chivalrous tradition of army aristocracy, at any time they could be evicted from their homes by a higher ranking officer. Frances Roe described this "bumping" system in 1877 when a senior officer appropriated the "chicken coop" she had just made habitable. At ten o'clock in the morning she was asked to vacate by one o'clock that afternoon. She protested: "And that means we have been driven out of our house and home, bag and baggage."[6] Regardless of Mrs. Roe's housekeeping and decorating skills, her domestic and social life depended entirely on her husband's rank. Still, then as now, the "true" army wife took pride in her faculties to adjust her life to her husband's career. In this respect she was no different from the devoted wife of a civilian pioneer. For frontier women, both their dependency and their responsibility were thrown into bold relief and exaggerated somewhat, since husbands invariably looked to their women to make comfortable homes under adverse conditions. In addition they were expected to pitch in when their men's work did not bring in enough income.[7]

From one makeshift arrangement to another, the camp-following housewife set up her pots in prairie schooners, tents, dugouts, sodhouses, and log cabins. From a wagon life without privacy she often moved to the other extreme, a remote homestead where female companionship and community life were totally absent. Commonly, female pleas for more time at the river for washing baby clothes or dust-encrusted dresses were treated with humorous indulgence by the men, themselves preoccupied with the dangers of the road ahead. Remorse and pity were reserved for those who were too weak for the demands of the road, and who, apologetic for holding up the group, expired quietly by the wayside. And one desperate frontierswoman, weary of gypsy housekeeping, set fire to the wagon in order to prevent her husband from going further.[8] But generally female reminiscences of pioneer life, like their male equivalents, herald the great survival experience. Recorded in later life for the benefit of the next generation, they stress physical hardship over psychological strain and success over failure.

Gentle Tamer versus Pioneer Drudge

Within this context, two types of women recur throughout the literature recounting the pioneer experience. One is the ready helpmeet, cheerfully wearing the mantle of the civilizing angel of the rough-and-ready West. The other is the disappointed, embittered woman who feels trapped and sometimes defeated by the terrible hardships that make up her daily life. Mary Ronan, the daughter of a pioneer and the wife of a printer-prospector who later became the agent of the Flathead Indian Reservation in Montana, fits the first description. Her daughter's biography of her reveals that she had a kinship with the frugal colonial manager, with the gracious plantation hostess, and with the romantic Victorian lady.

The log cabin served as a challenge to Mary Ronan's decorating skills, the winter isolation as an opportunity for cozy family intimacy. The journeys she undertook by covered wagon were adventures, her husband's business failures a source of renewed confidence in him. It never seemed to occur to her to be lonely or frightened when her husband worked far away at the mine, even when they lived near Blackfoot City, Montana, a notorious wild boom town.

When Ronan's husband took charge of the Indian agency in 1877, her new quarters were large enough for a parlor and a dining room. There, with the help of a Chinese cook and an Indian nursemaid, she entertained a continuous flow of official and unofficial guests. The amenities were a large cook stove, where water was heated, to be carried to a tin bathtub off the kitchen. Cold water was piped directly into the kitchen sink and drained into an outside ditch, "a truly great convenience." Ronan made all her own clothes and the clothes of her eight children, but she "never felt overworked or abused or longed for my little children to grow up." To her there was "always something especially appealing about the worn little shoes scattered about in the evening [that] made my resolve that the next day I would try to be more patient and sweeter."[9]

The second type of female at the frontier was somewhat less romantic: "gaunt, grim, shrill, weatherbeaten women, with rough skin and unkempt hair and coarse hands, clad in soiled, crumpled calico or gingham dresses and sunbonnets. . . . Women such as these scarcely enter my mother's story," says Margaret Ronan, "except as creatures to be pitied." Nevertheless, accounts by frontier historians suggest that such women made up the real majority of the pioneer wives. In the reminiscences of suffragist Abigail Scott Duniway, hardship and drudgery characterize everyday existence on the homestead:

> To bear two children in two and a half years from my marriage day, to make thousands of pounds of butter every year for market, not including what was used in our free hotel at home, to sew and cook, and wash and iron; to bake

and clean and stew and fry; to be, in short, a general pioneer drudge, with never a penny of my own, was not pleasant business for an erstwhile school teacher.[10]

Who were the drudges, and who were the heroines? Perhaps the difference was only in the eyes of the beholder. Duniway's own expectations, derived from her upbringing and her social class, informed her with particular values and prejudices that influenced not only her perceptions of others, but of herself. The drudgery which Duniway detested inspired other writers with a sense of awe. Like Catherine Beecher they remembered their mothers as superior home- and health-keepers on whom the life and happiness of the whole family depended.

Daily Life Reconstructed

Nowadays, one can hardly imagine the work involved in forging a new life from the bottom up. The frontier housewife reverted back to colonial conditions whether she liked it or not and whether she was used to it or not. "I looked after the weaving and spinning and all the house," recalled Mary Jones, who was born in Tennessee in 1825 (she died in California in 1918) and who took care of her nine brothers and sisters after her mother's death. "We wove all the cloth, such as jeans, table linen, sheeting, toweling, and we knitted stockings for all—both white and black. Yes, we made blankets too." Like many a daughter before her, she recalls her mother as a Western pioneer version of the domestic saint ministering not only to her own family, but to the whole community:

> Mother was always taking care of sick folks too. I remember many a night waking up and seeing her dressing by candlelight, getting ready to go on horseback miles away to help somebody that was hurt, or bring a new baby into the world. She was a born nurse, and she got quite a reputation as a doctor. There wasn't any real doctor any nearer than Napa [California] and there was lots of sickness. . . . Sometimes Mother's patients were brought to her; and our house became a hospital.
> She always kept herbs on hand, and buckeye bark to make salve, and wormwood to make medicines for swellings, and cascara bark for physic. . . . And tincture of iron for sore throats, and brandy mixed with camphor and button willow for coughs, and plenty of castor oil.[11]

For the less experienced housewife, cookbooks contained directions for sickroom care and recipes for fomentations (flannels drenched in hot water); poultices of yeast, mustard, and charcoal; and emetics and purgatives. *The Housekeeper's Companion* (1883), for example, contained recipes for a barber's shampoo mixture, cough syrup and paregoric, remedies for kidney and female complaints, and a "positive cure for Gonorrhea." The diseases, listed in alphabetical order, went from apoplexy to yellow fever.

Bertha Burkett's account of her childhood chores on a South Dakota homestead in 1893 affords us a rare insight into the general household duties performed in a frontier home. Again, the description might have been lifted out of an account of life in a colonial cottage in Abigail Adams's day:

> It was a ten to twelve hour job as we were kept clean. First off there was the water to get and heat over a mostly cowchip fire. There had to be a little lye added to soften the water, not the hands. Each piece big or little had to be rubbed on the board, then boiled. Then they had to be rinsed two or three times. Each time out of the water and through a hand turned wringer. And finally the starching and hanging. By this time the wind was generally blowing a gale so they dried. That is in summer. In winter the thinner and first washed things we hung out on the line when the weather permitted. . . . The other things we dried in the kitchen. And everything had to come in before night as a storm might come up anytime and we would have no clothes.

The water for this process was hauled in barrels from a surface well a mile away. Melted snow was used in the winter when the trace was icy or covered with snow. The job continued:

> We could not do the ironing all in one day. It took about five irons. Use one a few minutes and change for a warmer one. It wasn't so bad in the winter when the fire felt good. The summer, when there was more ironing to boot is when it was really bad. The kitchen floor was wide, soft boards, unpainted and had to be washed at least once a week . . . also the chairs and stairways were unpainted and had to be scrubbed. It took a lot of homemade soap. Another job that came about three timas a week was to clean and trim the seven lamps of different sizes and shapes. The chimney we washed every day with the dishes. Then there was that beastly pantry to clean. I'd rather do any job on the place than that and I generally managed to dodge it too.[12]

Bertha Burkett's father was a house painter, but obviously he found no time to paint his own floors and his furniture. He was inexperienced as a farmer, as many frontiersmen were, and had to take house painting jobs to make a living, although he had originally emigrated from the East to escape his unhealthy profession. His wife's health was also poor, particularly after the birth of her last child, which had not been attended by a doctor ("for birth control was a sin in those days and the stork never paused").[13] She raised popcorn to sell, tried raising a garden, cooked, milked, stacked hay, and ran the farm when her husband was away painting—all the while raising her flock of children. The family wondered how she lived through it.

Apparently, Burkett's mother did not complain or try to influence her husband to go back to civilization. Some women, defeated by the combination of loneliness and poverty and homesick or broken in body and in spirit, did urge their husbands to return to the East. One historian of the sodhouse frontier has suggested that the poverty of frontier life weighed especially heavily on pioneer women, and that these overburdened women were the inevitable casualties of the way of life they endured. They felt the tediousness of their existence particularly when their husbands were away at work, where they at least enjoyed the companionship of other men. The fastidious New England housekeeper did not adapt well. She was attached to the values of Victorian domesticity, which included the myriad supplies and services offered by the daily round of tradespeople. She was used to shopping city department stores. She did not know how to barter. She did not care to make the beds with a hoe—stuffing the bedticks with "prairie feathers" (hay) which had to be replaced often if the mattresses were to stay soft. Straw or hay on the dirt floor of the sodhouse was a primitive substitute for a carpet, and cow chips often had to be used for fuel since wood was scarce.

Frontier life offered not only irritations, but overt challenges to the survival instincts. A multitude of difficulties presented itself that had never been heard of in the East. For example, nourishing a family in the prairie territories was no easy matter. Although the prairie cookbook offered 30 different recipes for preparing corn,[14] there was not much joy of cooking involved with the other staples, sorghum and salt pork. Worse, the monotonous diet was dangerously low in vitamins. Gardens were difficult to establish in the harshness of the plains climate. One had to learn about the indigenous plants, for instance that wild greens such as buffalo peas and sheep sorrel were available in summer, that wild plums and nut trees only grew where streams were close.

Practical considerations aside, the psychological aspects of pioneer life were subtle and complex. For Easterners transplanted to the Midwest, living without trees in the vast expanse of the prairie was both frightening and unsatisfying. The frontier idyll might suggest open space and healthy country air to modern readers, but subfreezing cold and blizzards in winter and extreme heat in summer forced families to spend a great deal of time indoors. Accounts of pioneers in Kansas tell of the cold penetrating indoors. Apparently it was not uncommon to find two to four inches of snow on the floor and on the beds. One housewife recounted freezing both her feet indoors in a well-built, cellared house during her first Kansas winter.[15] The extreme heat and cold, the perpetual wind, the flies and mosquitoes, and the scarcity of water were accepted facts of frontier life—no use having "hypos" about it. The average pioneer housewife was as anonymous as her predecessors in Abigail Adams's or Harriet Stowe's time. She was inspired neither by the zeal of the crusader nor by the ideal of the gentle tamer. Her sole motivation was the critical necessity for making a new home. Her letters to relatives were generally unemotional, registering another birth, another death, with little explanation of why and how. For example, a Swedish woman in Texas wrote, "When this letter arrives, you will doubtless have heard that I have lost my husband, the loving father of my children," omitting the fact that the man had been killed in a fight with a neighbor.[16] The diseases that claimed the lives of dear ones were described merely as chills and fevers. The minds of these writers seem preoccupied with matters of survival. It was left to unconventional women, such as Abigail Duniway and Anna Fader Haskell, to reflect on the details and the emotional quality of frontier life.

Independent versus Dependent Pioneer

For Abigail Duniway (1834–1915) homesteading was not a pioneering venture, because her mother had worn herself out with "just such drudgery." Like Elizabeth Stanton, Duniway was able to relate her own life to that of women in general and her own problems to those of society as a whole. She started out under the typical circumstances that forced women to take on men's roles: her husband through an accident became physically incapacitated. She had to go to work to support him and their six children. She began in the traditional way, by taking in boarders and by teaching school. To make more money, she set up a millinery shop which earned her enough to begin what was really to become her path-breaking venture—the establishment of a weekly newspaper, *The New Northwest*. Based on her experience that the protection of a man was unreliable, particularly in the frontier environment, where physical danger and financial disaster were daily risks, she used her newspaper to encourage women in seeking better means to earn their own living and stand up for suffrage. In describing her pioneering work she admitted: "It is true that I did not encounter the diseases and deaths of the desert, in making that venture, nor meet attacks from wild savages, but I did encounter ridicule, ostracism and financial obstacles."[17]

Although Anna Fader Haskell (1858–1942) experienced many of the same obstacles as Abigail Duniway, she never translated her personal struggle for independence into political activism. One reason was perhaps that she married the socialist lawyer Burnette Gregor Haskell and poured her energy into supporting his radical newspaper, *Truth*. What made Anna Haskell a dependent pioneer was her total yet reluctant involvement with her husband's political career and her own introspective personality, which compelled her to fill every page of her pocket diary for 66 years of her life. With uncommon candor she recorded her emotional ups and downs along with her daily struggle to keep house and to supplement the dwindling family income. Unlike the proud reminiscences of other pioneer women, the Haskells' failures appear with regular frequency together with Anna's comment: "Blessed is he who expects nothing, for he shall not be disappointed."[18] Her ill-fated union with Burnette Haskell started rationally enough with a marriage contract, signed by both parties on July 21, 1882 (unrecorded in the diary), and a New Year's resolution to stop smoking. But at the end of the year Anna writes ominously: "I suppose I ought to say something pathetic about the old year.—But I have nothing to say. . . . For better or for worse . . . I have set my life upon a cast—and I will stand the hazard of the dice." And then in December 1883: "I care as little for the new year as I care for the one that is now breathing its last sigh. Whatever it has brought I have been ready for, whatever the next shall bring—I will be ready for and I ask no odds. 'LONG LIVE THE SOCIAL REVOLUTION.' "

During this first year of marriage Burnette was totally involved in San Francisco with organizing the International Workingmen's Association. Anna had to spend many evenings without her husband and many days working for his cause: setting type, editing, and answering mail for *Truth*. The words "alone again" appear with regular frequency from now on. *Truth* went bankrupt in 1884, but by then Burnette was busy with his plans for a socialist utopia in the Sequoia forests.

To what extent Burnette's politics contributed to the marital rift and to what extent the young couple suffered from the union of two strong individuals with volatile temperaments will never be known. When Burnette returned from a campaign trip to Oregon on February 21, 1886, Anna writes sarcastically:

Well, Mr. Haskell arrived home this morning. He condescended to come in and kiss me several times and recount his triumphs. . . . He is wrapped up in himself—some men care for their wives, simply because they are their wives—but not him—he will not even address letters to me as Mrs. B. G. Haskell—for fear—I perceive that I might detract something from his glory—not that I would accept even that from him—I believe maybe, I am a little out of humor.

The reason for ill humor was possibly that she was eight months pregnant. The next day her mood has changed, and she is full of praise:

Burnette was so good to me tonight—so kind and loving that I can't help but love him. He did not go downtown this evening. . . . I forgive him as long as he is good to me. I pasted a lot of scraps in a book for him, items about his business in Oregon. They devoted many editorials to him in their papers.

On March 7, 1886, she did not write. But later she fills in the news:

I did not know this morning when I arose that when another day should dawn I should be a mother. I felt badly all day—Mr. Gilfrid was here and we all played faro until 12 on. I smoked and smoked and smoked.—No one will know how I have struggled against smoking and it seemed impossible for me to give it up. I am up and around now for a long time—and it seems strange to look back upon the time when there was no baby in the house, everything is so different now in some ways—"A baby in the house is a wellspring of pleasure." How strange it all seems.

The new parents take their role seriously. Proudly they assemble an elaborately decorated scrapbook with pictures, poems, congratulations, and childhood ancedotes entitled "A History of the Babyhood of Victor Verulam Astaroth Haskell." In the scrapbook Burnette keeps track not only of Roth's progress but also of his own. Here he records important political rallies. But politics drains the family budget. They can only afford a new house if she takes in boarders once again: "We shall have to have some roomers or boarders if we shall be able to get them . . . then I shall have to work—but I don't care and working hard is about the best thing there is—I guess—after all." Yet the next day she laments:

> There will be an awful lot of work to do keeping things clean. I don't know how I shall be able to do it. I don't want to keep any more boarders—but I don't mind having two or three roomers. Oh—dear—this everlasting scrabble to make ends meet is enough to kill the strongest person in the world.

Her hard work is only beginning. Nine months later they move from San Francisco to the California wilderness in order to homestead the new socialist colony near Kaweah. Again she follows her husband's lead. Together with his friend James Martin and other former IWA members Burnette Haskell had created a Co-operative Land Purchase and Colonization Association in order to file for land which was then available for claim in the sequoia forests forty miles east of Visalia. The group intended to purchase the land and harvest the timber cooperatively. They wish to practice socialist principles as an alternative to the capitalist economy. For Anna the work load increased as their funds dwindled in the failing pioneer venture. Besides keeping house under primitive conditions and helping Burnette in the office, she added school teaching to her exhausting duties. On New Year's Eve 1891 Anna celebrates

> the dismissal of '91—bad luck to it, by sitting up around our own fire place, if you please—which has no chimney—it is true but holds a glorious fire nevertheless—and makes even candy. . . . Well good bye '91—the most miserable year I ever passed. If '92 is no better I have no use for it. Selah!

A vicious newspaper campaign and a trial in 1891 which charged the trustees of the colony with unlawful cutting of timber put the already tenuous community under so much pressure that it could not survive.

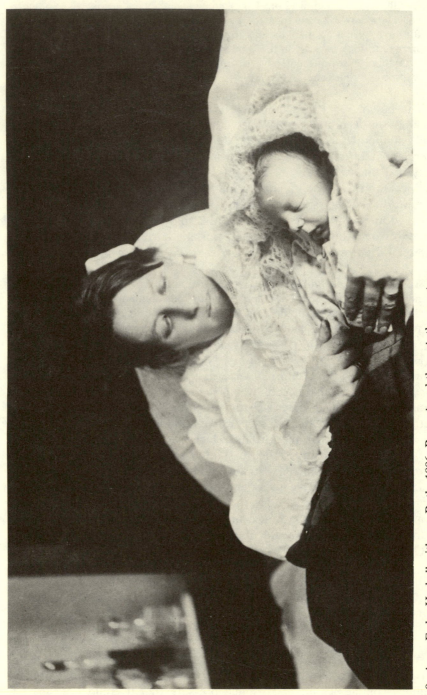

9. Anna Fader Haskell with son Roth, 1886. Reproduced through the courtesy of The Bancroft Library, University of California, Berkeley CA 94720.

Eventually the hardships of life at the colony and the recriminations in the community take their final toll on the marriage. Anna's exasperated comment at the end of 1893 expresses the mood of a weary pioneer wife: "I am tired of striving for what it seems I have no power to accomplish. I lack even determination and persistence—I am sick of trying to be good and I suppose I have never even really tried." The last words reflect her sense of guilt for not living up to the ideal of the cheerful camp follower. The Haskells held on until 1895, but the colonists disbanded having lost not only their investment but also their faith in social cooperation.

In April 1896 Anna separated from Burnette. Increasingly despondent over his failure, he turned against her in his alcoholic rages. She felt that the New Year could be "no more bitter than this has been. I have born this, but how can I bear another." However, this is only volume 20. Although she does not know it, she has 42 more diaries ahead of her, and increasingly they will describe good years. In 1898 she resumes her teaching that she had started in Kaweah. For the next 23 years her classes take her to various counties in Northern California. In 1909 she earns her permanent teaching diploma and in 1928 an annual pension of $383 for her retirement.

Anna Fader Haskell's diaries document the life of an unconventional woman who tried to live up to the standards of domesticity that even radical politicians espoused. Her daily reckonings clearly show the eroding effect of poverty on a marital relationship: the wife senses her double dependency, both financial and emotional, and feels guilty for expressing her needs. In this regard the most telling entry appears where she talks about not being able to have her teeth fixed:

> Then there is another thing that makes me feel bad—a little vain thing this is. My teeth are all broken and decayed in front. I who used to be so proud of my teeth, and it really has affected me so that I hate to go where there is any one—I hate to laugh or talk, because they show—I am morbidly sensitive on that point, because decayed teeth are to me the most disgusting thing in the world. Well I have spoken about having them fixed until I am ashamed, every time Burnette says very indifferently, you can have them fixed anytime. But never anything more than that.[19]

The Haskells' experience in Kaweah must have occurred in many parts of the country where high hopes ended in bitter disappointment when the immigrants did not find what they were looking for in the promised land. Still, Anna Fader Haskell's pioneer spirit was never broken. Writing about her son, she found him strong-headed and hard-willed, adding, "I suppose he must work out his salvation in his own way—as I have had to do, only I haven't worked it out yet by any means—but I will always keep trying."

THE IMMIGRANT HOUSEWIFE IN THE URBAN GHETTO

"Yes, we were poor," said Bertha Burkett at the end of her reminiscences, "but there was no running to the W.P.A. or anything else. We lived and grew and kept self-respect on what we had and we had many good times besides."[20] Always poor, she contributed the welfare payment to "somebody who really needed it." The immigrant housewife, following her husband to the promised land and finding herself in a tenement jungle, had to work harder for self-respect, because urban poverty and ethnic discrimination always threatened her sense of dignity. Americans have long been neglectful in giving immigrants from abroad as well as from distant rural parts of the U.S. their due in forging new ways of surviving in the life-challenging cities. A pilgrimage to the old Irish homestead is one thing, to the old Irish ghetto quite another. A grandmother who sold butter and eggs is no blemish on the family tree. Her family's poverty has become a record of pride. But the immigrant mother who scrubbed somebody else's floors or sat for hours on end behind a sewing machine was rarely asked to reminisce about her pioneer woman's past. On the contrary, she herself would hide this aspect of her past family life in shame, because one of the most basic requirements for middle-class respectability was that a mother did not work outside of the home.[21] Nevertheless the women of urban immigrant families, more characteristically than Western frontier women, were the prototypes of the wage-earning housewives of our own time.

Tenement Life

Whatever their reasons for uprooting themselves and making the hard journey to New York or Chicago, the immigrants inevitably found conditions of poverty and an endless cycle of work. Polish and Italian families who settled in rural America at first faced a ghetto in that they were excluded from the Anglo mainstream culture. But they were able to use their skills as farmers, and once they grew accustomed to the climate and soil they prospered. But for those who settled in the tenement districts of the Eastern cities, living conditions were so ghastly that merely keeping the apartments sanitary and livable was a crushing labor.

The tenement flat of the urban immigrant resembled the sodhouse or shanty in the limitation it imposed on family living standards. It offered no amenities, and did not even meet the basic requirements for the health and safety of its occupants, which generally far exceeded the number for which it was intended. Like the pioneers' first houses on the frontier, the tenement apartment was a shelter, no more, no less. Yet for hundreds of thousands of people it was all the home they had. The following description of an immigrant home in Lawrence, Massachusetts, in 1912, conveys a sense of the primitiveness involved and, again, harks back to the colonial era and Abigail Adams's first cottage in Braintree:

> The kitchen more than any other spot provided security for the frightened and lonely immigrant. Needing a place where all could go to perform the simple rituals, they turned to the kitchen. . . . Since it was the only heated room, it was ordinarily in the middle of the tenement with two rooms in front and two in back. Here, instead of the peasant hearth, was the stove that warmed the cold, fed the hungry, and cheered the unhappy. And here, too, were beds because the room was warm, the household large, and the apartment small.[22]

Other characteristics of typical immigrant housing conditions reinforced the resemblance to housing in the colonial era. An average of seven to nine people, some of whom were lodgers, packed into three or four rooms was common in both periods. The boarding of lodgers was the traditional method of increasing the family income in both eras as well. The high birth and infant mortality rates in the tenement ghettos were also similar to rates a hundred years earlier despite the application of sanitation principles and medical knowledge in other social spheres. The outdoor hydrant and yard toilet, the standard convenience in the nineteenth-century inner cities, were part of eighteenth-century living as well.

The crucial difference between the two eras, as noted earlier with respect to rural pioneers, lay not in primitive housing per se but in the historical contexts of daily life. In colonial times, all people lacked modern appliances and improvements. By the late nineteenth century, however, such lacks were associated only with extreme poverty. Like illiteracy, they afflicted only the very lowest class of American; the top of the class structure had by then grown high. In Lawrence, Massachusetts, even the Irish, traditionally considered to be at the bottom of the barrel by many Americans, had moved to the hills and to political prominence by 1910, leaving the shantytown to the incoming southeastern Europeans and Blacks. In the words of social historian Cole, quoted above, "the characteristic immigrant movement between 1845 and 1912 was set up from the bottom of the bowl."[23]

Regardless of whether future generations of Italians or Poles would reach the rim of the bowl, which was the lure inherent in the dream that had brought them to America originally, the first-generation immigrant housewife had to create her home at the bottom, and she knew it. While upper-rim housewives installed gas lights, water closets, bathtubs, Turkish parlor suites, sewing machines, and Acme kitchen ranges, along with other essentials ordered from the Sears, Roebuck catalogue, immigrant women had to content themselves with the amenities, such as they were, more typical of colonial times.

By the turn of the century the principles of domestic hygiene had been implemented in new housing developments, but new immigrants could not afford to live in them. Sanitation in the tenements was nonexistent. In 1920, for example, 80 percent of the families in a Slovak district of Chicago still used cellar or yard toilets. A yard toilet might be used by five families, or 28 persons.[24] Privies were used on farms, but were outlawed by city health authorities, although sewers were only partly underground at the turn of the century. The latter made outdoor play a health and safety hazard and forced the tenement mother to keep her children indoors when she could not tend them.

The typical tenement flat, where all but one window opened into an air shaft, contributed to the high incidence of tuberculosis suffered by the immigrant populations. The sharing of toilets and water spigots among several large families and lodgers helped to spread all contagious diseases. The urban pioneer housewife had no control over the health hazards under which she and her family lived, even if she kept her flat as clean as possible. Invariably, the immigrant woman threw herself into the disheartening activity of keeping her home clean, though sometimes she would inadvertently make bad things worse by adhering to Old World cleaning methods— for example, by pouring buckets of water over the floor that would drip through the ceiling of the flat below.

Mary Antin, author of *The Promised Land* (1911), describes her mother's part in the Russian-Jewish family's struggle against poverty as the most difficult one played in the family:

> Perhaps my mother's pack was the heaviest to lift. To the man of the house, poverty is a bulky dragon . . . and it is possible to give him knightly battle, with the full swing of the angry arm. . . . To the housewife, want is an insidious myriapod creature that crawls in the dark, mates with its own offspring, breeds all the year round, persists like leprosy. The woman has an endless, inglorious struggle with the pest; her triumphs are too petty for applause, her failures too mean for notice.[25]

Antin's family moved from one tenement area to another, each slightly poorer than the one before. In each location, the father's store stood a smaller chance of succeeding, since in each neighborhood the customers were poorer than the last. The situation was not untypical. Like a homesteader defeated by failing crops and the lack of skills and seed money, urban pioneer families were often forced to retreat from bad to worse, vainly battling against the press toward downward mobility. Confined to her private sphere, the wife had to depend on her husband's success. Regardless of her housekeeping capacities, the quality of where and how she and her family lived depended on her husband's work, for at first it was he alone who "made the living."

It was an irony of fate that placed the European peasant woman in the urban environment rather than in the sodhouse on the western frontier, which would have more closely resembled her native home. Just as the frontierswoman found herself out of her element, all her skills useless in her new environment, so the urban immigrant wife suffered the fate of the displaced person, forced to combat conditions for which she was totally untrained. Thus, a Polish housewife, for example, would complain that in America the cleaning of woodwork, hardwood floors, and windows was too laborious. Housekeeping on the Polish farm had been relatively simple: the women needed only to sweep the dirt floor, shake the featherbeds, and serve the same stew or soup from the same pot for each meal. Such women were used to focusing their energies on hard outdoor labor, and they had trouble with the complicated American diet with its individual dishes. Not only did this sort of meal involve more preparation, but it produced more dirty dishes for washing. In this context, the most defeating blow of all was the fact that the transplanted housewife had nothing to teach her daughters, since the homemaking skills she learned from her mother were worthless in the consumer-oriented society in which she found herself.

Basically, then, an immigrant wife had to learn how to cook and keep house all over again. The typical tenement kitchen had no storage space; therefore, the woman was forced into a daily shopping routine, and this too involved the development of a new skill. Somehow she had to learn how to make her husband's pitiful wages feed the entire family, by finding her way through the bewildering system of shops and districts that make up a city's consumer resources. With respect to the availability of food, the frontier pioneer was often in a comparatively enviable position, for at harvest time, at least, food was plentiful.

American currency was as foreign to the immigrant housewife as was the consumer economy itself. Labor in the old country had been paid for in meat and grain or land and living space, not in money. But in America the husband's weekly earnings were pledged to the landlord and grocer even before he brought them home. Cast into this morass, the meaning of which she could barely discern even though survival depended on her outwitting it, the immigrant woman did what she could to keep afloat. Barefoot, she walked the streets of the city (the family could only afford shoes for the husband and school-age children) searching for scraps of wood and bits of coal, for she was used to collecting her own fuel as part of her household duties.

Immigrants who did find work earned pauper's wages. In 1885, the average yearly salary of white-collar and professional families in Boston was $1,151. Rentals for high-quality apartments ranged from $250 to $420 a year, and middle-income housing was available for from $132 to $204 a year. In comparison, the immigrant paid from $96 to $112 a year for the worst kind of tenement flat, whereas 40 percent of Boston's wage earners, roughly approximating that city's immigrant population, earned less than $500 a year, and 11 percent made less than $250.[26]

One more similarity with the rural pioneer way of life—the frequency of working accidents, incapacitating the husband as wage earner—combined with general economic conditions to force urban immigrant women into going to work. The immigrant wife took this step out of necessity; her family simply could not survive on one source of wages, even when the husband was healthy and working. By forcing themselves to enter the alien world of manufacturing and retail trade—even under prevailing sweatshop conditions, these women laid the groundwork for the modern wage-earners who must combine housework and paid work. However, with respect to breadwinning wives ethnic heritage had a strong influence. Irish women most frequently left home to save the family from starvation but Italian mothers were not allowed to do so.[27] Where cultural restrictions prevailed on married women, sons and daughters were taken out of school to add a few dollars a week to the budget, rather than risk a loss in status for sending Momma out to work. Jewish wives were more likely permitted to work in Jewish stores, but family pride did not allow them to work in factories. From the beginning, women with family obligations were restricted in their efforts to earn a living by the type of jobs they took on, by the amount of housework they had to keep doing, and by the degree of hurt they could inflict on the family's pride if their culture prohibited mothers from working for pay outside the home. Keeping boarders or doing piece sewing work at home remained the most acceptable and least acknowledged method for a married woman to supplement the family income.

Our culture evinces nostalgia for the rural pioneers, but it was the urban pioneer women who contributed most to the modern work pattern. Working mothers from the poor urban subcultures were the role models for today's working women, though they would have been amazed to learn that fact. By acknowledging their contribution, we can identify the origins of some characteristic and often troubling attitudes that modern women hold toward work. One such attitude is that women's work is never permanent, that it serves as a temporary stopgap to be discontinued when conditions improve. Many modern working women dream of the day when they will stop working and resume their full-time homemaker role.[28] This thinking, particularly common among working-class women, originated among the poor who worked under sweatshop conditions.

Few women in the nineteenth-century labor force imagined that they would be wage earners for most of their lives. The haphazard methods with which they sought employment when their husbands got sick or when financial ruin threatened revealed that they unconsciously feared acknowledging the reality of poverty. In their minds, they were only helping out when they accepted the first job at the corner laundry. Often, they chose to forego training that would lead to a better-paying position, since they held that the training would be wasted or that they were too old to learn.

For these tenement-dwelling working wives, personal success was based not on advancement at their jobs but on their household activities, where duty and service to others was rewarded while personal aspirations were frowned on and even ridiculed. Working mothers, therefore, were seldom promoted even when they had the chance to earn more pay. Instead, their temporary jobs characteristically ran into years of monotonous work at laundries or in sewing sweatshops. Within this framework, they took pride in their stable work records, which they viewed as proving their faithfulness and industry. As on the frontier, women's willingness to stick to their work whether they liked it or not was seen as a virtue, not a lack of ambition.[29] This same mentality, of course, was—and has always been—applied to household and office drudgery.

Two other factors contributed to the tentativeness with which women identified with their work. The first, and most obvious, was that the kinds of work available to women were odious. In 1900, besides working at home or in laundries and sweatshops, most immigrant and Black women found employment in domestic positions. Servants were in as short supply as ever in private households, and wealthy people competed with the hotels and laundries for cheap labor from the immigrant population. But even there, there was prejudice. The following advertisement echoes an old aversion to the Irish, expressed a century earlier by Abigail Adams: "Woman Wanted.—To do general housework. English, Scotch, Welsh, German, or any country or color except Irish."[30] Domestic service also drew a lot of second-generation Americans: half of the 1.2 million maids, cooks, and charwomen had immigrant parents. Besides yielding low wages and a 16–hour workday, a job in a wealthy home offered a woman the opportunity to learn about setting a table for a 12–course dinner and cooking with 50 eggs at a time—a skill of questionable value for a tenement-dwelling house-wife. In spite of their complaints about bossy housewives, long hours, and lack of freedom, domestic service remained the top occupation for women— by frequency, not pay—until 1940. The double dilemma of serving two sets of families and mothering two sets of children—her own and her employer's—added to the frustration of married domestics. As one nanny explained in 1910:

I see my own children only when they happen to see me on the streets when I am out with the children, or when my children come to the yard to see me, which isn't often, because my white folks don't like to see their servants' hanging around the premises. You might as well say that I'm on duty all the time—from sunrise to sunrise, every day in the week. I am the slave, body and soul, of this family.[31]

This particular nanny had advanced over the years to a weekly salary of $10; although she slept and ate at her employer's home, she paid the rent for her own house. Factory women earned between $5 and $6 for a 60–hour week; then as now they were paid lower wages than men for similar work.

Although even under repressive conditions women took pride in their work, too often work was a grim necessity whose sole reward was a pitiful sum of money that might pay the landlord. In this fact lies the origin of the stigma against working wives commonly found among people who have managed to climb above that necessity. Here also lie the beginnings of the generation gap that opened up between immigrant parents and the children they boosted into better homes and jobs.

However, the most important factor that prevented all types of working women from committing themselves seriously to their work was the continuous pressure of their household responsibilities. A man at the end of his workday could stop off at the corner bar before going home to his meal and a well-deserved rest. His wife, however, having worked all day, would come home to attend to her regular cleaning duties, which included boiling laundry over the kitchen stove and ironing with a coal iron at night. Usually, the laundering and ironing had to be done two or three times a week, since the children had only one change of clothes. Some mothers kept their children home from school when their clothes had not been readied in time.

Because of her staggering responsibilities, the mother of small children who had to earn money often preferred to work at home as the tenement janitor or by taking care of other working mothers' children or by boarding lodgers. For two dollars a week, a lodger could expect his bed to be made and his food cooked. For the woman, these expectations often meant a complicated, task-juggling schedule when the men of any household worked on different shifts or adhered to different national diets. But because male lodgers contributed to the income, she had to meet their demands before meeting those of her family.

Immigrant women generally offered little resistance to such expectations. Often they were used to them, since they reflected Old World images of women. According to Mary Antin, immigrant men "rated the mental capacity of the average woman as only a little above the cattle she tended."[32] The following description of second-generation Irish and German immigrants on New York's West Side in 1904 indicates that the old native attitudes died hard, if at all:

> The husband comes home at night, has his dinner, and goes out with the "men," or sits at home to read his paper. She keeps house for him and bears his children. . . . He does not ill-treat her unless he is a brute or habitually drunk, but there is little spiritual comradeship. . . . The husband does not

MAYER'S PLACE

Unique for its grass plot. Janitress in the doorway

10. Janitress at Mayer's Place. From MOTHERS WHO MUST EARN by Katharine Anthony. © 1914 by The Russell Sage Foundation. Reprinted by permission of Basic Books, Inc., Publishers.

help the wife in the duty of childrearing. He does not heed her physical weariness. . . . There is little respect. They refer to each other as "Her" and "Him."[33]

Although this statement might reveal more about the observer's value system than about the true quality of individual relationships, it does suggest that the tenement housekeeper received little understanding from her husband, regardless of whether she expected it or not. How much compatibility was possible under the pressure of day-to-day adverse conditioning in the tenements is a matter of conjecture. The dynamics of frustration and defeat, too, are familiar to us in modern time. We can recognize the implications when wage-earning husbands under threat of debts, illness, and total ruin turned to alcohol for escape, and, in the age-old pattern, deserted their families altogether. The wives bore the brunt of these reactions. Many women interviewed by social workers from 1902 through 1904 in New York tenements expressed the hope that their daughters would not marry.[34] They attributed their own plight to marriage, expressing strong resentment against their husbands, almost as if the men had misled them by enticing them with false expectations. But they also felt that they had had no choice but to marry their particular husbands at the particular times they did. Overall, in these interviews, the women exhibited a total lack of self-determination. Pioneering under these conditions then meant keeping your head above water in order to survive. Reminiscences of urban frontier women are much fewer than from the West. In cities where success was measured by where you lived and what you could buy, survival alone did not count for much.

Adapting to the New Life

The Americanization of the immigrant housewife was a slow and often painful process. Here again, with respect to acculturation, the urban pioneer housewife had an even more difficult time than the rural pioneer woman. The latter saw herself as bringing refinement and "civilization" to a crude mining camp or a barren plain, while the immigrant woman found herself adrift in an intimidatingly complex culture with few means of buoying up her self-esteem. Under pressure from husband and children, who had regular contact with Americans at work and school, as well as from "helpful" volunteers who went to the immigrant settlements to teach the newcomers how to cook and save and keep baby from getting sick, the alien homemaker was made to see her old ways as wrong. The changes required of her to adapt to American standards involved more than household techniques, since she could not change her "odd" or "ignorant" methods of housekeeping without relinquishing part of her identity.

Mary Antin's account of her Russian-Jewish mother sheds light on the culture shock all immigrants experienced. For Antin's mother, religion was not confined to the temple or to Sabbath, but was integrated into her housekeeping procedures. In breaking one routine, a woman risked the eventual erosion of all the old values, including her own position in the family structure.

> My mother . . . had not the initial impulse to depart from ancient usage that my father had in his habitual scepticism. He had always been a nonconformist in his heart; she bore lovingly the yoke of prescribed conduct. Individual freedom to him was the only tolerable condition in life; to her it was confusion. My mother, therefore, gradually divested herself, at my father's bidding, of the mantle of orthodox observance; but the process cost her many a pang, because the fabric of that venerable garment was interwoven with the fabric of her soul. . . . On Sabbath eve my mother might believe and worship as she pleased, up to the point where her orthodoxy began to interfere with the American progress of the family.
>
> The price that all of us paid for this disorganization of our family life has been levied on every immigrant Jewish household where the first generation clings to the traditions of the Old World, while the second generation leads the life of the New.[35]

Antin's mother came from a world where women were judged not as individuals but as performers of certain tasks within the family and the orthodox community. These tasks had been fixed by traditional rituals passed on from mother to daughter for generations. For such a woman, the act of thinking for herself was a revolutionary concept. It took Mrs. Antin years to learn how to distinguish between "the husk of Judaism," which might be dropped, and the kernel without which her life would be meaningless. The experience was typical of people from many different cultures: it took most immigrants a lifetime to sort out those American ways that were necessary for survival in the new culture from those destructive to their rightful heritage and personal identity.

The Russian peasant woman who left her national costume behind arrived in America without a means of establishing credibility. In the Old World system, her dress told at once who she was and where she came from. With new clothes purchased in a New York department store she exchanged her cultural identity for a new anonymity. Further, what made her respectable at home did not necessarily make her so now, particularly if she had to begin her Americanization at the bottom of the melting pot. As we saw, poverty and respectability were no longer compatible as they had been in the eighteenth century. At the turn of the century, the foreign immigrant woman, like the Black woman from the rural South, had to adjust to the fact that she was the lowest of the low while at the same time she was learning to subscribe to the values of the "real" Americans, the middle class.[36]

Immigrants attempting to acclimatize themselves to the new culture faced formidable resistance from the outside. While they were trying to convince themselves that they deserved the same middle-class amenities that every other American seemed to be striving for, quotas were being established by the immigration authorities in an attempt to stem the tide of foreign "undesirables." Competition for jobs and space was fierce, and the struggle resulted in open discrimination against minority ethnic groups. Newspapers pitted groups against each other by periodically publishing statistics that supposedly revealed which nationality spawned the worst troublemakers, the most illiterates, or people with the dirtiest habits. The nation's population as a whole responded to these pitches, and rampant social discrimination swept the country, not only in the overpopulated areas, but also in the open prairie and the Far West. Clearly, the pressure on individual immigrants to become acceptable to "regular Americans," if for no other reason than to gain fair treatment, was immense.

The housewife felt deeply this pressure to acculturate, since she was responsible for her family's appearance. Teachers, immigration officials, social workers—the representatives of the American establishment—divided the immigrants they saw into two categories, the "deserving poor" and the "undeserving poor," on the basis of the appearance of their clothes and their apartments. Mothers had good reason to keep their children home from school rather than send them in unkempt clothes.

The first social workers—representatives of private charity organizations—were particularly attuned to superficial appearances in making judgments that determined a family's eligibility for assistance. These "friendly visitors" as they called themselves judged a mother by the cleanliness of her flat. In their reports, they listed such information as number of children or number of boarders, but the officials who read them rarely saw these factors as excusing a woman's disheveled appearance or the tattered condition of her children's clothes. To explain the shockingly high infant mortality and frequency of children who were maimed by accidents or were undernourished, the friendly visitors also dutifully reported mothers' ignorance regarding proper food or feeding schedules and their lack of knowledge regarding budgeting and hygiene.[37]

Social workers noticed that children slept two and three in a bed in windowless rooms and were not taken for walks. They shook their heads when mothers called the priest instead of the doctor when baby was sick. Few cited the awful housing conditions as the causative factor. A mother's ethnic background did count as a reason for her superstition or ignorance. Indirectly or directly officials tended to blame the mother for shirking her responsibility.[38]

The benevolent societies created for the "deserving poor" inevitably cast poor women in the role of "creatures to be pitied." Privileged women traditionally did charity work on behalf of the underprivileged, and these efforts were fraught with misunderstanding on both sides. Inadvertently charity workers judged these toiling housewives by their own standards of cleanliness and good taste. Miraculously they found exemplary women who did in fact manage to accomplish the superhuman job of keeping their children's clothes washed and mended, keeping the flat sanitary, and even finding the resources for children's piano lessons. The latter, however, was judged as an extravagance. Covertly, they thus concluded that the job could be done by those who really tried. Further, they recommended that domestic skills could and should be taught. Teaching tenement housewives how to manage their homes became the goal of the settlement workers— social reformers whose special focus was to better the living conditions in the urban slums.

Such intrepid reformers as Jane Addams and Sophronisba Breckenridge drew a family's bill of housing rights, which guaranteed each citizen access to adequate space, sunlight, sanitation, and safety. Housing standards which are now legally enforced were born on the urban frontier. The founders of the settlement houses in Chicago and New York learned to differentiate between personal and social shortcomings. Teaching immigrants to become good Americans according to their principles meant first of all treating them as citizens and giving them a decent place to live and work. Like the lady activists of previous decades, it was the middle-class daughters and wives, rather than working mothers themselves, who took on the public housecleaning at the turn of the century. Their achievements were significant: they created child care centers, Montessori schools, mothers' workshops, health clinics, and adult education classes. But though the settlement movement helped women acculturate, poverty housewives remained reluctant to organize in order to improve their lot, except on an informal, personal basis within the family or the religious or ethnic community. In this respect the toiling tenement housewife stood far behind single, full-time women workers, who had been organizing for self-help and labor improvement since the 1840s. Even the now famous Mother Jones favored working men over working housewives in her campaign to stamp out the exploitation of laborers.[39]

The immigrant housewife was the last in her family to avail herself of what educational advantages were open to her in America. Too often she was left looking backward, like Lot's wife, as her family moved on at work and at school, marrying second-generation Americans and identifying with the established American community. Her response to the American dream was to push her children relentlessly toward all the possibilities for a better life—toward any type of job or schooling that would take them out of the tenement environment. The irony was that by encouraging them she was losing them, not only as loved family members but as individuals at home who could share the household responsibilities. As she succeeded, so she was left behind. All the social forces at work in the tenement districts and immigrant settlements conspired against her adaptation to American life.

Caught in a strange environment but cut off from it by language and location, the immigrant wife struggled to become a *real* American—that is, a middle-class American—by buying American products from the street peddlers and the corner grocery stores. Even without the power of modern advertising, such luxuries as coffee, white bread, and canned goods attracted these poor women as symbols of America's good life. Moreover, these commodities were readily available and fresh produce was not. When the Russian housewife in Boston replaced the traditional thick vegetable soup, which had always simmered on top of the stove in the Old Country, with a pot of coffee, she was depriving her family of their much-needed nourishment, for all the pleasure they may have derived from the coffee. But she acted partly out of necessity in doing so, since she was often totally unaware of how to find familiar vegetables. Fresh produce was plentiful in the Italian section of Boston, but the Italians and the Russians lived at opposite ends of the city. And besides, even if she found the produce market, how could she make herself understood or trusted enough to gain credit? Better to stay home and feed her family white bread.

Although immigrants lived for the most part in the "melting pot," little interchange took place among the cultures. The Italian housewife might share her strong sense of family with the Russian Jew, but the two remained segregated because of religion. The Italian woman shared religion with the Irish Catholic but disapproved of the looser Irish family structure. The idea that since immigrants or minorities share problems they might pool resources to solve them has never been borne out in reality. Rather, the segregation of different immigrant groups has contributed to the assimilation problems and the lack of control that each group experiences in the mainstream environment.

If the immigrant housewife had difficulties in adapting, her husband's prospects for living up to his hopes were also slim. Although the work ethic was reinforced popularly in the nineteenth century by Horatio Alger–type stories, opportunities for the urban pioneer, as for the rural pioneer, were limited by the nation's economy in general and by racial discrimination in particular. According to Pleck, "the Irish, once the most downtrodden group in Boston, had climbed the social ladder by the turn of the century, whereas black Bostonians remained at its bottom rung."[40] Those immigrants who did manage to succeed sometimes built their enterprises on the exploitation of newcomers belonging to their own ethnic group. Bondsmen of every nationality, for instance, imported cheap laborers for handsome fees from their native lands. The foreign immigrant wife came to America as an appendage to her husband, and remained in the ghetto as her children left the nest to enter the new culture—a displaced housewife with no real hope for forging a new identity of her own.

In general, both rural and urban pioneer housewives belonged to social groups in which the chances for self-determination and self-improvement were severely limited. But, as in any group, the spirit of certain individuals proved irrepressible, and through the efforts of such people new possibilities were created.

Strong women such as Abigail Duniway followed the urge to explore and act in spite of the limitations imposed on them. In their own time these women were viewed as rebels; we see them now as innovators and trail-breakers. The dependent pioneer was an accepted paradox as long as the female experience was defined by traditional role divisions. The pathbreakers were in time duly noticed, but the ordinary homemakers who pioneered within the walls of their homes were recognized only by their children. Sons and daughters such as Mario Puzo or Mary Antin wrote about them, but generally they remained anonymous.

Some immigrant women learned to read and write in middle life, even though they had been brought up to believe that women could not or should not be literate. These late scholars were real pioneers in their own way: they were able to transcend the stereotypes that had pressed down on them throughout their lives.

But the most fundamental contribution of America's pioneer women to the social fabric was the wage-earning housewife who left the physical confines of the home to work.

By 1900 almost 50 percent of all the female wage earners were immigrants or daughters of immigrants, another 15 percent were Black women, and a significant proportion had to both subsidize their family's income and attend to their normal household duties. Their pioneering contribution was obscured at the time by the shadow of poverty under which they toiled. For the next decades, the need of women to go to work was viewed as a hardship. Most women who could avoid working by virtue of their husbands' or fathers' incomes remained firmly entrenched in the home. The home was the first, and often the only, symbol of prosperity. At all social levels, it was through her home that a housewife was judged as a worker, and, among the upper classes, which set the standards for the rest, the total immersion in domesticity was coming to be seen as the greatest virtue of the wife.

Thus, the skills that many immigrant housewives finally managed to acquire in the New Country, and many that they brought from the old, were lost to their daughters. The new generation of women, if the mother had succeeded at all, was assimilated into the American culture more completely than anyone had imagined was possible. These daughters—when their American dreams came true—lived in houses with more con-

veniences and fewer children than their mothers had ever dared hope for.
Just as earlier generations of native daughters had aspired to refine their
houses to ladies' homes, the daughters of the pioneers disdained household
drudgery and had no desire to go back to work for a few dollars in a shop
or a garment factory. If they married well, they saw their role as displaying
the home in light of their husbands' wages earned away from home. If
they had higher ambitions they worked for the public good. If they were
educated and leaned toward the sciences, they took up what came to be
called scientific housekeeping.

NOTES

1. "The Pioneers," address delivered in 1902 at unveiling of the Monument to
the Pioneer Woman, *Contributions of Historical Society of Montana*, vol. 4, p. 134,
quoted in Margaret Ronan's *Frontier Woman: The Story of Mary Ronan As Told
to Her Daughter* (Missoula, Mont.: University of Montana Press, 1973), p. viii;
Mario Puzo, "Choosing a Dream: Italians in Hell's Kitchen," in *The Immigrant
Experience* (New York: Dial Press, 1971), p. 35.

2. Robert L. Griswold, *Family and Divorce in California, 1850–1890: Victorian
Illusions and Everyday Realities* (Albany: State University of New York Press,
1982), pp. 24–47, shows that divorce was not a middle-class phenomenon and that
working-class couples not only filed more often, but also adhered to middle-class
ideals of companionate marriage and sanctified motherhood reflected in contemporary newspapers and magazines; Elizabeth H. Pleck, *Black Migration and Poverty: Boston 1865–1900* (New York: Academic Press, 1979), compares Irish and
Blacks from the South with Northern Blacks, who "were bourgeois in deed and
in thought but not in economic assets" (p. 200). More wives from this group filed
for divorce because of a husband's poverty, desertion, and sickness, and their own
capacity to support themselves. Other contributing factors in Boston were child-
lessness and diminished attachment to Black church and family.

3. Julie R. Jeffrey, *Frontier Women: The Trans-Mississippi West, 1840–1880*
(New York: Hill and Wang, 1978), pp. 28–29.

John Faragher emphasizes the idea of the passive pioneer:

> The psychology of social dependency, with its costs and rewards, was the result of
> the systematic oppression of women of which their marital relations were the key link.
> Their induction onto the trail, not as full and willing participants but more as reluctant
> draftees, was the cause not of rebellion and resistance, although there were occasional
> examples of those, but of self-denial, a kind of active passivity and endurance.

(John M. Faragher, *Women and Men on the Overland Trail* [New Haven: Yale
University Press, 1979], p. 178).

For a refutation of this image and a closer look at the working women outside
the middle class see "Women in the American West," *Pacific Historical Review*,
vol. 49, no. 2 (May, 1980). The entire issue is devoted to that topic. Sandra L.
Myres, *Westering Women and the Frontier Experience 1800–1915* (Albuquerque:
University of New Mexico Press, 1982), offers a tapestry of experiences that supports both the active and passive image of the pioneer.

4. C. W. Drepperd, *Pioneer America: Its First Three Centuries* (Garden City: Doubleday, 1949), p. i.

5. Different ethnic groups can be traced through recent publications on their separate pioneer experience such as Rudolf M. Lapp, *Blacks in Gold Rush California* (New Haven: Yale University Press, 1977), and Douglas Henry Daniels, *Pioneer Urbanites: A Social and Cultural History of Black San Francisco* (Philadelphia: Temple University Press, 1980).

6. Quoted in Annegret Ogden, "Queen or Camp Follower? The Life of the Military Wife in Early California," *The Californians* (March/April, 1984), pp. 11–16. For further study see Patricia Y. Stallard, *Glittering Misery: Dependents of the Indian Fighting Army* (San Rafael, Calif.: Presidio Press, 1978).

7. General Custer's widow and General Fremont's wife, Jessie, had to support themselves and their families by writing reminiscences because pensions were low or, as in Fremont's case, lacking altogether.

8. Nancy W. Ross, *Westward the Women* (New York: Knopf, 1944), p. 7.

9. Ronan, *Frontier Woman*, p. 90.

10. Abigail Scott Duniway, *Pathbreaking: An Autobiographical History of the Equal Suffrage Movement in The Pacific Coast States*, 2d ed. (Portland, Ore.: James, Kerns & Abott, 1914), pp. 10–13.

11. Mary A. Jones (1825–1918), "The Story of My Life" (manuscript in Bancroft Library, Univ. of Calif.).

12. Bertha Burkett, "My Early Life on the South Dakota Prairies" (manuscript in private family, lent to author), p. 45.

13. Ibid.

14. Everett Dick, *The Sod-House Frontier, 1854–1890* (New York: Johnson Publishing Co., 1954), pp. 270–271.

15. Ibid., pp. 222–223; for more information see Joanna L. Stratton, *Pioneer Women: Voices from the Kansas Frontier* (New York: Simon and Schuster, 1981), which contains good documentation of housekeeping.

16. Elise Waerenskjold, *The Lady with the Pen: Elise Waerenskjold in Texas* (Northfield, Minn., Norwegian-American Historical Association, 1961), p. 67.

17. Duniway, *Pathbreaking*, p. 42.

18. Anna Fader Haskell, unpublished pocket diary, 1876–1942, 65 vols. in the manuscript collection of The Bancroft Library. See also Annegret Ogden, "Sixty-five New Year's Eves," *The Californians* (November/December, 1984), from which part of this information has been taken.

19. Ibid., March 15, 1884.

20. Burkett, "My Early Life," p. 45.

21. Susan E. Kennedy, *If All We Did Was to Weep at Home: A History of White Working Class Women in America* (Bloomington, Ind.: Indiana Univ. Press, 1979), pp. xiv-xvii, a trend that lasted until the 1940s. Lynn W. Weiner, *From Working Girl to Working Mother* (Chapel Hill, N.C.: Univ. of North Carolina Press, 1985), p. 85.

22. Donald B. Cole, *Immigrant City, Lawrence, Massachusetts, 1845–1921* (Chapel Hill, N.C.: Univ. of North Carolina Press, 1963), pp. 107–108.

23. Ibid., p. 109.

24. "Chicago Housing Studies," *American Journal of Sociology*, vol. 20 (September, 1914), p. 154. See also Margaret Frances Byington, *Homestead: The*

Households of a Mill Town (New York: Charities Publications Committee, 1910; Arno Reprint, 1969).

25. Mary Antin, *The Promised Land* (New York: Houghton Mifflin, 1911), pp. 310–311.

26. Lloyd Rodwin, *Housing and Economic Progress: A Study of the Housing Experience of Boston's Middle-Income Families* (Cambridge, Mass.: Harvard Univ. Press, 1961), pp. 133–134. In 1885, a man "earned $500 a year for 250 days' work (because of frequent lay-offs). Since his total expenses were over $600, he could not survive unless his wife worked." By 1893, when wages dipped below $300, rents were often $200 a year. "By this time a man had difficulty surviving unless his children as well as his wife worked"; Cole, *Immigrant City*, pp. 118–119. By 1970, the average blue-collar income was $9,500 (before taxes)—the average income of a Black worker was still 30 percent less. The lowest family budget to meet living expenses was $6,960 (the affluent family required $15,950). By then "more than anything else, it is the working wives who have made possible even the modest standard of living workers enjoy"; Andrew Levison, *The Working Class Majority* (New York: Coward, McCann & Geoghegan, 1974), p. 39. By 1980, the wage-earning wife becomes a middle-class necessity.

27. Kennedy, *If All We Did Was to Weep at Home*, chapter 3, pp. 48–67, "Immigrant Women from Several Cultures," explains different attitudes about married women as compared to unmarried daughters. For southern Italians it was important to keep women under supervision of relatives; Jewish girls were permitted to work in order to put their future husbands through school, but wives were expected to stay at home or operate the family business only. See also Jacob R. Marcus, *The American Jewish Woman, 1654–1980* (New York: KTAV Publishing House, Inc., 1981), pp. 105–109, which points to class difference between German and East European Jews as well as to frequent incidents of desertion by husbands who no longer wanted to be associated with their "old country" wives (p. 144).

28. Ibid., p. 131. A *Los Angeles Times* poll (August, 1984) reported that 24 percent of the female wage earners versus 14 percent of the males would stop working if they could afford it. See also Chapter VII of this book.

29. Interviews with working mothers show this mentality (O. G. Cartwright, *The Middle West Side: Mothers Who Must Earn* [New York: Russell Sage Foundation, 1914]).

30. Kennedy, *If All We Did Was to Weep at Home*, p. 102; Alice Kessler-Harris, *Women Have Always Worked; A Historical Overview* (Old Eastbury, N.Y.: The Feminist Press, 1981), pp. 80–81.

31. W. E. Brownlee and Mary M. Brownlee, *Women in the American Economy* (New Haven: Yale Univ. Press, 1976), p. 246.

32. Antin, *The Promised Land*, p. 246.

33. Elsa G. Herzfeld, *Family Monographs: The History of 24 Families Living in the Middle West Side of New York City* (New York: J. Kempster Printing Co., 1905), pp. 50–55.

34. Ibid.

35. Antin, *The Promised Land*, pp. 247–248.

36. Pleck, *Black Migration and Poverty*, pp. 75–85, points to Northern Blacks' prejudice against Southern immigrants, even segregated housing, partly by choice of Southerners who like white immigrants lived together in order to help themselves.

Northern Blacks took pride in their advanced education and middle-class respectability. The same was true for the Black establishment in New York and San Francisco.

37. The *Jewish Settlement Cookbook* excluded pork, but included recipes for lobsters and frogs' legs, according to Marcus, *The American Jewish Woman*, p. 100.

38. Roy Lubove, *The Professional Altruist: The Emergence of Social Work as a Career, 1880–1930* (Cambridge, Mass.: Harvard University Press, 1965), pp. 22–54.

39. Kennedy, *If All We Did Was to Weep at Home*, p. 115.

40. Discrimination for Blacks worsened with each decade. Pleck, *Black Migration and Poverty*, p. 41, states:

> Once blacks had stood side by side, in the same kind of poverty as the Irish ... but by the turn of the century, the distance between the groups had widened: a growing disadvantage in health and inequality in property ownership, income and occupational status.

For a comparison of kinship and wage-earning patterns see Michaela Di Leonardo, *The Varieties of Ethnic Experience: Kinship, Class and Gender among California Italian Americans* (Ithaca, N.Y.: Cornell University Press, 1984).

5

From Scientist to Consumer, 1900–1950

> Household problems, large and small, became invested with entirely new interests and new possibilities. Instead of being something upon which to slave, they became objects of keen mental interest—quite the same ...as the tasks of the business and industrial world which men tackle with zest and results.
>
> —Christine Frederick, *The New Housekeeping: Efficiency Studies in Home Management*, 1914[1]

By the beginning of the twentieth century, the two images of women that had been forged during the last decades of the nineteenth century were firmly established in American society. The first image was that of the ladylike homemaker, totally immersed in the domestic arts and fully responsible for the well-being and comfort of her family. Such a woman was a middle- or upper-class lady who, by virtue of her husband's earnings, inhabited an insular world, separate from the employment market, that represented a haven from the commercial society outside her door. But the saintly homemaker was not a wilting violet. As encouraged by such writers as Catherine Beecher and Harriet Stowe, she applied her wit and intelligence to fashioning a retreat she could rightfully take pride in.

The second female image to which Americans had grown accustomed by 1900 was that of the poverty-stricken woman, often an immigrant or an immigrant's daughter, who had been forced to take a paying job. At this time, the taboo against women going to work was broken. Gradually during these early decades of our century society became accustomed to the idea of unmarried females, supporting themselves in respectable careers, who chose to remain unmarried. Gradually, too, married but childless women found an accepted place in newly developing professions. Thus, by 1910 both the single and the childless working life represented true alternatives

·THE·WOMAN·WHO·WILL·READ·

11. "The Woman Who Will Read." Reproduced from Marion Harlan, *House and Home: A Complete Housewife's Guide* (Philadelphia: J. H. Moore, 1889).

for ambitious women to keeping house for a supporting male. Without bearing the onus of failure or poverty, women who chose this path inspired young girls of all classes to pursue the respectable careers of nursing, teaching, clerking, and telephone operating in increasing numbers. The mother of children, of course, except in conditions of necessity, remained firmly at home.

So strong was the appeal of financial independence that even girls who did not need money went to work willingly wherever they could find jobs. However, employers considered the wages of females nothing but "pin money" and established their pay rates accordingly. Rightfully they assumed that their young women workers would all marry and leave and that it was not worth the effort to train them; moreover, that it was therefore legitimate to pay them far less than men and to give them those jobs that men did not want. Therefore, though the lure of a job might redirect a girl's ambition from marriage to work, then as now marriage served as an escape from terrible working conditions and unfair treatment.

In the early years of the decade, the impulse toward female independence was accelerating in every area of public life, not just employment, but also volunteer activism culminating in the Nineteenth Amendment, which finally gave all American women the right to vote. Although World War I would claim its toll in human suffering, it would offer women an opportunity to test and prove their new strength in public. The period between the two wars—though domesticity throve and most of our homes and our current domestic standards date from that period—would become a showcase for a string of female public figures, from pilot Amelia Earhart and swimmer Gertrude Ederle to social reformers Jane Addams and Lilian Wald, which in sheer numbers alone represented an historic first. The public would laugh at the parade of 10,000 umbrella-carrying women who demanded the vote before the 1920 Republican National Convention and watch skeptically as suffrage veterans Jeanette Rankin and Frances Perkins stepped into public office. The citizenry would look on with some surprise as Pulitzer Prizes were awarded to Clare Boothe, Zona Gale, and Edith Wharton, and would wonder with alarm whether Dorothy Thompson and other peacemongers were perhaps anti-American. Through it all, society's privileged young girls, dressed as flappers, would tumble through the social scene like glittering clowns, while sober brigades of club women continued their battle with white slavery, alcoholism, and child labor, and for the first but not the last time took on the Equal Rights Amendment. Even the women's magazines carried the torch for women in business and politics. *Good Housekeeping* offered advice on how mothers could help their working daughters to get ahead and featured regular reports on legislative progress on women's issues.

But for all the ramifications of the independent spirit, these new kinds of women were not wholly free of the more traditional feminine values.

WESTERN WOMAN

Vol. 1. No. 14.   SAN FRANCISCO, OCTOBER 1907.   Price 10 Cents.

MRS. WILLIAM KEITH

of Berkeley, California—Good college woman, good wife, good friend, good citizen and good suffragist

12. Mary McHenry Keith graduated from the University of California College of Letters in 1879 and from the University's first law department in 1882. She abandoned her profession in probate law after one year's practice to marry the painter William Henry and to support his career instead of her own.
Reproduced through the courtesy of The Bancroft Library, University of California, Berkeley CA 94720.

With the exception, perhaps, of the most avant-garde career women, most of them harbored desires for husbands and children and homes and gardens while they worked, and most did eventually become homemakers. Women in the early decades of the new century wanted the vote, jobs, peace, birth control, and education. But they also wanted families and stable homes. They wanted to wear sports clothes and business attire, but they also wanted alluring evening gowns and fashionable "at-home" wear. Women began to pay millions of dollars for makeup from Elizabeth Arden and Helena Rubenstein, new companies that took advantage of the advertising machinery originating in the ladies' magazines of the late 1800s. Most American women, regardless of socioeconomic class, partook to one degree or another in the general trend toward self-expression outside the home, if only by appreciating accounts of other women in the press, but the majority continued to feel safest inside the traditional female territory: the household and nuclear family.

But though they married, many middle-class women had tasted a lot more freedom before they became brides than either their mothers or their grandmothers. Their chances of growing restless or depressed increased as they looked for the same kind of challenges in homemaking that they had experienced studying or working. Furthermore, for the first time in women's history housewives found themselves in competition with working women who were receiving recognition outside the home—recognition that until now had been a man's prerogative.

Ironically, a development that had its roots in the ghettos of the urban frontier now came to the rescue of middle-class women in the better neighborhoods. This was offered in the settlement houses, to help immigrant women run their households in the new land. If the immigrant homemaker could profit from instruction on diet, sanitation, and efficiency, why not the middle-class housewife? After all, her self-esteem depended on the excellence of her homemaking abilities, but in the first decades of the new century she was still steeped in the domestic traditions of the past.

The development of domestic science was a natural outgrowth of industrialization. New information was surfacing in matters of sanitation, medicine, nutrition, and many other fields affecting the well-being of the human race. Technology for production and concepts regarding production efficiency were becoming highly sophisticated by the early 1900s. Certain women of the new century saw how the new information, technology, and patterns of thinking could be applied in the home. The result was a new approach to housework and a new kind of housewife—the domestic scientist. By incorporating the latest scientific information into the methods for running her own home, she could change the humdrum kitchen into a laboratory. Moreover, she could view herself as a bona fide worker with a respectable career without renouncing the traditional values of wife- and motherhood. As we shall see, practitioners and theorists of the new field worked hard to refashion the middle-class homemaker into the domestic career women they envisioned.

Industrialization had another effect that contributed to what we might call the new consciousness of turn-of-the-century middle-class housewives. The Industrial Revolution was creating a new kind of poverty—the sufferings of sweatshop workers, destitute city children, and immigrants whose hopes were defeated by tenement living stood out in bold relief against the accelerating productiveness of the society in general. Ladies had always carried breadbaskets to the poor, but exposure to the effects of industrialization jolted many middle-class Americans into public action. One important impetus was the publication of muckraker Jacob Riis's articles, photographs and commentaries as in *How the Other Half Lives* (1890).[2] This journalist, himself an immigrant become citizen, described the slums he saw as police reporter with camera and words. Not only did he make a profound impression on the general public, but he motivated social reformers to devote their lives to improving the cities' urban blight. The more pervasive contribution to the new public concern was the steady evolution of the settlement movement, epitomized by Jane Addams's Hull House in Chicago (Addams was greatly moved by Riis's work) and the lectures and writings of activist-writers within the movement on society's responsibility to improve conditions in the inner city.

Well-off women across the nation responded to these calls for action in droves. They redirected their altruistic impulses away from individual charities and toward public-welfare efforts, freeing themselves from their domestic cares to join clubs, attend meetings, and draw up proposals and petitions. One reason for the response was that here, at least, in the world of social activisim, a woman could gain the kind of public recognition denied to her as a hostess or a family matriarch.

In the process of becoming educated to the effects of an increasingly industrial society on the less fortunate, white and Black middle-class women began to see that their own lives were influenced as well. They saw, for instance, that poor schools were affecting the development of their children and that unsanitary conditions in the food industries were affecting their families' health. Unsanitary conditions were having adverse effects on the nation's health in general, and unjust taxation was cutting into the monetary resources of middle-income families. Women with a social conscience began to feel that the time had come to take action against the external forces undermining their efforts at home. Consequently, the membership of women's clubs with social-reform goals reached a peak between 1915 and 1925. The net result of these associations was a new consciousness among the nation's women of the need for better homes in better communities. A significant secondary effect was an increase in the self-esteem of club members who felt themselves having an effect, both in their homes and in society at large. Such women were eager recipients of the kind of information that the avant-garde of domestic-science educators was attempting to convey.

SCIENTIFIC HOUSEKEEPING: THE EARLY VISION

Ellen Richards

The first educator to perceive the relevance of science to homemaking was Ellen Swallow Richards (1842–1911), the first female graduate and the first female faculty member of the Massachusetts Institute of Technology. Richards saw the need to use the scientific discoveries being made in the new century to improve human life and the environment. For seven years she taught without pay in MIT's Woman's Laboratory, which she helped to found and to support financially. In 1884, she was appointed instructor of sanitary chemistry at MIT, a position she held for 27 years. Her painstaking reseach in food and water analysis did not win her the PH.D. she desired, but it did earn her a place in the vanguard of the public health movement, which was just beginning to surface.

At a time when women's education was still either oriented toward the arts or narrowly confined to domestic skills, Richards advocated the teaching of chemistry to women as a defense against food adulteration and consumer fraud. She believed that the housewife armed with scientific knowledge would overcome the monotony of housekeeping with "the zest of intelligent experiment." Such a housewife would control her work rather than be controlled by it and control the consumer market rather than be victimized by it. Scientific housekeeping as perceived and practiced by Ellen Richards (she ran her own home as a laboratory for experimentation in plumbing, heating, and efficiency methods, employing interns rather than servants) was the end result of practical technique combined with an inquisitive state of mind. Richards saw scientific housewifery as a career and a total way of life that embraced both the private and public sectors and enabled the housekeeper to participate in each.

In retrospect, it was significant that Ellen Richards was happily married but had no children. If she had, perhaps she would have foreseen that later housewives would direct what she called their zest for intelligent experiment almost exclusively toward child development. As a childless wife and professional educator and scientist, Richards believed that informed, scientific housekeeping could be a satisfying career in itself. But her vision was never realized as fully among the women of America as she hoped.

Richards's ideas were by no means isolated, however, and they were consistent with other developments around the country. In 1898, Richards initiated the first Lake Placid Conference on Home Economics. The stated goal of the conference was to enable housewives to base their decisions on "intelligent direction from within," not simply on tradition and methods rooted in the past. Richards and the other participants never intended to start a domestic revival movement. Their interest lay in improving the social conditions on which domestic concerns rested. The overall idea of the conference—and of the new domestic-science movement in general— was to free the housewife from trivial household matters so she might tend to significant activities concerned with social reform.[3]

Many participants at the conference gained their training in the settlement movement. In dealing directly with the housing and dietary problems of the immigrants, they became aware that it was economic pressures rather than dust and dishes that led to the most serious difficulties in the home. They saw domestic issues as reflections of more general social conditions. Thus, while later practitioners and domestic educators stressed the word *home*, these early social-science pioneers stressed *economics*. They knew that household technology would only be effective if people could afford to buy and use it. The important issues to be addressed, as they saw domestic science, were such matters as industrial pollution, which brought dirt and poisons into the home; unsanitary waste-disposal methods, which caused typhus; the contamination of milk, which caused tuberculosis; and unemployment, which caused poverty.

Even Ellen Richards, a committed academic, knew that the social and economic change necessary to solve these problems would not be accomplished by educators alone. Thus, as the first president of the American Home Economics Association, founded in 1908, she set about creating a network for communication among professional home economists, community leaders, educators, and householders. She adamantly refused to see the new association as a woman's group or a group addressing female householders alone. Home economics involved both sexes, she argued, as it involved every social class and every degree of education. She saw home economics courses—which, in her vision, would be included in all school curricula, from primary school through university—as a means of making available critically important information in such areas as nutrition to all people for their own well-being. For Richards, the culmination of the science was *euthenics*, the science of improving human living conditions, which she conceived of as a university-level specialty.

Richards's influence was far-reaching within the fledgling field of domestic science. Laboratories similar to the one she ran at MIT sprang up under the leadership of professionals who had either studied with her or had been inspired by her pioneering work. Marian Talbot (1858–1948), for example, taught sanitary science for 19 years in the Department of Household Administration at the University of Chicago, founded in 1906. Sophronisba Breckenridge (1866–1948) and Edith Abbott (1876–1957) taught courses on the legal and economic position of women, cooperative housing, marketing, and consumer protection there. Isabel Bevier, a student of

Richards's who succeeded her as president of the American Home Economics Association, became professor of chemistry in the Department of Household Science at the University of Illinois. Other women inspired by Richards carried out private experiments in kitchen design and time and motion studies. One such disciple, Christine Frederick, was to have a profound effect on the metamorphosis of domestic science into the study of consumerism.

Martha Bensley Bruère

In 1916, Martha Bensley Bruère wrote *Increasing Home Efficiency*. In that work she stated outright her belief that the home should be made more efficient to enable the housewife to engage more freely in social action outside the home. Like Ellen Richards, Bruère lectured and wrote prolifically with the intention of convincing the modern educated American housewife that she could find outlets for her energies more gratifying and having more enduring results than bread and butter making. Bruère showed none of the nostalgia for the old country ways that many women indulged in as she described her ideal: a sophisticated woman who lived in a cooperative apartment building with meal and maid service and ample time to function as a responsible citizen, an attentive mother to her single child, and a good companion to her husband.[4]

Two key ideas for Bruère were cooperative housekeeping and cooperative marketing, both based on the notion of pooling resources to free the participants for other activities. The former notion had already flared up in the nineteenth century when educated housewives saw themselves as trapped by the pressure they were under to play many roles at the same time, compounded by a shortage of servants. As early as 1868, an article appeared in the *Atlantic Monthly* claiming that the American housewife was neither a professional cook nor a seamstress nor a musician nor a student nor a fine lady, but merely a "patchwork apology of them all."[5] If the hours she was forced to spend in the kitchen or sewing room were reduced, a woman would have enough time to participate in philanthropic endeavors or even in the retail trade. The concept of cooperative housekeeping—which was developed in the nineteenth-century communes, for example—was posed as a means of freeing the woman for more worthwhile pursuits. The proposition itself implied that, given the time, women did not have to function in servitude, but could be worthwhile contributors to society.[6]

Charlotte Perkins Gilman

Ellen Richards believed that industrial society had much to offer the housewife in terms of information and technology, but Charlotte Perkins

Gilman (1860–1935) saw the American household as the distorted end-product of a greedy, class-conscious society and the housewife to be society's victim. In *Women and Economics* (1898) and *The Home, Its Work and Influence* (1903), she described a utopian ideal in which the home would function as a private retreat. The physical needs of the family would be supplied by communal kitchens and cleaning and child care services, as in many modern senior citizens cooperatives. There, in an environment taken care of and monitored by the domestic service agency, family members, none too dependent on another, would be free to rest and share social, political as well as emotional concerns. In contrast, the contemporary household as Gilman painted it was a food and comfort station, with the housewife an overburdened buyer and caretaker of *things*. The whole, imperfect as it was, was supported by a male breadwinner whose salary was always inadequate to the task. The children of such a household, used to consuming their mother's energy and their father's money, would continue to feed their enormous appetites for goods in adult life by endlessly consuming goods and services, depleting the earth's resources, and failing to share what was available with the poorer nations of the world.

Gilman was not as fortunate in her choice of a husband as were Richards and Bruère, both of whom married men who supported their outside interests, and in order to pursue her speaking and writing career she had to strike out on her own, leaving husband and child behind. The unhappiness of her own stifled domestic life led her to consider the contemporary home as a lost cause and to put all her hopes in the future—after all, she was grandniece to Catherine Beecher, and thus perhaps a born idealist. Gilman was extremely critical of the past and overly optimistic about what was in store for women. In 1903, she wrote this projection of the progress she saw as inevitable:

> The girls today, in any grade of society, are pushing out to do things instead of being content to merely eat things, wear things, and dust things. The honourable instinct of self-support is taking the place of the puerile acceptance of gifts, and beyond self-support comes the still nobler impulse to give to others; not corrupting charity, but the one all-good service of a life's best work.[7]

Gilman's analysis of domestic problems even now might be considered a sophisticated assessment. Thus, it is not surprising that by 1927 her ideas had been accepted by only a small group of progressive home economists. Nearly 30 years after the Lake Placid Conference, domestic-science experts met once more at the Conference on Homemaking at Columbia University Teachers College, to debate the question of whether housewives could ever forge a professional image for themselves as long as their income and status derived from their husbands. A number of speakers at the conference concluded that modern woman's discontent was related to her economic dependence and the difficulty she had in pursuing her own career, which forced her toward outside activities that were all basically avocations or leisure-time enterprises, whereas a man's outside activity was his profession.[8]

As Gilman had earlier, this minority argued that the married woman still suffered from her "dependence upon the largesse of her male supporter" in her personal development. Once more this faction advocated that women be encouraged to keep up with social and economic changes and that domestic science should function to free women from rigid, housebound roles, not serve as a new cult of domesticity that glorified housework in order to keep women at home. But the majority of conferees reiterated the traditional opinion that women should be educated because educated women made better wives and mothers. They saw domestic-science education as a means of training modern homemakers to deal with the increasingly complex conditions affecting the American family. They believed that the American home would always be the focal point of society, and that the role of domestic science was to bring to the home the highest level of sophistication in scientific management, technology, and emotional support.

Needless to say, the majority ruled. The voices of Gilman and the others who saw the need for fundamental changes in the social structure were drowned out by those who believed that improvements of the housewife's lot lay in efficiency studies and sophisticated technology. Over the years, the gap between the professional domestic expert and the American family home grew ever wider until the professional home economist worked in industry, far from the domestic scene and the problems that the field originally addressed.

For the next decades, the remnants of Ellen Richards's vision narrowed in scope within secondary and community college education. Often they served as a limp counterpart to the more trade-oriented "boys' courses" such as welding and auto repair. Prestigious universities that once supported pioneering research in the economic and social aspects of the home gradually dissolved their Departments of Household Science or divorced home economics courses from sociology, anthropology, and economics, where they had originated. During this period, the domestic-science educator struggled with the image that had transformed her from a social analyst into a home ec. school teacher, a "female, not too bright, who prepares other females to be wives and mothers."[9]

One might wonder what would have happened if the pendulum had swung the other way and the vision of the Richardses, the Bruères, and the Gilmans had taken precedence over the more technology- and efficiency-minded activists in the movement. In 1974, *Scientific American* asked the age-old question once more: Why do American women spend so much time doing housework?[10] Neither home economics nor kitchen technology

13. American Home Economics Convention Banquet, San Francisco, 1925. From the author's collection.

had liberated the modern housewife; the typical white middle-class woman still worked as many hours in the home as her grandmother did.

THE HOUSEHOLD ENGINEER

In the years following the Civil War, industry mushroomed throughout the nation, as it did in all the prosperous nations of the world, and with the growth of industry competition became ever more intense. It didn't take long for the heads of industry, under pressure to increase production, to concern themselves with reducing waste, both in materials and time. Factory production in particular was a natural laboratory for studying efficiency-production ratios. Thus, with the invention of the assembly line and mass production, the efficiency movement was born. Experts, at first self-taught and self-identified, studied each stage in a production process to identify essential motions and pinpoint those that resulted in wasted time. Appropriately, such intensive observations, conducted under controlled conditions, were known as time-and-motion studies. Machines were analyzed in the same way, and their productivity was measured against the materials necessary to build and fuel them.

It was with reference to such studies that Martha Bruère responded to such housewives' laments as the following:

> I run up the family bills one month and pay them the next! I buy what the stores have to sell at the price they choose to set,—I pay rent for a house somebody else had chosen to build,—I send my children to the sort of school the town has happened to establish,—I dress, and come, and go, and read, and see, as other people have arranged for me! What have I to do with it all? Merely to pay the bills with money I haven't earned. I don't control a single thing that goes into housekeeping, yet I know that unless I see to it that we have what it is best for us to have, I am not running my home efficiently.[11]

Those in the domestic-science movement who put their faith in technology and American ingenuity wanted to lift whole techniques and bodies of data from industry and business and apply them to the home. They hoped to streamline housework, and thus put the housewife into control of her sphere of interest as a business manager would be, the way Henry Ford controlled the assembly-line production of automobiles. Martha Bruère was a visionary and one of the minority who viewed domestic science as a liberator of women. But she was also a believer in efficiency and had a place among those who attempted to apply the results of time-motion research to the home. In fact, Bruère translated her efficiency expert husband's principles in industry into a gospel of efficiency for the home. Her objective, however, was not to improve housework for its own sake, but to enable the woman to dispatch her domestic responsibilities quickly so she could engage in social action outside the home. In the introduction to her book *Increasing Home Efficiency* (1916), she asks, "Is there any way to judge of the home's efficiency except by its social product?"[12]

Mary Church Terrell

"I studied all the new notions, attended Mrs. Rorer's lectures on cooking, and made a business of keeping up with the housekeeping times," writes Mary Church Terrell (1863–1954) in her autobiography *A Colored Woman in a White World* (1940).[13] Educated Black women embraced the same ideals in private and public housekeeping as their white counterparts with whom they participated in settlement kitchens and housing reforms on behalf of the underprivileged members of their race. Mary Church Terrell, the daughter of former slaves, graduated with honors from Oberlin College. Her father by then was a wealthy real estate owner in Tennessee, her mother a successful businesswoman in New York. As the wife of Robert Terrell, who for 20 years held the office of district judge in Washington, D.C., she immersed herself in social activism. After teaching in a segregated high school, she became the first Black member on the Board of Education and the first president of the National Association of Colored Women, founded in 1896. In her inaugural address she advocated better training for Black girls in homemaking and motherhood, and all her life she remained true to her precept to "ennoble the ideals and purify the atmosphere of the home."[14] Unlike Jane Addams, however, who invited the officers of the NACW to a much publicized luncheon at Hull House,[15] Mary Church Terrell experienced the same discrimination in every aspect of her private and public life as her less fortunate Black sisters. Rejected from prestigious women's clubs, shunted to the back of the bus or theater and excluded from Washington's hotels and restaurants, she increasingly devoted herself to the politics of racial discrimination. All of the high standards for housekeeping were irrelevant when confronted with blatant housing discrimination. Even a well-educated lady, respected by the Black and white communities of Washington, could not buy the home she wanted without resorting to subterfuges. Mary Terrell described her humiliating search as follows:

> When I started in quest of a house for the second time and asked several real estate firms to show me what they had on their list, I discovered they took me to see nothing but residences which had been discarded by discriminating people, because they were old-fashioned and devoid of modern improvements. Then it dawned upon me that, as a colored woman, I would be unable to SEE the kind of house I desired. I decided to devise some sort of scheme by which I would be able to look at desirable houses with modern improvements without benefit of real estate agents.

Previously she had been sadly disappointed when an agent had assured her that "anybody would be glad to live next to Judge Terrell and his wife," only to return her deposit, "because the owner had discovered that a colored family wanted it." Several other attempts failed until a white agent finally procured them a home in a street where some other Black families lived and a price "at least $2,000 more than a white purchaser would have been obliged to pay." The author goes on to explain:

> If colored people could find houses on a street restricted to themselves which were as well built and as up to date as are those in the white districts, they would make no effort to thrust themselves upon their fair-skinned brothers and sisters who object to having them in close proximity.[16]

Like Mary Terrell, who learned that her knowledge of Greek and Latin made no difference to those who objected to her color, educated Black women realized that the much heralded goal to "improve the race" went beyond better housekeeping, beyond better education, and even exceeded their own lifetime.

As white middle-class housewives involved themselves with household engineering, Black housewives could never deceive themselves about the forces that really controlled their homes: labor economics and racial discrimination. It is ironic that Mary Church Terrell died in the same year that the "separate but equal" doctrine of public education was struck down by the Supreme Court in the landmark case, *Brown versus Board of Education of Topeka*, 1954. Her autobiography closes with the words:

> While I am grateful for the blessings which have been bestowed upon me and for the opportunities which have been offered, I cannot help wondering sometimes what I might have become and might have done if I had lived in a country which had not circumscribed and handicapped me on account of my race, but had allowed me to reach any height I was able to attain.[17]

Christine Frederick

While Martha Bruère sought to free the housewife from scrubbing wood-work so she might devote herself to passing an anti-smoke ordinance, Christine Frederick (1883–1974) took on the task of improving house-work for its own sake, addressing her work to the refined family woman of "slight strength and still slighter means of whom society expects so much."[18] Her idea was that most homemakers were simply too busy to do all they had to do and too poor to hire help. At the time, only about one family in ten employed regular household help, and the quality of such help was, as always, a subject for constant complaint, particularly among those housewives who could only afford to employ the untrained and the

14. Mary Terrel's inheritors, following the pioneering path of Mary Terrel, 1964. Reproduced through the courtesy of The Bancroft Library, University of California, Berkeley CA 94720.

unwilling. Thus, Frederick's special audience as she saw it was made up of the majority of the nation's women.

Counting herself among the middle class, which had to keep up appearances, Frederick set out to show that work methods of proven efficiency could have the same results in the home that they had in the shop and factory. Since a regular breakfast on *Good Housekeeping*'s menu page during this period featured creamed codfish or fried chicken, and Fanny Farmer's cookbook prescribed 12 courses for a full dinner, Frederick's claim was bound to inspire interest. Six servants were still required to keep an affluent home running smoothly, and New York's better known hostesses needed at least 15 staff members to maintain their prestige. As household editor of the *Ladies' Home Journal*, Frederick knew that this elite minority set the tone for the aspiring middle class. She saw efficiency housekeeping as enabling middle-class women to meet unforgivingly high modern standards without working themselves to death.

Frederick used industrial terminology in discussing household matters: kitchen conditions were "standardized"; cleaning tasks were "scheduled" and "dispatched." Budgets were "planned" and records "maintained." Housewives were instructed to fill out purchasing orders and to compare the price lists of different stores by brand. She broke down all aspects of housework into specific tasks, adequately identifying and describing each as they might be by a personnel director. Furthermore, she analyzed all tasks in terms of efficiency equipment and time-motion studies. Under Frederick's direction, the white-enamel kitchen became a control station in which the household engineer, white-clad in keeping with the symbolism of sanitation, directed her operation. Through her attention to detail, Frederick gained credit throughout the nation for elevating housework from the status of labor to that of management. She seemed to have solved the problem that had dogged the housewife down the ages: how to eliminate the drudgery of daily life.

Although Bruère and Frederick advocated efficiency principles with equal enthusiasm, they differed sharply regarding the most important aspect of domestic industry, its motivation. Bruère wanted women to work efficiently in the home so they could finish and get out: "We have always had to go without the things we could not afford in money; we must learn to go without things we can not afford in time, and housework is the chief of these."[19] But Frederick viewed household problems, large and small, with new eyes: "Instead of being something upon which to slave, they became objects of keen mental interest—quite the same . . . as the tasks of the business and industrial world which men tackle with zest and results."[20] One might wonder to what extent Frederick actually did the work she romanticized in this way and to what extent she was experimenting for the sake of her career. She had a kitchen for the sole purpose of designing new products.[21]

Ironically, Frederick included a solemn warning by efficiency expert Harrington Emmerson in her introduction to *Household Engineering*: "I remember when sewing machines were first introduced, they made running of long tucks one hundred times easier. But this was made a reason for making seventy times as many tucks."[22] Efficiency housekeeping did indeed result in more tucks than time. The career housewife "scheduled" her time and "dispatched" her chores. But she was germ-conscious and nutrition-conscious as never before, and she was religiously obedient to her scientific manuals, which contained specific instructions for airing and dusting; washing down shelves, refrigerators, lamps, and woodwork; and preparing tasty snacks and balanced meals with special menus for children's tender digestive tracts. Thus, in spite of efficiency, the 12–hour workday continued to be passed from one generation of housewives to the next like an heirloom.

Lillian Gilbreth

So completely did efficiency expert Frank Gilbreth capture the imagination of his wife Lillian that she viewed motherhood as a rich field in which she and her husband could experiment for more productive living. Frank persuaded his intelligent wife not only to go after a doctoral degree at Brown University in 1915, when she was already a mother of five—they moved across the street from her classroom so that she could keep an eye on her children—but also to give birth to an even dozen and to become his partner as management consultant and designer of kitchen machines. As two of their children documented, often hilariously, in a pair of popular books, the first of which was the best-selling *Cheaper by the Dozen*, they raised their brood in accordance with Frank's highly innovative efficiency methods. The fact that Lillian never did much housekeeping and never learned to cook (they employed a staff of 12) only emphasizes the management aspects of their scheme.

Clearly, Lillian Gilbreth was committed to efficiency methods not only in her professional life, but in her domestic life as well. Like the home advocated by Richards, the Gilbreth household served as a laboratory for testing new domestic-management techniques. Clearly, efficiency did get Mrs. Gilbreth out of the house, for she added several more degrees to her name and continued the lecture and consulting circuit. But whether her methods helped other housewives to achieve the same goal is unlikely.

In 1954, Lillian wrote *Happier Living through Saving Time and Energy*. Here she reiterated an example used by Christine Frederick of a bricklayer who increased his speed by utilizing a scaffold and pulley. Both women focused on the increase in production, but neither asked whether the bricklayer's work was less tedious or whether he was able to go home any earlier in the evening. In fact, the profit deriving from the increase in his output went not to the worker but to the builder, who by virtue of the increase could ultimately produce more houses for less money. Since the housewife functioned both as bricklayer and builder, theoretically at least she had the option of deciding which gain was more significant to her: increased time for herself or increased production. Most women who employed efficiency methods, swayed by the social and cultural forces that had always influenced their decision making regarding the home, did so for the latter reason.

A comparison of the ideal housework schedule developed by Frederick in 1914 and by Gilbreth in 1954 reflects this bias toward increased production. Jobs that were done once a week in 1914 had become part of the daily routine by 1954, the availability of electric appliances having made the increase in performance possible. Although both Frederick and Gilbreth promised that efficiency housekeeping would result in more time for the housewife herself, neither writer allowed time in her schedule for self-improvement or self-indulgence. A total of two hours daily for rest and personal grooming were scattered among home- and family-care activities in a 12–hour day. Rest periods for the housewife, as for the bricklayer, were deemed necessary to insure the health of the worker and the quality of the performance; this requirement was a direct result of efficiency studies and production analyses in industry.[23]

Such time budgets, patterned as they were after the industrial model, implicitly justified a wife's full-time commitment to her home. The implied message in this businesslike treatment of housework was that such work was directly analogous to work in industry or business and that a homemaker could derive the same kind of satisfaction from performing housework that a wage-earner took in performing paid work. The proof lay in the fact that housework could be scheduled, broken down, and described, just as work in a factory might be.

The idea of career housewifery was bought whole by American women who were egged on, as usual, by the press and the magazines. The notion that a woman might perform her household chores and then go out to do some more significant work receded as efficiency housekeeping took hold. Simultaneously, the "lady of leisure" also became suspect—close to immoral, in fact. Only the busy housewife deserved a break. If housework was to be perceived as "real" work offering real job satisfaction, then women had better punch in with regularity along with the rest of the work force. The old Puritan work ethic—wherein people's worth was measured in the good works they performed—was reinforced during this period, and *work* and *virtue* became nearly synonymous. Since that time, the work ethic has continued to dominate the American psyche. The fruits of one's labor, in the shape of such products as houses, cars, boats, and swimming pools, still count much more heavily than the amount of leisure one might earn through hard work. The net effect of the efficiency movement for the American housewife, therefore, was actually to *increase* the amount of work she did and the amount of social pressure on her to do it. What woman would dare to worry about time for herself when one had to keep up one's end of the production line?

ELECTRICITY AND THE HOME

Industrialization produced more than efficiency studies, however. Perhaps its most fundamental contribution was the electric motor, invented in 1892. This development had a profound effect on the quality of housework at the turn of the century. Electricity might have been invented with the housewife in mind, so totally did it transform her work and so eager was she at the time to prove her worth as a worker in spite of it.

In subtle ways, the advent of the labor-saving device put women at home under more pressure than ever to prove their value. As more appliances became available, the task of proving that housework was bona fide employment became more and more difficult. Advertisements promoting electric gadgets showed the husband in the role of Lord Bountiful, showering his wife with vacuum cleaners, potato peelers, flatirons, milk sterilizers, shoe polishers, bed warmers, sewing machines, toasters, broilers, washers, wringers, choppers—relieving the little lady of every task that might cause her difficulty or discomfort. According to the *Manual of Electricity in the Service of the Home*, published in 1914, the magic of electricity would turn "a neurotic wife, worn out with the worries of housekeeping and domestic troubles" into "a loving woman, bubbling over with mirth and joy." With electricity in the house, the wife herself would serve as "a sure antidote for all the worries and trials which each man, more or less, has daily to encounter in this strenuous and competitive age." Moreover, she would cook her food properly with scientific control and thereby "aid in securing a race of more healthy and robust people."[24]

Thus, the message to the housewife was a double one: She was valuable, sophisticated, and productive as a worker, *but* if her husband could afford to supply her with the necessary technology, all she *really* had to do was monitor the health and welfare of the real American producers, the husbands and, potentially, the sons. Under these conflicting pressures to prove herself both as an efficient worker and old-fashioned hausfrau, it is not surprising that the old postwar fervor for independence and socially responsible action gradually dissipated.

By 1928, about two-thirds of the homes in America were wired for electricity. More than 13 million families cooked with gas or electricity, but more than 14 million still used coal, wood, or oil. An electric kitchen became synonymous with a high standard of living. It replaced the formal dining room as a status symbol except among the very rich, who could afford to maintain old-fashioned kitchens and hire the personnel necessary to run them. After a brief interruption, during World War I and the

Depression years, the home appliance business grew faster than the population. From 1923 to 1928, the sale of washing machines increased from 2,915,000 to 5,000,000; of vacuum cleaners, from 3,850,000 to 6,828,000; of irons, from 7,000,000 to 15,200,000, and of refrigerators, from 27,000 to 755,000.[25]

There is no doubt that inestimable hours of labor were saved by the new domestic appliances. But the electricity revolution was so successful from the producer's point of view that it even succeeded in bringing back into the home labors that had already been absorbed by the service industry. In the early decades of the century, for example, young city women had practically forgotten how to bake bread. The volume of bakery goods sold tripled between 1900 and 1925, while the population increased only by half. But electric mixers and modern ovens now enabled the housewife to bake as well as the baker and to use higher quality ingredients. Not only that, but the ambitious young wife could even outcompete her mother by producing a fresh homemade cake every day, rather than just once a week, as in the old days.

The laundry business, too, declined as washing machines became more popular. Before 1920, most households sent much of their washing out. Prices were low as long as sweatshop conditions prevailed. But, by 1929, the price of commercial laundering was four times higher than in 1915 and, though twice as many employees worked in the laundering business in 1929, the number of laundry establishments in 1915 and in 1929 remained about the same.

Thus, labor-saving devices actually brought new work into the home, or at least brought back work that had been let go by women of the preceding generation.[26]

In summary, then, the efficiency movement in combination with the appliance revolution finally managed to banish the old-fashioned drudge to the back woods and to the slums. "Without drudgery or effort," advertisers proclaimed, the glamorous button-pusher could set her mechanical servants in motion with the touch of a switch. But drudgery merely became unfashionable; it did not disappear. Not everyone could afford to employ the new methods; not everyone had the leisure or education to learn about them. And, of course, only the financially secure could afford the labor-saving devices that were being invented hand over fist. But even the housewife who had everything was hard put not only to apply her new knowledge of nutrition, sanitation, and efficiency principles, but also to find a need and fill it with the new tools appearing on the market. Frantically, she tried to employ everything the society made available to her. In the process, she adopted another principle from the industrial world, competition, and the notion of "keeping up with the Joneses" was born.

THE RISE OF MRS. CONSUMER

One way the housewife had of meeting expectations—heartily encouraged by advertisers capitalizing on the guilt bred through competition—was by buying what she was expected to buy. In 1928, America was riding on a high wave of prosperity. More people had greater incomes than ever before. Consuming became a national pastime involving, or at least attracting, almost everyone in the nation. The consumption of products reached its peak among the middle class, where people had both the need and the means to symbolize with objects their success as money-makers. In *Economic Principles of Consumption* (1929), Paul H. Nystrom, a professor of marketing at Columbia University, suggested that "consumption supplies an avenue through which to carry out one's desires for self-realization" and that "through consumption more directly than in any other way the individual determines and develops his social position and escapes from feelings of isolation and loneliness."[27] Consuming the products that American industry made became a socially approved means of self-expression.

If the new consumerism was based on increased productivity due to industrialization, the success of industry very much depended on the continued existence of the new consumer. It benefited industry that citizens were depending on American products not just for their face value but as symbols of their owners' self-worth. The giants of industry were intent on making sure that the trend of consumerism accelerated. To stimulate consumption, Henry Ford provided more leisure time to wage-earners by introducing the five-day work week and higher industrial wages. But the most effective method of guaranteeing that the new trend became permanent was to stimulate the appetite of the wage-earner's wife, Mrs. Consumer. The economic system that divided Americans into money producers (male) and money spenders (female) was working exceedingly well in 1928. Men earned about $92 million that year, while women spent $52 million on food, clothing and shelter.[28]

In 1928, 1,250,000 couples married, 2,500,000 babies were born, 400,000 high school students graduated, 2,000,000 families moved into new houses. Each event sent the housewife on a major spending spree. As soon as industry began to realize that 80 to 90 percent of the American retail dollar was in the housewife's pocket, advertising became a serious business. It sold the belief that American women did not want to make money but loved to spend it, that they did not want to work but longed for leisure. Businessmen argued that since women held the purse strings, women controlled the economy. Thus, American industry decided to pay homage to "the priestess of the temple of consumption . . . the limitless demander of things to use up," so labeled by social critic

Thorstein Veblen in 1899.[29] It was against this image of the female consumer invented by the advertisers that Charlotte Gilman did battle until her death in 1935.

But who was Mrs. Consumer? Christine Frederick, who had once concerned herself solely with efficiency housekeeping, applied Paul Nystrom's theories of consumption to the American housewife and produced a new book of her own, *Selling Mrs. Consumer*, in 1929. In this book, Frederick claimed that the new housekeeping revolved not around household engineering, as she had believed ten years earlier, but rather around shopping. Self-realization through consumption had always been a feminine occupation, allowing a woman to live up to the expectations of her husband's social status. But woman's power as consumer had never been officially recognized before, since the economic welfare of the nation had never been as dependent on the flow of consumer goods. Frederick now stated for all the world to read that a woman's task was to spend her husband's money wisely and to display her purchases to their best advantage.

Frederick went on to identify the typical housewife consumer not as the college graduate she had been interested in in her earlier publications but as a woman with a sixth-grade education, who did "not know more, intellectually, than the present 14–year-old adolescent, if as much." The typical consumer was a creature of instinct and practicality, not logic and mechanics. "One reason why so many women have failed to get a thrill out of scientific training in home economics or budget-keeping," wrote Frederick, "is because it is too strictly logical."[30]

In the woman of 1928, Frederick perceived a marked change from the previous generation of women, who were tradition- and religion-oriented. The modern woman, she said, was emotional but not sentimental or illogical, and she was sure of what she wanted. Moreover, she could be classified according to age, and her proclivities predicted according to age bracket. From 16 to 22, the female consumer was pleasure- and style-oriented; from 22 to 28, she was in a romantic home-building period and most interested in new ideas. From 28 to 38, she was settled in housekeeping and most generous in her family budget. After 38, the housewife was less apt to be interested in fads but was more in need of volume, comfort, and luxury. She wanted more of what she had rather than new products that might reflect new values. At any age, however, Mrs. Consumer was susceptible to manipulation by advertising.

Basically what Frederick did in her book was to create a stereotype and instruct industry on how to use it. What had happened to Frederick's high ideals of womanhood? Had the pioneer of efficient homemaking become disillusioned with her own sex? Had she given up measuring women's skills and expectations against men's? Leaders of women's clubs, former suffragettes, and pioneer educators frowned on the new selfish generation of hedonists characterized by Frederick's Mrs. Consumer, but Frederick was less critical of the self-indulgence of the housewife she depicted. She argued that women were simply demanding a place in the sun by expressing themselves in the marketplace. They were making their desires known "for more kinds of food, more leisure, more athletics and sports, more education, more travel, more art, more entertainment, more music, more civic improvement, better landscaping and city planning, more literature, more social graces, more social freedom and more cosmopolitan polish and smartness."[31] And in the America of 1928, the table appeared to be loaded with goods available in an unending supply. If the products she desired were there for the asking, Frederick queried, why should the housewife become a drone if she could be the queen bee? And, of course, society would be benefitted in turn by indulging the consumer instincts of Mrs. Consumer. The greater the demands made by women on industry the more products industry would be able to turn out. More production meant that more wage-earners would elevate their wives into the queen-bee category, and the nation would be enveloped in prosperity.

Perhaps it was ironic that *Selling Mrs. Consumer*, which was based on a blind faith in the country's healthy appetite and ample resources, was written at the dawn of the Great Depression. But Frederick's belief was actually vindicated by events, since the Depression and World War II only temporarily restrained the spending of American consumers. In 1932, *Good Housekeeping* magazine made a special appeal to women to keep on shopping in order to keep the men working and the dollar rolling; at the same time, the lifestyle of the rich who remained dominated women's magazines and women's sections of newspapers. The press seemed to assume that the poverty-stricken housewife could forget her troubles by escaping into the dreamland of affluence. Thus, the hunger for consumer goods was kept alive for better times ahead.

Despite the efforts of the press, however, the housewife had a difficult time forgetting that the Depression was affecting her buying power. In the 1930 census, Secretary of Commerce Lamont officially classified homemaking as an occupation. His announced intention was "to give recognition to women in the home who hitherto, unless they had some moneymaking employment, were reported as having no occupation."[32]

The census counted 23 million housewives and 10 million women in "gainful" employment. Together they made up 90 percent of the adult female population (ages 16 to 64). According to William M. Steuart, director of the Census Bureau, about 47 million people were at that time "gainfully" working to support America's population of 122 million, of which 41 million were under 16. In this light at least 64 million wives and children depended on 47 million breadwinners. Only 4 million homemakers listed also some "gainful" occupation. Clearly the burden of financial support rested with the 26 million male heads of families. When unemployment figures climbed from 8.7 percent in 1930 to 23.6 percent in 1932, naturally not only the employed but also the women outside the labor force were affected. Most of them were occupied as housewives who therefore relied on a paycheck from the gainful workers in the family. The Census figures only revealed the economic facts which, as Charlotte Gilman had already asserted, would "puncture that beautiful bubble"—the image of equality between women in the home and men outside the home.

The consequences of their economic dependence dawned on more than a million wives whose husbands lost their jobs and who had to learn to live without income. Forced to rely once more on their grandmothers' producer skills, housewives accepted the challenge valiantly and took a renewed pride in their work at home, since their efforts were obviously keeping their families alive. Women no longer viewed canning, cooking, and sewing as creative hobbies but as sheer necessities, as they had been in the past. Urban women became rural pioneers, managing to keep house without plumbing convenience, gas, or electricity. If the collapse of the stock market was to be blamed on businessmen, clearly the stretching of the dollar could be credited to women at home.

Women sought employment to supplement the dwindling family income, but the job market had decreased even more dramatically for women than for men, particularly in the skilled and professional categories. With one-third of the population under 16 years of age and domestic employment or elementary school teaching as the most likely job opportunity, women's work in the thirties revolved primarily around the home and the child. Women also replaced men in menial jobs, since employers felt free to pay women less. As had been the case since wives began going to work, wage-earning women continued to maintain their homes in addition to their outside responsibilities.

Gladys Caldwell conveyed a strong impression of what it took to work at home and at a mill to supplement her husband's weekly salary of $12.85.

> Yes, I have a husband and five children [Mrs. Caldwell told author Paul Blanchard in an article called "How to Live on Forty-six Cents a Day"], I'm a weaver, at least I work in the weave room fillin' batt'ries. I get paid by the day ($1.80). . . . I get up at four to start breakfast for the children. When you got five young'uns it takes a while to dress'em. The oldest is nine and she helps a lot. The others are seven, five, four, and three. . . . After I've got the children dressed and fed I take 'em to the mill nursery, that is three of 'em. Two go to school, but after school they go to the nursery until I get home. . . . We have breakfast about five, and I spend the rest of the time from five to seven gettin' the children ready and cleanin' up the house. That's about the only time I get to clean up. Ruby washes the dishes. . . . I work from seven to six with an hour for dinner. . . . At noon I run home and get dinner for the seven of us. . . . Of course I make my own bread. . . . After dinner I wash the dishes and run back to the mill. We don't have any sink but there is a faucet with runnin' water on the back porch and a regular toilet. . . .

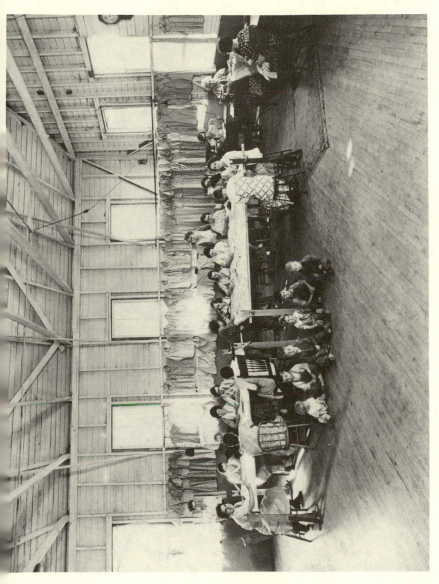

15. Sewing cooperative in Southern California Self-Help Movement, 1934. Reproduced through the courtesy of The Bancroft Library, University of California, Berkeley CA 94720.

When the whistle blows at six I come home and get supper. Then I put the children to bed.... When supper is over I have a chance to make the children's clothes. Yes, I make 'em all, and my own clothes too.... On Saturday night I wash the children in a big wash tub and heat the water on the oil stove. Then I do the week's ironin.' I send the washin' to the laundry. I just couldn't do that too. It costs nearly $2.00 a week.[33]

Regarding their financial expectations, women who went to the most prestigious institutions of higher learning were no more secure in their jobs than women with high school diplomas or factory jobs. Therefore they viewed marriage to a good provider as the most lucrative career they could pursue.[34]

WORLD WAR II AND BEYOND

From the turn of the century through the Depression, married women who left the home to work for money did so under threat of starvation. Though it had been attempted, the notion of working wives had never been validated by the society at large as desirable, and for low-income women the double work load did not make the prospect enticing. But during World War II the situation reversed itself. A large portion of the male labor force left work and went to war. Women found themselves being courted by business and industry as prospective employees. Child-care centers were established in factories to ease mothers' way into the labor force. Posters and advertisements showed attractive girls in overalls swinging hammers and operating heavy machinery. Out of necessity, the culture was suddenly bent on increasing the self-sufficiency of the women left behind. Carry-out food services and store hours were adjusted to meet their schedules. Evening schools offered courses to women in plumbing and home repair. The image of the helpless female became unpopular. Six million women entered the job market, and by the end of the war 36 percent of all women were wage-earners, but half were over 34 years old.[35]

Federal and local monies went to additional child care centers, although the supply never kept up with the demand for them. More than half a million children were estimated to have received child care at some time during the war, but only one-third of the children who needed day care were covered.[36] All but a few day care centers were dissolved after the war.

And as soon as the war was over the men returned to reclaim their jobs. "Help wanted" signs disappeared from office and shop windows and the media launched a vigorous campaign calling for the return of femininity. With wartime depriviations finally ended, both men and women craved the comforts of home. The result was a heavy demand for the old-time domestic virtues. The same women who had condemned the fascists for

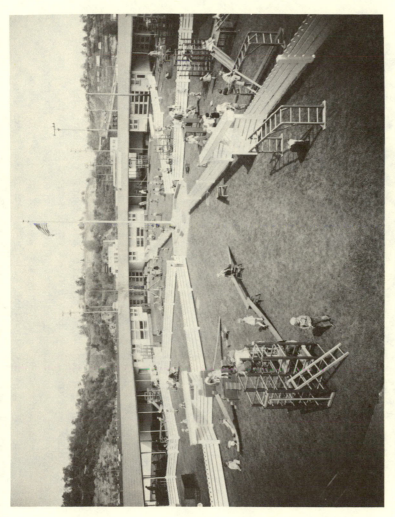

16. While makeshift conditions prevailed in California, Kaiser Shipyard Industries in Portland, Oregon (1940s) offered housing and childcare to their workers. The facilities featured the services of professional nutritionists, childcare workers, and family counselors. Reproduced through the courtesy of The Bancroft Library, University of California, Berkeley CA 94720.

17. Interior of childcare center offered by Kaiser Shipyard Industries in Portland, Oregon (1940s). Each child receives all the food he needs during his stay at the Center, including his daily requirement of cod liver oil. The children eat with their teachers in the familiar atmosphere of their playrooms. Each parent is given a weekly menu listing his child's meals at the Center. This menu includes suggestions for planning the child's remaining meals at home.

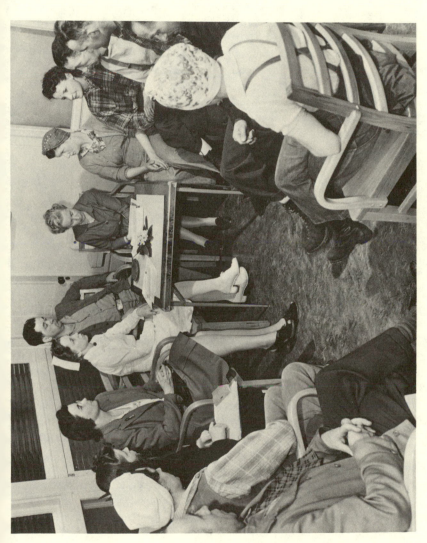

18. Parents and teachers discuss childcare and family relations at the childcare center offered by Kaiser Shipyard Industries in Portland, Oregon (1940s). Reproduced through the courtesy of The Bancroft Library, University of California, Berkeley CA 94720.

keeping women fenced in the kitchen and nursery were now ready to settle down to child rearing and homemaking. GIs returned home with European and Oriental brides because they considered these women feminine, complaining that American women no longer knew their place. Hemlines dropped below the calf to replace the short-skirt economy dresses, waists were tightened, and busts expanded. The greatest number of marriages in United States history was recorded in 1946. In 1947, the national birth rate increased by 5 percent and continued to climb after that.

As noted earlier, in the period following World War I, social and political activism among women had increased markedly, but after World War II such activity declined. Pioneers among the older generation continued to battle for economic equality, but the typical homemaker was encouraged to turn away from involvement in outside activities that did not directly concern her family. Women's clubs were now regarded as social diversions with little impact on social affairs, and serious clubwomen were subject to ridicule. Those women who persevered in their careers (there were many) were labeled sexless or abnormal. They were considered to be either incomplete women or aggressive competitors for the jobs that rightfully belonged to men.

It is interesting to see what happened to the young women who had been educated to the prewar ideals of social responsibility and efficiency housekeeping after these notions receded in the postwar era. At a class reunion in 1948, Vassar alumnae of 1934, who had been potential scientific housewives when they entered college, looked back at their alma mater with mixed feelings. They valued their education as a culturally enriching experience but felt it had left them "woefully lacking in knowledge" of those things that would make them better wives and mothers. "It seems to me college prepared me to be another female college professor," commented one alumna. Another added, "I have discovered in most of my friends and, I must admit, in myself, a feeling of frustration and of having been prepared for something better than the monotonies of dusting, sweeping, cooking and mending."[37]

Clearly, whatever the sights outside the home were that these women had set for themselves as undergraduates, a new domesticity set in after the war. Most of the interviewees were happily married, some for the second time. They averaged 2.16 children—later the college graduates of the prosperous fifties and rebellion-wracked sixties. These women admitted to having little or no political and religious involvement. Most were active members in bridge and country clubs. They indulged in regular but moderate smoking and drinking, and they admitted to feeling inadequate intermittently.

These Vassar graduates belonged to the highest income bracket in the nation. If anyone could have realized the ideal of the scientific housewife they could have. But as adults they were very different from the socially active women Ellen Richards, Martha Bruère, and Charlotte Gilman had envisioned, and they hardly even resembled Frederick's career housewife, who was to profit from time-motion studies and efficient kitchen designs. If domestic trials such as laundering without running water and cleaning without electric power had disappeared from the American home in the 1940s, so, apparently, had the "zest for intelligent experimentation."

The American home of 1950 was a hothouse in which the thermostat was fixed permanently on family happiness. Great stock was now placed on being "happy" and "fulfilled" at home, while the goal of realizing personal ambitions in the outside world had receded into oblivion for most housewives. Marriage per se became a focus of interest. One rated one's marriage on a scale from "about average happy" to "extraordinarily happy." It was dangerous to admit to unhappiness in marriage, since most women could not identify another arena in which they might seek personal fulfillment. Not surprisingly, "housewife's syndrome"—characterized by low self-esteem, emotional instability, and fatigue—was a common complaint.[38]

The remedy had been well tried on previous generations of immature complainers: rest and management skills. But contrary to Frederick's claim that the home was the best environment for self-realization, the full-time homemaker was set up for failure, since her work satisfaction remained inseparable from her personal life. Time had proven that her home could never function like industry because the private environment defied standardization.

In magazine stories and particularly on the Hollywood screen, the either-or decision between career and family—now seen as a choice between self-realization and love—persisted as a theme, often as a subplot to a Horatio Alger story of masculine success. In movie after movie, from *The Best of Everything* to *That Touch of Mink*, the male hero is rewarded for his toils in the labor force with the affection of a grateful family, and the female heroine gives up her career in exchange for love. Her decision is motivated by her fear of becoming the *Dark Lady*—"the lonely woman with the lonely heart who airily in her early twenties gave up home life for the baubles of a stage career, a business career or even a college career, and now, as the plaudits grow fainter, goes down toward the sunset alone."[39]

Thus, the true impact of the industrial age was the polarization of private home and public work place. Each sphere had separate standards, duties, and rewards, and, rather than influencing each other, the two spheres encouraged different value structures altogether. Neither the vote nor the vacuum cleaner had revolutionized the attitude of the housewife. She still remained dependent on the variable tides of her family's affection and her husband's income. He worked for money on the assembly line in the city. She worked for love by herself in the suburbs. But like an omen of what was to come, the divorce rate increased from 2.8 percent to 10.4 percent of all marriages between 1948 and 1951.

Still, though the white culture reendorsed the old domestic values after the war, with respect to working wives at least, not all that had been gained was lost. True, after the war most women invested their future in full-time motherhood and marriage, but 30 percent (and 22 percent of that portion had children) opted for a paycheck as well. Working wives clung to their new independence and respectability. "By 1952 some 10.4 million wives held jobs—two million more than at the height of World War II and almost three times the number employed in 1940.[40] Still, these new married workers tended to be mostly middle-aged women who had held jobs before.

In the postwar decades younger married women helped sporadically to pay the bills, but the supermothers of the fifties hovered over the family nest until it was empty.

NOTES

1. Christine Frederick, *The New Housekeeping: Efficiency Studies in Home Management* (New York: Doubleday, 1914), p. ix.
2. Jacob Riis, *How the Other Half Lives*; see also Gwendolyn S. Hughes, *Mothers in Industry: Wage-Earning Mothers in Philadelphia* (New York: New Republic, 1925), for detailed descriptions of housing and family conditions among the lower working class.
3. Frederick, *The New Housekeeping*, p. 234, quotes Ellen S. Richards's goals stated in 1899 at the Lake Placid Conference on Home Economics as: a. A home life "unhampered by the traditions of the past"; b. "The utilization of the resources of modern science to improve home life"; c. "The freedom of the home from the dominance of things"; d. "To free the spirit for the more important and permanent interests of the home and of society." See also Dolores Hayden, *The Grand Domestic Revolution*, chapter 5, pp. 183–205, "Domestic Evolution, or Domestic Revolution?" which summarizes the background for new home economics and professional domesticity.
4. Martha Bensley Bruère, "Twentieth Century Housekeeping," *Good Housekeeping*, vol. 58 (March, 1914), pp. 387–392.
5. "Cooperative Housekeeping," *Atlantic Monthly*, vol. 22 (Nov.-Dec., 1808), pp. 513–524, 682–689.
6. Hayden, *The Grand Domestic Revolution*, chapter 3, pp. 67–131. "Cooperative Housekeeping" offers history and sociopolitical framework of the movement.
7. Charlotte Perkins Gilman, *Women and Economics* (New York: Harper & Row, 1966; reprint of 1898 ed.), pp. 120–122.
8. Columbia University Teachers College, *Homemaking as a Center for Research: Report of Teachers Conference on Homemaking, 1927* (New York: Columbia Univ. Press, 1927), p. 88.
9. Ruth L. Bonde, "A Time of Growth, a Time of Decisions," *Journal of Home Economics*, vol. 68 (January, 1976), p. 30.
10. Joann Vanek, "Time Spent in Housework," *Scientific American* (November, 1974), pp. 116–120. According to a 1923 report in the October issue of the *Journal of Home Economics*, housework then consumed six or seven hours per day, or an

average of one hour and 30 minutes per family member. For full-time housewives the hours actually increased in later decades. See also Katharine E. Walker, "Homemaking Still Takes Time," *Journal of Home Economics*, vol. 61 (1969), pp. 621–624. For a detailed analysis of this aspect, see Susan Strasser, *Never Done*, which analyzes housework over the years from the aspect of continuous pressure to do more, rather than less. Ruth S. Cowan, *More Work for Mother*, proves the same point with her analysis of the effect of household technology.

11. Martha Bensley Bruère and Robert W. Bruère, *Increasing Home Efficiency* (New York: Macmillan, 1916), p. 2.

12. Ibid., p. 10.

13. Mary Church Terrell, *A Colored Woman in a White World* (New York: Arno Press, 1980, reprinted from 1940 ed.), p. 124; Bert J. Loewenberg et al., *Black Women in 19th Century American Life* (Philadelphia: Univ. of Pennsylvania Press, 1976), p. 23.

14. Terrell, *A Colored Woman*, p. 426.

15. Ibid., p. 154.

16. Ibid., p. 119.

17. Ibid., p. 427. P. Giddings, *When and Where I Enter*, p. 154, talks about Terrell's efforts to unionize Black women workers, and other political activities.

18. Frederick, *The New Housekeeping*, pp. 11–12.

19. Bruère, "Twentieth Century Housekeeping," p. 391.

20. Frederick, *The New Housekeeping*, p. ix.

21. Christine Frederick, *Household Engineering: Scientific Management in the Home* (Chicago: American School of Home Economics, 1919), pp. 70–72.

22. Frederick, *The New Housekeeping*, p. 87, and *Household Engineering*, pp. 88–89. See also Lillian M. Gilbreth, Orpha Mae Thomas, and Eleanor Clymer, *Management in the Home: Happier Living through Saving Time and Energy* (New York: Dodd, Mead, 1954), p. 26. The same figures pertain to the early thirties (Benjamin R. Andrews, *Economics of the Household, Its Administration and Finance* [New York: Macmillan, 1935], pp. 441–445).

23. The bricklayer image was also used in studies of women workers: Sue A. Clark, *Making Both Ends Meet: The Outlay of New York Working Girls* (New York: Macmillan, 1911), chapter 7, pp. 223–270, "Scientific Management as Applied to Women's Work."

24. Maud Lancaster, *Electric Cooking, Heating, Cleaning: A Manual of Electricity in the Service of the Home* (London: Constable, 1914), p. 2.

25. Paul H. Nystrom, *Economic Principles of Consumption* (New York: Ronald Press, 1931), pp. 352–370; Andrews, *Economics of the Household*, pp. 471–472.

26. Cowan, *More Work for Mother*, chapter 4, pp. 69–101, "Twentieth-Century Changes in Household Technology."

27. Nystrom, *Economic Principles of Consumption*, p. 249.

28. Christine Frederick, *Selling Mrs. Consumer* (New York: Business Bourse, 1929), pp. 16–17.

29. Thorstein Veblen, *The Theory of the Leisure Class* (1899); Charlotte Perkins Gilman, *The Home Its Work and Influence* (Urbana: Univ. of Ill. Press, 1972; reprint of 1903 ed.), p. 326–27.

30. Frederick, *Selling Mrs. Consumer*, p. 22.

31. Ibid., p. 31.

32. "Census Will Classify Women 'Home-makers,' " *The New York Times* (March 21, 1930).

33. Paul Blanchard, "How to Live on Forty-six Cents a Day," *Nation* 128 (May 15, 1929), pp. 580–581. For further reading see Jean Westin, *Making Do: How Women Survived in the '30s* (Chicago: Follett, 1976).

34. Lois Scharf, *To Work and to Wed: Female Employment, Feminism, and the Great Depression* (Westport, Conn.: Greenwood Press, 1980), chapter 7, pp. 139–158, "New Necessities and Old Traditions," offers a clear picture of the housewife who "was pushing her family into a comfortable income range." One out of seven wives belonged to that category, because the husband's income fell between $1,500 and $2,000 a year (p. 148).

35. Alice Kessler-Harris, *Out to Work: A History of Wage-Earning Women in the United States* (New York: Oxford University Press, 1982), p. 278, supports Scharf's statement that the emerging white working woman continued to be older: "By 1950 there had been a net drop in the rate at which married women aged 25–34 went out to work. Correspondingly, half again as many women aged 45–54 were working for wages as had worked in 1940."

36. National Manpower Council, *Womenpower* (New York: Columbia Univ. Press, 1957), p. 340. Childcare facilities varied greatly from one plant to another. On the whole there was never enough space for the number of children who needed day care.

37. John Willig, "Class of '34 (Female) Fifteen Years Later," *The New York Times* (June 12, 1949).

38. Abraham Myerson, *The Nervous Housewife* (Boston: Little Brown, 1920), pp. 77–81; and Gail Sheehy, *Passages: Predictable Crises of Adult Life* (New York: E. P. Dutton, 1974), p. 218 (data quoted from U.S. Dept. of Health, Education and Welfare, *Selected Symptoms of Psychological Distress* [1970]).

39. George W. Fiske, *The Changing Family* (New York: Red Label Reprints, 1928; 1st printing 1901), p. 102. Originally drawn for an earlier generation, the image gained new validity during this period of marital mass appeal.

40. *Women and the American Economy: A Look to the 1980s* (Englewood Cliffs, N.J.: Prentice-Hall, 1976), p. 17.

6

The Rise and Fall of Supermother, 1950–1970

As soon as I was visibly and clearly pregnant, I felt, for the first time in my adolescent and adult life, not-guilty. The atmosphere of approval in which I was bathed—even by strangers on the street, it seemed—was like an aura I carried with me, in which doubts, fears, misgivings, met with absolute denial. This is what women have always done.
—Adrienne Rich, *Of Woman Born*, 1976[1]

With the creation of the Mrs. Consumer stereotype, the housewife gained a new centrality in American society. But in the Cold War era, when nationalism and patriotism, not to mention rank suspicion, reached a high pitch, the housewife was seen as important not only because she spent her husband's money, but also because it was she who could shore up the family against liberalism, socialism, and communism. Mrs. Consumer became Mrs. America, and the experts turned their attention on her in earnest as Sputnik, Khruschev, and the Bomb loomed ominously on the nation's horizon.

It was no accident that the nuclear family became reinforced as the American norm in the 1950s. World War II had torn families asunder and put women to work, men to war, sometimes against their will. When the war was over, families became reunited and began having babies at a great rate, a trend that resulted in an unprecedented baby boom. And by 1950, conditions were ideal for starting and raising a family. A booming economy guaranteed enough jobs for men and women. The production of weapons, houses, furniture, cars, and appliances, and the proliferation of America's newest mass-marketing invention, the shopping center, had created enough jobs to send most Americans on a seemingly endless shopping spree. Never had consumerism been more representative of the American way of life.

One more development helped the new wave of domesticity become a way of life. Improved health conditions and a housing boom in the semirural areas gave even the traditionally disadvantaged families a chance to own detached, single-family homes on their own bits of land. The suburbs were born, and the great exodus from the cities began.

The future looked great for those who reached the suburbs in the early fifties, but it looked best of all for the daughters of white middle-class families, especially when their prospects were compared with those of young women a century past. Not only did they have the right to vote, the opportunity to study for a degree, the chance to take a job or pursue a career. They also kept the old option of gaining status and security as the wife of a steady money earner, or better yet as a supermother.

Marriage was the key to the housewife role in the 1950s. And marriage brought with it an unchallenged dependency that would not openly trouble American women in such relationships for roughly another decade and a half. Without a regret for the independent spirit that had flashed out proudly in the twenties, thirties, and forties, women of the cold-war age happily allowed themselves to be whisked off to the suburbs. There they voluntarily traded loyalty to home and husband for financial security and a share of their husbands' prestige. Thus, when teenage girls watched Grace Kelly's romantic wedding in movie theaters, and when college girls throughout the country admitted that they had no plans for life beyond marriage, they were dreaming technicolored dreams of their own romantic courtships and repeating to themselves the vows they would make to the breadwinner of their dreams.

American culture reinforced and validated these goals. Girls were often sent to college on the premise that they would find a husband there and drop out. Or, if the plan was to send a daughter to college for a full four-year course, frequently the rationale was—that old, familiar song—that educated women made better wives and mothers than uneducated ones. Women who actually specialized in a particular field of study often did so "to have something to fall back on"—that is, in case, heaven forbid, the husband should die.

Though the suburban wife presiding over home and children—in the old Beecher-type "refuge" from society at large—became the ideal, another reality was influencing the context in which the ideal flourished. In the *Journal of Home Economics* in January, 1952, Dr. Drusilla Kent marked a landmark in women's history, noting that the American economy would be unable to sustain its productivity, much less expand it, "without the increasing number of women in the labor force." Kent called on communities and the government to recognize the fact that for the first time in American history more married women than single women were employed. The working wife had finally gained the respectability associated with sheer numerical superiority—or so one would have thought. In fact, society conveyed two powerful but contradictory messages to American women concerning the goals that were considered acceptable for them. One message was, *Be a wife and mother and gain your fulfillment at home*. The other was, bluntly, *Get a job*.

Early in the 1950s, the experts specializing in how women should live their lives attempted to resolve the contradiction. Often they took pains to show that a working woman's job did not automatically exclude her from the ranks of acceptable homemakers and satisfactory mothers. Even the old, often-cited argument that working mothers had more delinquent children than mothers who stayed at home was laid to rest by the ever more authoritative social scientists: only *part-time* working mothers had more troubled children, new demographic evidence showed, and this finding was said to be related to the fact that such mothers had histories of alcoholism, delinquency, mental illness, or financial deprivation, not to the fact that they worked.[2] At the Annual Congress on Industrial Health in 1952 the theme "Occupation Housewife" focused on 66 percent of the employed women who were also housewives and needed the support from government and industry. Childcare and cooking classes at the workplace were recommended by home economists. Far from rushing out to buy herself an automatic washer or dryer, the typical employed wife was said to invest her money in the family budget for a new home, a new car, or the children's college education. Although she spent only 34.4 hours a week on housekeeping, compared with the average of 56.4 hours spent by the full-time homemaker, her home, according to eye-witness reports, did not show the difference. Furthermore, the defense continued, children in homes where mothers divided their energies between family and job even seemed to prosper from the situation. They were described as self-starters, well-adjusted, and confident that they were well-loved, since their mothers valued the time spent with their children more than full-time mothers did. Thus, the official conclusion of the fifties appeared to be that women could carry the double burden of household and job.[3]

Between 1956 and 1958, every major women's organization and employment organization as well as the National Manpower Council made active efforts to credit the working women of America with valid concerns and serious problems. These groups called for more and better child care centers, higher salaries for women, more part-time jobs, and equal-rights legislation to increase womanpower in the labor force. Nevertheless, the working mother did not capture the sympathy of the public in the 1950s. Rather, the suburban housewife and the more fully realized version of her, the supermother, served as the norm for women throughout that decade and well into the next. As Lois Scharf concludes in *To Work and to Wed* (1980), "The gulf between the reality of the working wife and the ideal of the married woman as wife and homemaker continued to grow. In accepting dual roles, the married working woman also accepted dual burdens, and the voices of concern and protest were barely whispers."[4] Working women, single women, divorced or widowed women, suffered the self-consciousness of the not-quite-right in a media-controlled society whose watchword had become nuclear family conformity.

SUPERMOTHER: THE RISE

The renewed focus on domesticity and homemaking led naturally to the evolution of a role that complemented and completed that of Mrs. America. The wife of the 1950s saw herself—and was encouraged to do so by the media and the pressure of society—as supermother, pure and simple. Once the image makers in the magazines, on radio, and on television had guided girls toward their wedding days and their tidy houses in the suburbs, the experts in the universities began to convey information and advice that would make American women the most informed and sophisticated mothers in the world. If a majority of the young women starting families in the 1950s chose to have more babies than their mothers, and even their grandmothers, they did so because they believed that the children themselves would serve as their medium for job satisfaction and success.

The Child-Management Experts

The branch of domestic science that had taught American women scientific housekeeping now offered them the potential for producing scientifically programmed children. Child management all but replaced home management as a focus of interest. The idea of child management had been afloat since the turn of the century, escalating with the notion of household engineering, and like the home, the perfect child was seen as the product of good management. Moreover, the well-managed child promised to grow up into a punctual, time-motion-conscious adult well suited for the industrial environment. Research agencies and institutes gathered expert information to substantiate this prediction for conferences and foundations. The National Congress of Mothers, a small group of private individuals that had first met in New York in 1897 to discuss the "scientific" approach to motherhood, grew into the Child Study Association of America.[5] The experts had taken over. Having never been too interested in the problems of home management—women ruled that field—male professionals soon dominated the child behavior studies and controlled the mother's relationship with her offspring.

In the 1930s, Sigmund Freud's theories about early childhood influences had gained popularity and interested the experts in the darker, less-measurable aspects of emotional behavior. If mothers did not always understand psychoanalytical techniques, they did get the message that if something went wrong with their children, the cause could be traced back to themselves. Thus, Sigmund Freud vindicated those who had insisted all along that every moment of a mother's behavior during conception, pregnancy, and the daily nurturing process had to be monitored to guard against serious wrongdoing, however unintended. With Freud she became sure: Women really did rock the cradles that rocked the world. But what if they made a mistake? The other side of this new certainty regarding maternal responsibility was the rise of the overprotective mother. Everybody in the fifties knew about dominating mothers. These were the "vipers" who, out of boredom or frustration, interfered in everyone's life and who, during the war, had broken their soldier boys' patriotic resolve.[6] The movies were full of Mildred Pierce mothers who would not let go. Experts blamed mothers for the existence of war defectors and henpecked husbands. Doctors especially heaped blame on mothers for failing to recognize that they were obligated to raise their children by rules that were only now being elucidated. The doctors of the fifties had been exposed to Freudian theory to one degree or another. If they learned nothing else from Freud, they learned that mothers were responsible for their children's failures and that they walked a thin line between overprotectiveness and inattention. Thus, the young wives of the fifties inherited the guilt bred by Freud and his followers in the thirties. They had to be better mothers yet.

The culture responded to this new philosophy of motherhood by raising mothers onto a shining new pedestal—a fragile pedestal, as it turned out. The first two crops of children born in the twentieth century had been damaged by wars and depression—and matriarchs. But the children of the fifties, under the loving guidance of their psychoanalytically informed mothers, had the potential to become straight, tall, well-groomed, teeth-straightened, ambitious, well-educated, happy individuals, the pride and joy of their devoted parents. No wonder that when the results came in, during the volatile 1960s, the supermothers of the fifties were shattered by insecurity and bewildered by the fruit of their labors.

In the early 1950s, when the supermother was just coming into vogue as the favored housewife model, it became unthinkable to bring up children without expert advice. Psychologists and sociologists in academic settings devoted ever more scholarly research to children. Once again, as in the late 1800s and early 1900s, the female mind and body, particularly as they influenced childhood, became topics of endless study and discussion by the newly popular social sciences, psychology and sociology. Their findings now filtered down into undergraduate courses and high schools and found their way into households via magazines and advice books. Chief among these topics was the fast-growing field of child development.

Young mothers who learned experts' opinions in college conscientiously followed the advice of such formidable taskmasters as Erik Erikson. Like Freud, Erikson based his theories mainly on his own experience in counseling mothers of disturbed children. And, like Freud, he saw the mother as the main shaper of the adult personality, though he did sympathize with her heavy emotional burden. In his classic work *Childhood and Society* (1950), Erikson demonstrated the necessity of a mother's "untiring attendance" on the young child. To demonstrate the need, however, he cited the case history of a schizophrenic girl. The girls' mother, who had tuberculosis, had been forbidden to touch the infant. At age three, the disturbed child was brought to Erikson, who recommended that she be allowed to nurse at her mother's empty breasts and spend as much time as possible on her lap. The treatment was sustained for years and was apparently successful. But at one point the mother had to leave the child in the care of others, and the daughter regressed completely to her schizoid stage.[7] Thus, Erikson's "proof" of the need for a mother's untiring attendance rested on a pathological situation far removed from the experience of most people.

Not surprisingly, mother's reminiscences of the fifties are filled with expressions of their fear of failure. As daughters, women now bore the weight of their own mothers' remorse over having failed to turn into perfect daughters, since these women had not turned out as planned on the parental blueprints. As new mothers, they already felt guilty for resenting children who demanded "untiring attendance," which they knew they could not give. Adrienne Rich focuses on these feelings in describing her own experience of becoming a mother in the early fifties:

> I could not possibly know then, that among the tangle of feelings between us [her mother and herself] . . . was her guilt. Soon I would begin to understand the full weight and burden of material guilt, that daily, nightly, hourly, Am I doing what is right? Am I doing enough? Am I doing too much? The institution of motherhood finds all mothers more or less guilty of having failed their children; and my mother, in particular, had been expected to help create, according to my father's plan, a perfect daughter.[8]

Experts had many ways of deepening the sense of obligation to produce perfect children among America's mothers. They took every opportunity to point out to young mothers that they ought to be thrilled and excited at each change in their children's behavior, from nursing to finger painting to graduation from college. Child development might be viewed as a detective story, the experts suggested, with the solution to the mystery lying in the mother's own behavior. If she treated her children in accordance with the rules, everything would come out all right. A program of tests was devised by Arnold Gesell's institute at Yale, where children played behind glass, to guide mothers in their expectations of what was to come.

By 1984 the experts at Yale were to add another dimension to her nurturing role—a career. Both parents will be needed to ensure full-time nurturing care. Both provide models for achievement-oriented boys and girls, but according to Professor Ritvo: "It's important that the mother be a good nurturer first, if the mother is a good achiever and not a very good nurturer, this has a much bigger impact on the young child than if the mother is a good nurturer and not a very good achiever."[9] Now as twenty years ago the effect of such ambiguous counsel is guilt for mother.

As the social scientists grew more confident, the old nineteenth-century optimism blossomed once more. Behaviorism—the belief that if you start manipulating the behavior of the human animal at birth, you can shape it to fit your expectations—came to dominate child psychology. The implication was politically similar to the earlier fascination with eugenics, where social scientists had sought to improve the human race before birth genetically.[10] In the behaviorists' view, although the cultivation of the individual had long been accepted as the American way of life, mothers were still only incubators of the future generation. The more dominant the belief in behaviorism became, the less value was invested in women as individual human beings. Thus, ironically, the role of supermother, in which the women of the fifties put so much stock for personal fulfillment and social recognition, was really the role of an obedient child following rules drawn up by someone else—an authority figure in a far-off university laboratory.

Still, women sought out the role and agreed to stick to the rules. Implicitly, they agreed that in the mother-child relationship the child was the central figure, probably because they remembered being the centers of attention in their own mothers' lives.[11] Mothers of the fifties saw themselves as tenders of little martinets to be fed on demand. Painfully, these women learned to give up their illusions of individuality and self-determination. Grandmothers, who had fed their children on rigid schedules and took a stern view regarding youngsters' need for discipline, accused their daughters of spoiling their children. Fathers, on the other hand, were not expected to participate much. They were absent for most of the day, and the idea that they might adapt their work patterns to baby's arbitrary rhythms never entered anyone's head.

Given her isolation as well as her sense of responsibility in child rearing, it is easy to see that what the supermother needed even more than instruction was reassurance—that she had the power to do the "right" thing and that it was all worthwhile. The work of pediatrician Dr. Benjamin Spock reflected the perfect blend of comprehensible instruction and understanding reassurance. These qualities met the needs of mothers in the postwar era so well that his *Common Sense Book of Baby and Child Care*, first published in 1946, was reprinted year after year to become the all-time American bestseller. Most children born from 1946 on were raised with strict reference to its pages. He is often considered to be the spiritual father of the generation that reached majority in the 1960s.

Spock led this generation not only literarily but literally as well—he was a leading activist in the anti–Vietnam War protests of 1967. His trial for Anti-Americanism in 1968 was symbolically the trial of an entire generation of rebels, a group marked by individualists and pacifists. As children, these people had been brought up in accordance with the anti-authoritarian principles elucidated, step by step, in Spock's book.[12]

Spock's theories on child development did not differ greatly from those of Erikson and Gesell, and did not even stray far from Freud's in stressing the importance of mother's influence on baby's first years. But his tone was soothing rather than accusing. Mothers felt that Dr. Spock was on their side. By telling mothers that the next stage was easier and just around the corner, he cajoled them into bearing with baby, giving him or her that untiring attendance that scholarly experts still proclaimed as essential. Mother must rest; mother must make time for herself, crooned Spock. His point, however, was not so much to insure the health of the mothers. Rather, the benefit of mother's rest, like mother's milk, accrued directly to the baby.

Once supermothers had been conditioned to accept their state of dependence—from their own accounts a spirit-breaking ordeal—they became adept people tenders. They adapted both to the demands of a husband's career and to their children's unfolding personalities. "He was on the road a good deal of the time," writes Pat Loud about her way of life in the fifties. "There I was, home with the babies. That was all right; that was fulfillment. He was doing his thing and I was doing mine."[13]

The new domesticity of the fifties was not unlike that of Catherine Beecher's and Harriet Stowe's time. But a significant difference marked the housewife's role as it was manifested a hundred years later. The supermother's daily routine still involved putting food on the table and cleaning up after other people, but now, as Harvard sociologist Talcott Parsons pointed out in *Family, Socialization and Interaction Process* (1955), her major role evolved in building egos, in keeping domestic peace, and in maintaining the family's emotional stability. Obviously the focus of the housewife's job description had once more shifted from the more controllable task of keeping house to the totally uncontrollable Victorian assignment of keeping people happy.

The Government's Version

When one looked from the outside into the home, the comparison with the domestic revival of a century before held true. In 1963, in a report called "The Modern Task of Homemaking," the President's Commission on the Status of Women spelled out almost to the letter the ideals Catherine Beecher had expressed in 1843. The report summed up the developments that had been taking place in the typical middle-class American home over the past decade and basically endorsed the role of supermother. Psychology had replaced God as the supreme authority, but mothers at home still served as role models for their daughters and as moral counselors for their sons and husbands. The children's early years had gained significance in the later model, since "modern psychological knowledge . . . added its force to the traditional conviction as to the mother's role."[14]

The commission by no means viewed the mother of 1960 as dismissed when her children left the nursery. "The responsibilities of the home during the child's later years may be even more demanding," concluded the commission. The charge continues in true Beecher style: the responsibility of the modern homemaker was to make the home "a place where all members of the family can find acceptance, refreshment, self-esteem and renewal of strength amidst the pressures of modern life."

Thus, in 1963, the government officially sanctioned the homemaker's role as conceived in 1843. The supermother of the 1960s fit beautifully into the century-old dream of home as haven. Further, modern plumbing and ranch-style exteriors camouflaged what was essentially a Victorian home: a place in the suburbs that made up for all the shortcomings of city life; a place which the father, absent by day, could enter and forget his worldly cares; a place from which mother could venture forth for the things she needed to perfect her family life and entertain the children.

In the sixties, as in Victorian times, this type of life was made possible only by the strict distinctions that existed between the roles of men and women. One suspects that the commission mentioned the father only in order to indicate that the subject at hand was not the fatherless home. As in John Adams's time, Dad became important in later years, when child rearing "may be even more demanding of the best knowledge and understanding that both parents can bring to their task." But the real key to the task of homemaking lay in the mother's role: "The security given by the mother figure during infancy can have a lifelong impact on the personality of the individual and his ability to cope with life." Thus, from the government's point of view, the father was largely absent, the mother singlehandedly providing the security that young children needed.

The commission concluded pointedly that families flocking to the newly developing suburban communities accounted for two-thirds of the total increase in American population. Between 1950 and 1960, the major cities showed only an 8.7 percent rise in population, but the rise in suburban communities was a whopping 47 percent. These communities, the report noted, were "the domain of women and their children." More significantly, the recommended type of mothering had the affluent homemaker in mind, who had not only the time, but also the means, to drive her children from one enrichment program to another.

Commission members did not feel the need to add that not just any women could claim the suburban turf as their own. Rosie the Riveter might briefly have been considered as a model for mainstream Americans, but she did not belong in suburbia, where mainstream America lived. Rosie belonged with the "other Americans," those who stayed behind in the inner cities because they needed jobs or because they were too old or too poor to move. The "others" were also those who stayed behind because they were black or Puerto Rican or members of any number of minority groups that, through social pressure or overt discrimination, were forced to remain within the boundaries of their particular urban ghettos. By 1960, the battle lines had been drawn between traditional, "normal" Americans and everyone else. Thus, inner-city people faced suburbanites, and super-mothers faced welfare and working mothers, over barriers whose strength would be tested in the decade to come.[15]

The Sociologists' Version

Whereas fragmented families were often the rule in the overstressed, economically depressed areas of the cities, they were the horror of the suburbs. After all, if the vocation of a wife and mother was to create a haven for her husband and bring up her children to realize their full po-tential, a broken family was the most obvious form of failure. Talcott Parsons, who became the classic authority on the family, went further; he viewed the broken family as downright pathological. Moreover, he sug-gested that the "failures and casualties of American family life" were "rather heavily concentrated in the lower-income groups, and complicated there by racial and ethnic problems."[16]

Parsons expressed a popular view that the nuclear middle-class family represented human life as it was meant to be and stood therefore as a model that eventually all Americans would come to inherit. Along with most middle-class people, Parsons believed that the healthy middle class would absorb the problem people and that the nuclear family represented the fittest of the species, favored by the process of natural selection. In white suburbia the nuclear family had indeed replaced the extended family of the past, but to Parsons no loss was involved, since he believed that the intimate family circle provided the best conditions for emotional enrichment.

The modern family as Parsons saw it was a voluntary organization, with its members constantly reevaluating their commitments to each other. The mother's role in this setting was that of adjuster. She functioned to help husband and children work out their conflicts with each other and with the outside world. In brief, the supermother was the adjustable spring that held the family machine together.

Another sociologist, writing somewhat later than Parsons, took a more analytical look at what was called "the typical housewife." Helena Zanieki Lopata made a detailed study of 571 urban and suburban housewives from the Chicago area, and reported her findings in a book called *Occupation: Housewife*.[17] In her interviews and questionnaires, Lopata found that the "typical American housewife" was differentiated along ethnic lines to some degree. For Jewish mothers, their principal function was to be loving, warm, and understanding; for Catholic mothers, to keep their children out of trouble; and for Protestant mothers, to guide their children through a normal development into individuality. Level of education seemed to have a stronger influence than ethnic background, however: less-educated women were generally task- and possession-oriented, while more-educated women gave more importance to personal relationships. Finally, location had an effect on the housewife's role. Lopata felt that the urban women in her study benefited from a great choice of role models and more outside stimulation than those in the suburbs living out the American ideal.

Overall, both in the suburbs and the city, Lopata found an astonishing agreement among the women in her sample. All stated that being a mother came first; next in order of importance, they ranked being a wife and being a housewife. And in almost all cases the husband's job defined the status of the woman and determined whether she remained at home or went to work.

The sociologists went a long and politically divided way toward describing the form and function of the American family and the role of the woman in that configuration. But to learn what most women playing the supermother role were actually told—and to get an intimation of why the role eventually failed to satisfy—we must turn once more to the advice literature of the day.

The Challenge of Being a Woman: The Popular View

Keeping the house sealed against conflict—that was the major responsibility of the housewife of the late 1950s. Nevertheless, the dust of emotional conflict tended to settle unobtrusively in the cracks and corners of suburban homes and had to be dealt with around the clock. Irrepressible dissatisfaction, the old "housewife syndrome" that had surfaced in the late forties, had never gone away. Now, however, active efforts were being made to eradicate the feelings of anger and frustration, dissatisfaction and irritation that surfaced into her consciousness, despite all her efforts to deny them, during the course of the housewife's day.

In 1955, marriage and parent counselors Helen Sherman and Marjorie Cole wrote *The Challenge of Being a Woman*. In this work, they promised that every women could find greater fulfillment as a wife and mother "by developing a concrete daily philosophy for mature self-realization, in which such typical sources of irritation as housework, negative emotions, and disappointments are viewed in a challenging new perspective." Basically, the book was a lay introduction to self-psychoanalysis, an offshoot of the Freudian approach that was very much in vogue during the 1950s. A basic premise of both psychoanalysis and the method advocated by Sherman and Cole was that negative feelings were symptoms of repressed childhood traumas. The authors advocated positive thinking, religion, creative hobbies, and, if all else failed, professional counseling, to help the wife and mother "recondition" herself to self-acceptance and to happiness.

This book and the scores of others that took the same cheerful, practical outlook and sported similar titles swamped the market during the 1950s. Simultaneously, advice similar to that offered in the books appeared in column after column of magazine print. Written by the various brands of authorities on marriage and children surfacing at the time—psychologists, psychiatrists, marriage counselors, family counselors—this literature skillfully combined optimistic common sense with the latest "scientific" ideas. But even more fundamental to these books and articles was the fact that they steered the reader away from economic or political sources of discontent toward the inner sanctum of herself. If her marriage was not working, if the children were not learning—why then, she had only to look to herself. And once she did so, by following the simple rules set forth in the book or article at hand, she could reason herself back to equilibrium. A happiness quiz, a popular gimmick at the time, began Sherman and Cole's book, and it differed little from the quizzes on readers' behavior that are still a popular feature of women's magazines.

As was typical for the fifties, the advice literature did not challenge the nature of housework per se, but rather focused on the nature of the reader. Are you glad to be a woman? they asked. Do you enjoy children? appreciate men? get on well with other people? Do you feel sorry for yourself: often, seldom, never? Do you "accept philosophically and courageously the bad things that can't be changed?" Clearly, some women would have to answer "no," or the authors would not have written the book. In answer to these responses, the message came across loud and clear: if you want your family life to change, dear woman, *you* must do the changing. Sherman and Cole seemed to suggest that if the reader just shaped up and *tried*, balance—and family happiness—would be restored.

> You can change your attitude if you are determined to, sometimes by simply improving your techniques. . . . If you play the part of a woman, you will be able to enter the sex act with warmth and receptivity. . . . The good wife encourages her husband to enter into family activities not by demonstrating to him how naughty the children can be and how tired she is but by planning her work so that when he comes home both she and the children are relaxed and at their best. . . . If your marriage isn't yet all that you want it to be, new psychological insights can help you.[18]

The "psychological" approach was touted as new and enlightened, but in fact it was grounded in the undying sex-role division that nineteenth-century social analysts had made much of. Women look inside; men look outside. Men, however, had changed, at least in the eyes of family counselors. A century earlier, they had been viewed as insensitive, rapacious fighters struggling to bring about the Industrial Revolution. Now they were seen as fragile growing boys whose power to survive could be too easily crushed and who needed as much nurturing as their own toddlers. Thus, the advice the experts offered for mothering applied equally well to the wifely art of husband tending. Whenever a child stepped aside for one moment, the husband stepped in, and vice versa. Switching from one to the other and catering to each at the right moment with the right measure of care was part of the challenge of being a woman.

The Retirement of Supermother: The Empty Nest

According to the sunny, psychological approach, the woman who met the challenge would be a fulfilled homemaker with only one thing to fear— the premature death of her husband. This attitude toward life reflected the traditional white middle-class pattern, but with an added dimension: the acknowledgment that within each individual family things could not go on as they were forever. Children grew up and left home; husbands died faster than wives. In ethnic groups the old extended family still allowed women to participate in its endless permutations, but in a nuclear family a mother's central activity could last for the limited period of only about twenty years.

The experts grew interested in the plight of the older woman. The "empty-nest syndrome" had been incorporated into the jargon of counselors and analysts, like menopause, with which it was closely connected, in their view. The experts saw this condition as a threat to the peace of husbands and grown-up children, and it was not long before these family members saw themselves as the potential victims of over-dependent wives and mothers with nothing to do.

If the challenge younger women faced lay in tightening family ties, the challenge to older women lay in letting go. Writers in the advice literature treated this subject as just another adjustment women had to make. Way back in 1914, Dorothy Canfield Fisher, who introduced American mothers to the Montessori method of early education, had warned mothers, in *Mothers and Children*, that "maternity is not the occupation of a lifetime." And in 1952, in *The Many Lives of Modern Women*, Sidonie Gruenberg advised women to prepare for the end of child-rearing. Drawing on her experience as director of the Child Study Association of America, Gruenberg encouraged her readers to seek part-time jobs throughout their child-rearing years, particularly in time-flexible professions such as real estate, academic research, architecture, and politics. The most popular advice was given by such writers as Ardis Whitman in *How To Be a Happy Woman* (1952), where homemakers were told to treat housekeeping as an interlude and to keep a job waiting on "the horizon of middle life." Looking forward to that horizon, dreaming about it while doing the dishes would help her get through the years of drudgery. There was no doubt in the author's mind that opportunities to work for satisfaction and for pay were waiting for the middle-aged homemaker like tickets at a travel agency. During the expansion-oriented fifties, such suggestions seemed feasible, and the inevitable conflicts that working mothers face today were anticipated only by those early "women watchers" who saw that more than wishful thinking was needed to prepare supermothers "for discontinuity in their married lives."[19]

In 1955, to educate home economists in this neglected area of family living, Michigan State University's College of Home Economics invited the experts to a Symposium on "Potentialities of Women in the Middle Years."[20] Much was made of women's changing roles. The questions raised are still being discussed on college campuses today: Can one be a housewife and a career woman too? Can the middle-aged woman go back to school or return to her former vocation? What support will she find in the community and in colleges? What are the implications for women's education in general? The answers posed—continuous education, part-time jobs, volunteer-career combinations—all are still valid today. In fact, they are offered as new solutions to the problems of today's displaced homemakers, who at that time were building careers as full-time wives and mothers.

What happened? Why did the brides of the fifties drop college and career ambitions? Why did the wives and mothers not prepare for post-motherhood? One answer came from an ex-supermother who did get ready for life after motherhood. Betty Friedan began her landmark book *The Feminine Mystique* in 1957. She said later:

> Until I started writing the book, I wasn't even conscious of the women problem. Locked as we all were then in the mystique, which kept us passive and apart, and kept us from seeing our real problems and possibilities, I, like other women, thought there was something wrong with me because I didn't have an orgasm, waxing the kitchen floor. I was a freak, writing that book.[21]

The feminine mystique was aimed directly at Mrs. Supermother, who was none other than Mrs. Consumer dressed in her new identity. It took Betty Friedan five years to write her indictment of the consumer industry. While she was writing *The Feminine Mystique* to destroy its power, a second author was telling advertising giants how to use it as a sales pitch to Mrs. Supermother.

The Selling of Supermother

In 1958, Janet L. Wolff published *What Makes Women Buy*, another book, like *Selling Mrs. Consumer*, directed at businesses and advertisers minutely describing their target. The book portrayed the typical housewife of the fifties as an unfulfilled, bored, insecure isolate who believed she could buy happiness and would never give up trying. Wolff advised the advertising industry that "the term housewife no longer carries prestige."[22] It was self-indulgence and self-reward that motivated housewives these days, she said, not those admirable qualities of self-sacrifice and a sense of duty that had inspired women in days gone by. Instead of slaving in the kitchen or saving for the future, the new consumer housewife as portrayed by Wolff bought herself status by keeping up with what the Joneses were buying.

Wolff suggested that a new image had emerged as well. The fifties housewife now wanted to appear attractive, warm, youthful, and feminine. Even the term *lady* now had wrong connotations, sounding stuffy and old. Wolff told the consumer industry that homemakers wanted to be distracted from the ordinary, drab reality of their home lives with products that would build up their fantasy life, products that would convince them of their worth as feminine wives and superior mothers. The business of identifying the consumer target and matching the product to a sales image was and is a multimillion-dollar enterprise. By 1979, Pillsbury had invested $25 million in its "doughboy" symbol, a doll which sells frozen dough on the television screen.[23]

It was true that the fifties housewife had an even more central role in distributing money than Mrs. Consumer of the twenties. While men continued to evaluate their personal worth in terms of their material success, women still practiced the lady's art of acquiring and displaying possessions. Never mind that 38 percent of all American families were officially considered poor—with "poor" defined as having an income of less than $3,000 per year. The general belief that this was an affluent society, bolstered by Kenneth Galbraith, who coined the phrase, held firm throughout the fifties and sixties, and the business sector did everything to reinforce that belief.

The advertising industry might have used Wolff's book as a bible. The industry fed what she identified as a need to buy happiness, pouncing on television as the perfect medium to reach the housewife right in her own home. There, presumably dissatisfied and lonely among her children and her possessions—the very things that she had counted on for fulfillment—television promised her new ways to make herself happy: buy our soap and look young, buy our cereal and make your children into Olympic athletes, buy our vacuum cleaner and never do housework again.

Nor were working women of America left out of this advertising barrage. What business could afford to ignore 22 million potential buyers who earned money of their own? But the 5.5 million single women, the 7.5 million widows, the 1.33 million divorcees, and the countless older women in American society in 1958 *were* ignored by the manipulators, and this might have been the most grievous insult yet. According to the advertisers, these women did not wish to exist as they were. The implication was that the

only *real* woman in America was the middle-class, affluent, supermother—
and grandmother. She belonged to the happiness club that every woman
wanted to belong to. The primary requirement for entry into the club
was—as ever—a husband who could buy the membership.

Five years after Wolff's book came out, in 1963, Betty Friedan published
The Feminine Mystique. After having played the role of supermother in
suburbia for a decade, she now declared herself duped by the sales pitch
for total home involvement. When *The Feminine Mystique* appeared, it
marked a turning point in the passive victim role that women had been
accepting at the hands of the consumer industry. Friedan acknowledged
that unhappy women made good consumers, but she exhorted these women
to pull themselves out of the race and see what was really happening to
them. New babies created the need for paper diapers, she said. Lawns
required lawnmowers; women afraid of growing old needed products they
believed would keep them young. Friedan accused the consumer industry
of manipulating women into staying home to have babies they did not
really want and to spend their lives buying products they did not really
need. The basic message in Friedan's book was that supermother in the
suburbs was nothing but an advertising dummy. But the dummy was held
up by the giants of the consumer industry. To declare war on the supermarkets was to declare war on the American economy.

Although during the 1960s supermothers began to leave their suburban
homes, they again acted out of private, unpolitical concerns. For some,
playing dollhouse no longer captured their imaginations. For most, however, the dream of family togetherness was shattered by divorce. While
the marriage exodus had not reached the proportions it would attain in
the seventies, women even in the best of homes underwent painful transformations. Quite obviously, the suburbs had been designed for *young*
parents, and in spite of the propaganda regarding the joys of the period
following motherhood, there was not much left in the empty nest after the
children went their ways. Often, a greying supermother found herself quite
alone to pay the mortgage and mow the lawn.[24] Contrary to earlier predictions, superfathers did not always stay around for renewed togetherness.
The wide gap between a couple created by different lifestyles—one connected with family, the other with business relationships—would often not
close after so many years, especially if the children had been the only
remaining link.

In a last-ditch effort to convince reigning supermothers that they had
nothing to fear from the empty-nest syndrome, male supporters of the
feminine mystique such as Morton Hunt and Allan Sinclair gallantly explained *Her Infinite Variety* (1962) and affirmed the superiority of *The
Better Half* (1965), applauding women for their many past and present
contributions at home and everywhere. But these books, supposedly reflecting a new, liberal attitude, even toward women in the labor force,

depicted women primarily as wives: educated wives, to be sure, with-it wives, financially and mentally stable wives who would not drag their feet behind their husbands and children, but still wives.[25] Such wives carefully adjusted every step to the progress of husband and children. In this vision of the new helpmate, women's efforts in the labor market would always remain supplementary to those of the chief breadwinners. Quite obviously too this image showed a middle-class wife who could count on a good and solid breadwinner. The gracefully aging helpmate therefore was seen as standing firmly behind an aging husband, nursing him through job crises and retirement traumas. These seductively attractive perceptions amounted to a denial of economic reality, which perhaps explains why society continued to evince an almost total lack of concern for the inequities suffered by wage-earning women. Despite the prevailing bad conditions, however, an increasing variety of women and a greater number of "better halves" were entering the labor market at a rapid pace.

SUPERMOTHERS' COMPETITION: WAGE-EARNING MOTHERS

Since the war women from all levels of society had been joining the labor force in significant numbers. The picture of working women in America at the close of the 1950s differed radically from that of even 20 years earlier. At the beginning of the century, most of the nation's working women had been single and under 25. Now, for the first time in American history, family women who were neither widowed nor destitute were returning to or beginning to go to work after age 30. Mothers over 45 made up the fastest-growing group of working women in the nation. Though this fact diverted the attention of family and labor experts, younger mothers too were significantly represented in the labor pool. In 1948, one-quarter of all mothers with school-age children had worked. In 1958, the number had increased by 80 percent.

In a collection of statistical evidence entitled *The Employed Mother in America* (1963), editors F. Ivan Nye and Louis W. Hoffman duly evaluated the testimony of psychologists, economists, and child development experts from 1957 to 1962 and came up with a relatively optimistic diagnosis: There was nothing wrong with a mother who worked for wages. Her marriage and her children prospered to the same degree as those of full-time homemakers. Her personal satisfaction with life in general and the family budget in particular increased. Her husband helped more with the housework and still maintained the same amount of power in the relationship because her position and her salary were considerably lower. The information was gathered in response to negative reports from psychologists and "interested laymen, always alert for a simple explanation of the numerous and complex social problems of our times, [who] speculated that the employment of the mother was the principal cause of current social problems." If Nye's words have a modern ring, so does his admission that one research project was "financed by a social agency which expected to obtain data which would justify its insistence that mothers leave employment."[26]

Obviously the results of *The Employed Mother in America* never reached the public ear, because, despite the new employment trends, by the early sixties working women were all but forgotten. Both the real and the potential wage-earning housewife were receiving little or no media coverage. Apparently nobody wanted to read magazine stories about older women working in supermarkets or dead-end offices. *Woman's Day* had other things to do besides interviewing divorcees who supported their small children on starvation wages or public assistance because the fathers would not or could not pay their shares.

Redbook continued to give cautious advice to tired, housebound young mothers in suburbia, but the magazine devoted no space to the 8 or 9 million working mothers who had children under eighteen. The fact that the number of totally unsupervised children had increased dramatically and that publicly supported childcare had deteriorated markedly since the 1940s caused no general outcry. Instead, what little became known of the situation fueled an antagonism growing between mothers who stayed at home and mothers who did not. "How could they leave their children?" frowned the suburban mothers. Most wage-earning mothers would have replied: "How could I not?" Few people pondered the implications at the time, because women tended to keep quiet, lest something wrong might be revealed about them. Such was the power of the feminine mystique.

The statistics describing the working-mother population emerged at appropriate times, and the needs of working mothers were cited occasionally by politicians, but in 1965 even the official advocates of women and of labor causes still pictured working mothers as the exception, with the "normal" mother staying home. It is significant that the term "working mother" always applied to wage earners, though, and not to homemakers who without paychecks worked for their families in the home.

Neither the Women's Bureau, which had protected female workers since 1928, nor the Commission on the Status of Women, established by President Kennedy in 1961, offered fresh solutions to what by now were the same old problems. Ten years earlier, champions of working mothers had pressed for more flexibile working hours, employer- and government-sponsored child care, social security and equal wages for women, equal training and promotions, and in 1961 these same demands reappeared in the form of recommendations by the commission. The few programs that gradually moved out of planning agencies and into funding agencies merely accommodated the abnormal wage-earning housewife to the prevailing system, where men figured as primary and women as supplementary breadwinners. Finally, in 1964, under pressure from the Children's Bureau, Congress appropriated $4 million to establish and expand childcare services in 41 states. At that time, 9 million mothers were employed in the United States. The gesture was made in the time-honored tradition of charity which had characterized the government's treatment of the poor since 1776.

In 1966, a group of activists, disillusioned with the president's commission, took its complaints to the meeting of the Equal Opportunities Council. They claimed outright that the continuous delay in public support for issues of concern to working housewives amounted to sex discrimination. When the council refused to deal with the complaints, declaring that sex discrimination was not a civil rights issue, these new feminists created the National Organization for Women, which they patterned after the National Association for the Advancement of Colored People.

The founder of the fledgling organization was Betty Friedan, a disillusioned bride of the early fifties who like many ex-supermothers got her divorce in 1969. Friedan's words written a decade after the publication of *The Feminine Mystique* echoed Elizabeth Stanton's basic reform of marriage and divorce: "I think the next issue for the woman's movement is the basic reform of marriage and divorce."[27]

Due to the efforts of the newly minted feminists, women workers now captured the interest of the American public. Women's struggles for job training, equal pay, quality childcare, and adequate child support made television news and magazines headlines. Even in suburbs Americans began to realize that only if these long-standing demands were met would women become independent of a husband's or father's paycheck.

By the last few years of the sixties, the public could hardly avoid these issues. The female labor force now contained many former middle-class housewives who had either been displaced from their suburban homes by divorce or widowhood or who had escaped from those homes voluntarily, spurred on by dissatisfaction and disenchantment. These women were unrecognizable as the suburban supermothers of a few years earlier. Having left the protected isle of their husbands' financial security, they became the victims of the social conditions that had earlier supported them. Between 1960 and 1970, the number of women who alone supported their families grew by 1.1 million, but only 9 percent of the total had incomes over $10,000. By 1973, more than half of all the children living in poverty depended solely on their mothers for support.[28] Clearly, the transition from supermother to single mother invariably meant downward mobility, if not outright poverty.

Under the circumstances many women did not dare to go out to work. Even if their image of supermother was shattered, they remained in the suburbs and underwent painful transformations at home. Even those women whose central ambition in life had been to reach the suburbs and run homes of their own found themselves rethinking their values and doubting their choices by 1967 or 1968. But the conflict between the way women were expected to see themselves and the ways in which they were actually starting to see themselves did not spring up without reason. Nor did it arise spontaneously in the breasts of middle-class women simply because they were dissatisfied with housework. Rather, the conflict arose when these women slowly became aware that they had no power to control their own destiny because they depended totally on their husbands' income. Worse, as mere wives and mothers they no longer stood on a pedestal, but were denigrated as gullible consumers of American products. Typically for the new consumer society, the divorced supermother no longer qualified for a credit card. If the homemaker's identity was being challenged as a wife, she was equally troubled as a mother. The revolution in values among middle-class children forced her to re-sort her own values and to reestablish her priorities. Many a carefully monitored offspring simply did not turn out according to plan. All that clinically tested advice had come to nothing, as children became runaways and drifters by the thousands; took drugs; listened to and developed their own wild, inexplicable music; and strangest of all, cast their loyalties with the minoritites and working class, openly and sometimes bitterly challenging their middle-class roots. Clearly, a mother who had been groomed by the old Freudian interpretations of her responsibility would have been forced to do some serious introspection in view of the paths her children were following. According to the old principles of domestic sainthood as well as modern popular psychology, she had only herself to blame. With all the security pulled out from under her, the falling supermother was terrified.

NOTES

1. Adrienne Rich, *Of Woman Born: Motherhood as Experience and Institution* (New York: Bantam, 1977), p. 26.

2. Elizabeth S. Herbert, "When the Homemaker Goes to Work," *Journal of Home Economics*, vol. 44 (April, 1952), pp. 257–259.

3. F. Ivan Nye et al., *The Employed Mother in America* (Chicago: Rand McNally, 1963), chapter 27, pp. 384–399, "Adjustment of the Mother: Summary and a Frame of Reference," reviews attitudes of social sciences to establish a framework for "a sociological conceptualization of maternal employment." Nye compares negative attitudes of psychologists who interpreted her motive as rejecting wife- and motherhood and of social workers who blamed mothers for child neglect with positive positions of economists.

4. Scharf, *To Work and To Wed*, p. 158.

5. Barbara Ehrenreich and Deirdre English, *For Her Own Good: 150 Years of the Experts' Advice to Women* (New York: Anchor/Doubleday, 1979), p. 208.

6. Philip Wylie, *Generation of Vipers* (New York: Farrar & Rinehart, 1942).

7. Erik Erikson, *Childhood and Society* (New York: W. W. Norton, 1950), p. 198.

8. Rich, *Of Woman Born*, p. 223.

9. Anita Shreve, "The Working Mother as a Role Model," *The New York Times Magazine* (Sept. 9, 1984).

10. For a mother's struggle with Doctor Spock in the sixties read Jane Lazarre, *The Mother Knot* (New York: Dell/Laurel, 1977), pp. 130–131.

11. Nancy Chodorow, *The Reproduction of Mothering: Psychoanalysis and the Sociology of Gender* (Berkeley, Calif.: University of California Press, 1978), gives a new interpretation of Freud's early childhood theories which predestines women to recreate their mothers in their own motherhood experience; thus the mother-daughter tie can never be broken and continually reproduces old values, regardless of social conflict.

12. Maxine L. Margolis, *Mothers and Such: Views of American Women and Why They Changed* (Berkeley, Calif.: University of California Press, 1984), pp. 67–79, "Spock-marked Mothers and 'Moms': 1940–1960," chapter 3, "Mothers Descend," shows the development from controlled to permissive, child-psychology-oriented mothering.

13. Pat Loud and Nora Johnson, *Pat Loud: A Woman's Story* (New York: Bantam, 1974), p. 54.

14. "The Modern Task of Homemaking," in U.S. President's Commission on the Status of Women, Report of the Committee on Home and Community, October, 1963 (Washington, D.C.: Govt. Printing Office, 1963), p. 3:

> Modern psychological knowledge has added its force to the traditional conviction as to the mother's role in the child's early years. All studies tend to confirm the hypothesis that the security given by the mother figure during infancy can have a lifelong impact on the personality of the individual and his ability to cope with the demands of life. The responsibilities of the home during the child's later years may be even more demanding of the best knowledge and understanding that both parents can bring to their task....
>
> Furthermore, our highly mobile society of today requires her to provide both stability and adaptability to new situations. She must make of the home a place where all members of the family can find acceptance, refreshment, self-esteem, and renewal of strength amidst the pressures of modern life.

15. Nancy Rubin, *The New Suburban Woman: Beyond Myth and Motherhood* (New York: Coward, McCann & Geohegan, 1983), pp. 58–61, "History of the Suburban Woman."

16. Talcott Parsons and R. Bales, *Family, Socialization and Interaction Process* (Glencoe, Ill.: Free Press, 1955), quoted by Jessie S. Bernard in *Women, Wives and Mothers: Values and Options* (Chicago: Aldine, 1975), p. 228.

17. Helena Znaniecki Lopata, *Occupation Housewife* (New York: Oxford University Press, 1971), pp. 108–111, 152.

18. Helen Sherman and Marjorie Coe, *The Challenge of Being a Woman* (New York: Harper, 1955), p. 52.

19. Ardis Whitman, *How To Be a Happy Woman* (New York: Appleton, 1952). "Wives today must deliberately set out to make their marriages successful." "Practice daily habit of tenderness."

20. Irma H. Gross, ed., *Potentialities of Women in the Middle Years* (East Lansing: Michigan State University Press, 1956).

21. Betty Friedan, *The Feminine Mystique* (New York: Dell, 1974), p. 1. Reprint of 1963 ed. with new introduction.

22. Janet L. Wolff, *What Makes Women Buy* (New York: McGraw Hill, 1958), pp. 9–16. The author quotes *Retailing Daily* (January 3, 1955), which estimated that a typical housewife cooked more than 57,000 meals in her lifetime, washed 26,200 dishes a year, and walked 300 miles a year in her own home. Working housewives spent almost as much time on housework (pp. 212–215).

23. R. Parker, *The Myth of the Middle Class* (New York: McGraw Hill, 1958), pp. 9–16.

24. Rubin, *The New Suburban Woman*, p. 37, looks at the greying of suburbia.

25. Morton M. Hunt, *Her Infinite Variety* (New York: Harper & Row, 1962).

The thesis of this book is that in the modern world woman functions most adequately and has the best chance of happiness when she defines femininity in terms of a multiplicity of roles, finding ways to handle them more or less simultaneously with a minimum of inner conflict, sudden shifts or unpreparedness. p. 154

26. Nye et al., *The Employed Mother in America*, pp. 6–7.

27. Friedan, *The Feminine Mystique*, p. 379, "Epilogie." Summarizes development of NOW and author's role after publication of *The Feminine Mystique*. For detailed accounts see her *It Changed My Life* (New York: Random House, 1976).

28. Nona Glazer, *Woman in a Man-Made World* (Chicago: Rand McNally, 1977), p. 383, for feminist interpretation of this period.

7

The Displaced Homemaker: She Doesn't Do It Anymore, 1965–1975

I was in the condition of anybody who has lived forty years on a certain set of concepts only to wake up one morning and find them blown to bits. Was it possible that people were not made to stick together all their lives? Could it be that even if you married somebody you loved very much it might just somehow end, leaving you lost in space? Then what do you do?

—Pat Loud, *A Woman's Story*, 1974[1]

With the publication of *The Feminine Mystique* and the formation of the National Organization of Women, in 1963 and 1966 respectively, the new American women's movement was launched in earnest. Over the course of the late 1960s, the movement pushed its way into the nation's consciousness. Feminists began to appear on talk shows; feminists began national magazines; feminist civil rights and anti-war activists began to consider their positions within their organizations relative to the male leadership. Consciousness-raising groups and women's literature and art seminars mushroomed on college campuses. Advocacy groups for women workers surfaced. Women in the print and electronic media began monitoring women's images in textbooks and magazines and on television. In 1970, some 35,000 women marched down Fifth Avenue in New York to demonstrate their solidarity.[2] In short, women began forging new self-images that more closely matched their own understanding of themselves than the pictures created by a tradition-bound consumer-oriented society. If the sixties had been shaped by rebellious students, the seventies belonged to rebellious women who refused to act out their sex roles. Sex roles victimized women, claimed feminists. Sex roles prevented women from developing their potential as human beings, as students, as workers, as artists, as citizens. A new wave of feminist scholarship began to reveal the effects of sex-role divisions on the American culture and economy. Novels and poetry, and eventually even movies and television, reflected the theme with various degrees of honesty.

Through it all, suburban housewives across the country felt the rumblings though they were far removed from the centers of activity. They continued to question their old values, and divorce statistics alone during the period show that in increasing numbers they found the marriage-home-children model lacking. But the burgeoning women's liberation movement did not lend much overt support to the suburban woman's struggle in the early days. It gained its energy from angry women who had already thrown off conventional roles and from the new generation of single women who defied the marriage-family pattern *before* being drawn into it. By them, the middle-class housewife was treated as a lost cause-when she was treated at all. Like the rest of the nation, the more radical feminists still believed in the media's image of the happy homemaker who had barricaded herself into suburbia against the threatening forces of the "women libbers." But economist Kenneth Galbraith, as always au courant in his diagnosis of American society, called the seventies housewife "a cryptoservant . . . to almost the entire male population."[3]

On her own, as we saw in the preceding chapter, the troubled housewife had been rethinking her commitments to the traditional family values and was beginning to doubt that she would reap the rewards that had been promised to her in the fifties. In 1972, she did finally expose her condition to the scrutiny of the public eye, most appropriately via the medium of television.

BREAKUP OF AN AMERICAN FAMILY

In 1972, public television presented a 12–part series called *An American Family*. Over the course of the series, many millions of viewers were transfixed by the daily comings and goings of a "typical" American family. The series was a *cinema-verité* view of a middle-class Santa Barbara family—affluent father, capable mother, and their five children—simply living their lives, day after day. About two-thirds of the way through the series, Pat Loud, the wife, calmly announced to her husband—and to millions of thunder-struck viewers—that she was arranging for a divorce.

In suddenly turning *An American Family* into the record of a family breakup, Pat Loud had created a dark mirror for many viewers following the series. Since 1960, the nation's divorce rate had doubled—that is, it had increased 100 percent in four years. Statistically, any family in the viewing audience had a good chance of going through an experience similar to the one that the series promised to document. Psychologically, most of the housewives who tuned in had a great deal in common with Pat Loud.

What had happened to Pat Loud to bring her to the moment of truth

19. Pat Loud and the American Family.

already happened to feminist writer Betty Friedan, to feminist poet Adrienne Rich, and to countless women who had gone to college in the early fifties and then followed a new husband to a suburban paradise. Friedan jolted herself out of the backwaters and into political leadership, and Rich hung onto her poetry throughout a long, sad marriage. Both women, publicly at least, emerged strong. But not Pat Loud. As she wrote in her own account of her metamorphosis from wife to divorcee, *Pat Loud: A Woman's Story* (1974), she came out of her 20–year marriage "a washed-up harridan." In a reversal of the Pygmalion story, the beautiful Stanford graduate had permitted Bill Loud to dismantle her until she was nothing but an empty pantsuit. Why had she let it happen? Why, for that matter, had Betty Friedan switched from Karl Marx to Doctor Spock? Why had so many female college graduates given up their careers for the chance to push a baby carriage? How, in short, had so many intelligent, well-educated women—who eventually found the strength of purpose to leave home, go to work, write books, and organize others—allowed themselves to believe, even for one minute, that they were the suburban housewives, the self-sacrificing supermothers, and the avid consumers that America's experts had told them they were?

In her book, Pat Loud tackled the latter question directly. She described herself as having been programmed for marriage. "They all were," she said. "Those who went to college and those who did not." In her case, the brief exposure to Stanford and her equally brief infatuation with archaeology seemed unreal compared with the life she had spent at home, where "Dad ran everything" and "Mama and Grandma cooked like mad . . . tending the family heirloom, a house that had belonged to great-grandmother with . . . basement shelves of gleaming jars of fruits, relishes, and sauces." Her father treated her mother, her brother, and herself as his "most priceless possessions."[4]

Pat goes on to describe the glamor of the boys returning from the Korean War and the chain of weddings that followed. Pat herself simply stepped into line, seeing her future as inevitable. She married a gregarious ex-soldier with leadership qualities and drive who began to make money while she made babies. "One of the things that gets you the most points is having a baby," she said, echoing the quote by Adrienne Rich in the preceding chapter, "because then everybody forgives you for everything." Pat and her husband followed the blueprint to the last detail. They had five children and reached the top level of the American middle class in prestigious Santa Barbara. They lived in a large, sprawling house with a swimming pool and a three-car garage, and Pat cooked in a designer kitchen hung with copper pans. She cooked and cooked and cooked, until her children were teenagers. One day, watching them from across the top of the stove, she realized that it would not be long before they would get up from the table, walk out the door, and never come back.

What Went Wrong?

When the American dream family fell apart before the eyes of millions of television viewers, the general consensus appeared to be that Pat was at fault. Television critics threw the first stones, and the public followed with letters. Critics and viewers alike blamed many factors for the breakup: the lack of communication among the Louds, their shallow emotional life, their preoccupation with material things, the parents' tendency to buy off the teenagers with trips and ballet lessons and horses and guitars, family members' general lack of values, their habits of drinking and smoking for escape, and their intentional avoidance of confrontation. The most frequently made comment, however, was that intelligent, affluent, privileged Pat Loud had simply not tended to her own house. From the outset, though the program's director had argued that he was completely unbiased, the camera focused on the mother's trouble spots. Although 268 hours of film had been shot of the Louds, Pat and Lance, her frankly homosexual son, came out as the center of attention. Mother and son were set up through the editing as the maker and her flawed product.

Above all, detractors blamed Pat for taking the initiative in obtaining the divorce. The fact that she announced her intentions on the air, and did so in a cool, unruffled manner, offended the audience further.

Pat simply informed Bill that she had arranged a divorce, as if she were telling him she had made a doctor's appointment.

But off camera, as we learn in Pat's book, she was anything but cool and calm. She vacillated between blaming Bill and blaming herself. Bill had been a liar and a cheat for years, she says, but she played that old ostrich game to the fullest. When it came to admitting that he had been unfaithful in the past, she stuck her head in the sand, since confronting the truth would have meant packing five children into the car and heading toward the unknown. Bill was a philanderer, true, but he was nevertheless charming, and he always paid the bills. Besides, putting up with his infidelities meant not having to admit that she had failed to hold him. Women have played the ostrich game for centuries. Novels and plays throughout history have shown that it could be played tastefully, in the aristocratic tradition, and without tiresome scenes.

But Pat could not quite play the game all the way through. Bill encouraged her to have affairs to even the score, but Pat did not like his ideas on "open marriage" at all. She had been brought up to be a good girl. On the other hand, she just could not play the proverbial good woman who "lives with it." She wavered. Her anger dissolved into a chronic case of self-loathing.

In reviewing her history, Pat Loud realized that she had been counting on enjoying the traditional satisfactions of middle life: watching the children grow into productive adults, luxuriating in a debt-free, possession-studded home and the renewed companionship of a husband in retirement who was glad to have withdrawn from the rat race. Instead, what she wound up with was a husband who preferred the companionship of independent women over her own, and who loved the rat race and had no intention of withdrawing. And, far from anticipating the pride she would take in her children's success, she had no idea what her children would be after they emerged from their rock-music phase and their flirtations with unorthodox lifestyles. What, after all, she finally had to ask herself, would she have to show for her 20–year investment if she stuck around?

Like Betty Friedan, Pat concluded that the Hollywood movie-makers, the novel writers, her parents, and the experts had fooled her with half-truths and sold her on bogus, easy-to-follow recipes for happiness. Her anguish over having been cheated was matched by her anger at having been a fool, a dummy who needed her husband to select her clothes for her and to give her a monthly allowance for groceries. She finally concluded that she had spent her entire married life indulging herself in a simplistic need to be needed.

Waking Up from the Dream of Supermother

Had she not been filmed for television, Pat Loud might have been one more good-looking Santa Barbara divorcee who dabbled in this and that until she married again. Instead, she had the opportunity to look at herself through the eyes of a television director who had a point to prove about the decay of the American family and who created a particular image of Pat Loud out of the fragments of her wrecked ego that would suit his needs. Pat did not like the image he created, but she did not like the true version of herself very much either. The unlooked-for boon, however, was her discovery that she was not alone. For, in addition to her detractors, a great many admiring viewers wrote in to express their feelings of empathy or kinship. In some cases, they expressed gratitude. Pat found that she represented a battered army of veterans who had all been told that, as wives and mothers, they had a special responsibility to save the American family dream. Pat Loud showed them on television that one can walk out of a losing battle even without knowing where to go next.

Pat Loud also demonstrated that it takes more than a wife and mother to keep a family intact. One of the many letter-writers who praised her honesty and courage wrote, "You are not so much in question as the whole of family life in general."

Pat Loud managed to break the hold of the family mystique on her heart and mind, but her notion of what to do next was anything but clear. What is the alternative, she asked, to hanging around "in enclaves the way women do, like tough old cornstalks left in a field at the end of the summer?" She decided to fly to New York—one more ex-supermother catching up with the growing number that had escaped from gilded cages. In reflecting on the point she had reached, she wrote,:

> All of us of my generation were propelled into marriage as the big panacea—the big cure-all. Since we can't go back and undo that, we now have to grow up at forty-six, and at forty-six you are a little stiff and tired from bringing up those kids and painting the dining room and driving one thousand miles a day and shoring up a husband in the throes of the male-menopause. It doesn't seem quite cricket, and society has dealt us a foul blow, but for God's sake let's not whine. As Miss Jean Brodie said, *I am in my Prime.*[5]

THE HOUSEWIFE-HEROINE: A NEW STREAM OF CONSCIOUSNESS

Pat Loud's story, written in a chatty, confessional style, served to document the classic struggle for self-discovery that was becoming a new convention in the suburbs in the early seventies. But a certain type of popular fiction—here termed antidomestic fiction—written during the period in which supermothers strained to see themselves through their own eyes explored the process more deeply. In retrospect, one could view the antidomestic novels of the sixties and early seventies as a single, slow awakening to the fact that princes make scullery maids out of princesses, not, as the advertisers would have it, the other way around. Romantic love had drawn masses of women into marriage and away from themselves. The new antidomestic fiction would show them the way back.

The first classic of the genre was Mary McCarthy's *The Group* (1963), an ironical, sometimes bitter view of a group of women educated at Vassar in the thirties and the hopeless discrepancy between their expectations and their fates. Another was Sue Kaufman's *Diary of a Mad Housewife* (1967), which showed the extent to which a woman could function with no real sense of her own identity.

Marriage as perceived by the anti-mystique authors could only follow along male definitions, because the male breadwinner holds the housewife in his power:

> I understand [says Bettina Balsam, the mad housewife], that unless I wanted to divorce Jonathan, or have Jonathan divorce me, I had to jump when he said Jump. Since the very word divorce brought on an avalanche of bewilderment (Why? How did we get here? What happened? etc.), and since I went into a tailspin at just the very thought of trying, in my current condition, to go it alone with the girls (provided, that is, I got them) and to cope with all the problems of existence by myself, I knew I would jump. And jump and jump.[6]

'Myth America:' The kitchen dummy revolts

'The shirts have ring-around-the-collar. The floor has yellow waxy buildup. And I think my husband has run away with Mrs. Olsen.'

Take heart, America, the days of anguish over "Ring around the collar" may be numbered.

Among the various forms of fallout from the women's movement has been a significant redesign advertising, particularly on the TV.

That picture may have come a long way, baby, in the last one or two years but there is still a long way to go, according to Joan Levine, president of Hall and Levine Advertising in Los Angeles.

Ms. Levine spoke recently on "Myth America — Women's Image in the Media" to a group at Mills College in Oakland.

"We've been being insulted for a long, long time but until very recently women didn't know they were being insulted," Ms. Levine said. "Women bought the cliche that a hot meal and a clean shirt was all there was to womanhood."

But that picture is changing, at least in the realm of TV advertising, and generally for the better.

At the request of the California Commission on the Status of Women, Ms. Levine participated in a survey of some 350 to 400 television commercials on the air and in the print media and compared the picture presented of women today to that in commercials from two years ago.

But before dissecting individual commercials themselves, Ms. Levine put the practical limits of television advertising into perspective to help the audience see why a TV ad was the way it was.

Most commercials run for 30 seconds with the last several seconds devoted to a picture of the product, and the middle devoted to delivering the commercial message.

This leaves something under 10 seconds at the beginning of the commercial to set the stage. Because of this

clean.

"I don't think women object to being depicted as housewives per se — it's the ecstasy they are showed as feeling over the clean floor that is so offensive," she said.

With this perspective, Ms. Levine turned to some current commercials which she felt struck a good balance between selling a product designed for women and portraying that woman in a human, reasonable light.

A current "Bold" commercial, for example, showed a woman and her daughter with the child roughhousing in the yard. The woman's voice explained that when she was a child her mother was always fussing about her getting dirty but today she doesn't have to worry about dirt because she has a good laundry product. The commercial ends with the mother and child happily playing together.

Ms. Levine contrasted this approach to the often-ridiculed "ring around the collar" ad for Whisk which showed a woman's life entirely falling apart because her laundry product failed to get her husband's shirts clean.

On another front, Ms. Levine took exception to the interaction between men and women in certain commercials. In a particular Alpo dog food commercial the woman — played by a actress — is accused by her husband of being an utter dummy (and an implied animal-hater as well) for buying brand X dog food instead of Alpo.

The old cycle of Mrs. Olsen Folger's coffee commercials, in which the husband says nasty things to his wife because she makes bad coffee, is another example of unpleasant portrayals of both men and women which are insulting and degrading to both parties. Ms. Levine feels, she noted the Folger's ads have been replaced with a new series in which the couple is making coffee together.

The old stereo...

20. Newspaper article reproduced from the Berkeley *Independent-Gazette*, March 18, 1976.

In real-life confessions, as in these novels, the husband's power is economic in the eighteenth-century sense, that is, absolute, authoritarian. The wives dress in clothes bought according to the husband's taste; they give parties for the husband's friends to impress them with his possessions, his children, his know-how. Although they realize that this is wrong, that they ought not to jump, they cannot change their enslavement, because they see no viable alternatives to their bondage. They are totally cut off from all ties to the outside world. They are trapped in the "feminine sphere," which has turned into their private hell, where they suffer endless trivial tortures. Almost as if the authors wanted to prove psychiatrist Helene Deutsch right, these heroines suffered the pains of penis envy: their husband out there did everything right while they persisted in bungling their way through dinner parties, errands, and half-hearted love affairs.

Love had long been the hallmark of the "woman's novel." But, though romantic fiction abounds to this day and is a formidable commodity at supermarket checkout counters, love is treated with irony at best, and with bitterness commonly, in the antidomestic novel. Rather than following heroines through love affairs whose basic value remained unchallenged, novelists describing middle-class life disillusioned the reader with shopping lists, household dirt, and an endless round of small, everyday defeats. Presumably the new heroines had already made the mistake of being swept off their feet and down the aisle. Now they dreamed of being set free from the tedium of married life. Concurrently advice columns in magazines were gluing real-life marriages together.

The heroines of the antidomestic novels of the late sixties were always more pathetic than tragic. They invariably set out to please outrageously demanding husbands and bratty children, seeming to suppress intentionally their own needs and desires. Their neuroses appeared to come out of a desperate need to achieve and an utter contempt for the materials and methods available that might at least have allowed them some fulfillment within the domestic trap.

"I have to make a pee pee, Mummy, Mummy! My pee is coming out!" Thus writes Sheila Ballantyne in "They Call Me Mummy" (1972) about a mother's major contribution to mankind, toilet training. She continues her account of this daily event:

> Into the bathroom we go, to sit again on haunches. Eternal Mother, waiting for the pee to begin. But wait. There in the bowl floats a little pair of pants—fetid, dead, languishing in a sea of golden excrement. "Wait a minute, dear. Mummy has to take care of your poopie."[7]

One overriding characteristic of the housewife-heroine was her penchant for waiting. She waited for the people she loved to get up in the morning, to come to the table, to finish eating, to come back home, to go to bed.

She waited for machines to complete their cycles, for repairmen to arrive, and for the telephone to ring. She waited in line at the supermarket and she waited at the doctor's office. She waited in parking lots and on the road. She waited for approval, for deliveries, for bowel movements, for decisions to be made. The process of waiting was not strenuous, but it drained her energy. Waiting, like seeping poison, immobilized the house-wife-heroine, rendering her incapable of acting on her own behalf.

The antidomestic novels of the sixties and early seventies concentrated almost exclusively on the slow awakening of Sleeping Beauty. In keeping with the standard advice of the time, self-awareness was seen as the house-wife's salvation. But one reading such novels today is not convinced that a newly awakened Sleeping Beauty will stay awake for long. Sometimes the novel showed the heroine shrugging off her old marriage only to walk away with a new prince, suggesting that the story was to start all over again. But if she was shown as emerging, like Pat Loud, alone, she was certainly not portrayed as knowing where she was going. The latter version was an accurate accounting of the housewife's situation. The reason for her passivity was precisely that she did *not* know where she was going. In *Kiss Sleeping Beauty Good-Bye* (1979) Madonna Kolbenschlag used fairy-tale imagery to describe women's self-liberation from Sleeping Beauty. The Frog Prince represents the needy patriarch who thrives on her need to be needed which, like an evil spell, can only be broken by throwing him out of her bed against the wall.[8]

By expressing their disgust with male oppression in a violent fashion Marilyn French and a number of feminist authors attempted in the late seventies to jolt the housewife-heroine out of the domestic trap. Ten years after Sue Kaufman portrayed her hopelessly mad housewife, Marilyn French wrote *The Women's Room* (1977), a new kind of antidomestic novel, named for the setting of the opening chapter, the graffiti-covered women's rest room at Harvard University. The novel's heroine has achieved her escape from suburbia, only to find herself "at the age of thirty-eight huddled for safety in a toilet booth in the basement of Sever Hall." The time is 1968 and the graffiti read, "Kill all fascist Pigs" and "Cunt is Beautiful." Self-analysis does not lead to liberation in this novel. Rather, French's technique turned to confronting the enemy: men.

In the first half of *The Women's Room*, French follows her central char-acter, Mira, into the suburbs and describes a group of women trapped in their own tract homes—death traps ruled by husbands wielding meaty, lethal fists. The blue-collar men inflict physical abuse on the women; the professional men employ more sophisticated means of defeating them. The women fight a losing battle. Only those who escape early manage to survive.

Thus, for the first time in domestic literature, a female author declared open, unmitigated war upon men, the oppressors. Analogous with radical feminists Brownmiller and Atkinson, French portrayed every male character without exception as the enemy, the rapist, the Nazi:

> My feelings about men are the result of my experience. I have little sympathy for them. Like a Jew just released from Dachau, I watch the handsome young Nazi soldier fall writhing to the ground with a bullet in his stomach and I look briefly and walk on.... Forever and forever I will hate Nazis, even if you can prove to me that they too were victims, that they were subject to illusion, brainwashed with images.[9]

Although literature records a long tradition of misogyny, or woman-hating, no equivalent documentation of man-hating exists. We do not even have a word for the phenomenon of man-hating. Female characters who hate men do occur throughout fiction and drama, of course, but usually as the very women—the whores, the witches—who conventionally disturb the peace of misogynists. Strains of man-hating could be found as the counterparts of saint- and angel-worship, which were rampant in Victorian fiction. For example, violent Victorian man-haters, though not identified as such, joined forces to fight intemperance and white slavery, the most dramatic manifestations of men's brutality toward women. The drunkard who murdered his son to punish his wife in Lydia Huntley Sigourney's *The Intemperate* (1848) matched any man in *The Women's Room* in cruelty. But such brutal villains were inevitably killed off in Victorian fiction. In French's book, they lived on to break the spirit of their wives.

Since Greek and Roman times, men have hated women for two intertwined reasons: as mothers, women had life-and-death power over the boy-child and could give or withhold their love; as lovers, too, they might give or withhold affection, but with their power now reinforced by sexual trickery. According to Katherin M. Rogers, in *The Troublesome Helpmate* (1966), woman-hating is a reaction against both idealization and sexual repression. As a reaction to the former, it is manifested as "a desire to tear down what has been raised unduly high." In response to the latter, as the man strikes out against a woman who has spurned his love, "it motivates attacks on woman's physical nature, such as Swift's nauseating descriptions of her flabby breasts and body odors."[10]

The man-hating theme in *The Women's Room* is motivated by identical power-play dynamics, though the roles of men and women have been reversed. Mother-power is replaced by an omnipotent husband-power—men exhibit a combination of patriarchal and sexual force that keeps their wives economically, physically, socially, and mentally dependent. Repeatedly in the novel, the distastefulness of the sex act serves as a symbol for men's power and women's vulnerability.

Whereas in Victorian novels the women are vindicated and happily widowed in the end, in *The Women's Room* the women are killed in action or condemned to suffer continually. Those women who manage to escape from their husbands' thrall enjoy only a brief period of freedom—sharing ideas and ideals with women like themselves—before they succumb to poverty and isolation. Near the end of the novel, Mira lives alone and bored near the campus of a small New England college. At night she has nightmares about being locked into an empty house that can only be opened from the outside. Nobody will come to let her out. "What prince is going to cut through the brambles to reach me?" she asks. Vestiges of fairy-tale love stories haunt her days; men with mindless, empty eyes terrorize her nights. Mira, like Pat Loud, faces the future alone. Still, according to French, it is better to be alone outside the house than alone inside. Outside, somewhere, lies a chance for a new life; inside, death is inevitable. The domestic madhouse of the sixties has become a tomb in French's vision.

French's use of the home as death house represents a new interpretation of an old convention. The home used to serve as a refuge and the condition of its interior as a symbol for the condition of the family that lived in it. As long ago as the 1860s, Catharine Maria Sedgwick celebrated family contentment as expressed around an ordinary supper table. During the same period, Harriet Beecher Stowe enshrined the joys of wifely living for all to experience vicariously. These novelists drew their readers' attention to simple foods and flowers in the manner of a Dutch still-life. Their heroines were examples of the sort of psychological adaptability women traditionally were good at: making the best of a bad situation. For a great many women of the past, interior changes have been the only changes possible, and turning inward the only response to domestic unhappiness. In a broad sense, even Marilyn French was participating in the tradition of turning inward, since words and the novelist's imagination have always been women's most powerful weapons.

The Women's Room was a political novel. Like *Uncle Tom's Cabin*, it focused on the abuse of power. The evil of Simon Legree was the evil of an entire system grounded in slavery. Regardless of the relative decency of individual masters, the men who owned, sold, or used slaves stood condemned in the novel. Stowe's book sold a million copies in the first nine months after publication. As a political propaganda piece, it aroused worldwide opposition to slavery, hastened abolition in the United States, and fueled the American Civil War.

The Women's Room did not incite another civil war, but the success of the novel was phenomenal. Nine printings of the paperback edition appeared in the first five months after publication. Published originally by a small feminist press, the book became a surprise best-seller nationwide. It is safe to assume that the public's response was linked to a reevaluation of the nature of marriage taking place in the minds of many more Americans at the time. Marriage had originally served as the exchange of the wife's services for support and protection by the husband. In French's novel, the women refuse their services and men refuse to give their support. The success of the novel coupled with the ever greater national divorce rate indicated that the war between the sexes had taken a serious turn.

In 1977, when Marilyn French left Mira walking alone on the beach, women who had escaped the suburban housewife role still had a lot of battles to fight. They also still had a lot to lose. Fiction writers, on whom we rely for new images of ourselves, had yet to devise a model that could capture the public imagination with a more conciliatory version of the struggling housewife-heroine. Marge Pierce, author of *Small Changes* (1973) and *The High Cost of Living* (1978), who was also one of the most widely anthologized feminist poets, wrote:

> I love people who harness themselves, an ox to a heavy cart
> who pull like water buffalo, with massive patience,
> who strain in the mud and muck to move things forward
> who do what has to be done, again and again.[11]

The theme of heroic persistence against all odds for survival emerges triumphantly with Alice Walker's bestselling novel *The Color Purple* (1984). Celebrating a Black woman's power to vindicate both sexual and racial oppression, the heroine resorts once more to the traditional sources of women's strength: love and compassion, which she sustains with guts and lust for life. Like the nineteeth-century domestic novel the book demonstrates women's superiority over men and women's talent for making the best of a bad domestic situation, but unlike its Victorian predecessors it openly expresses women's sexuality in their relationship with each other and with the men in their lives. As a feminist statement it shows how the heroine changes from victim to victor through her supportive contact with other women. Not surprisingly, Alice Walker won the Pulitzer Prize.

BEYOND SUBURBIA: THE BATTLES OUTSIDE

In 1966, when Betty Friedan founded the National Organization for Women, she declared outright that one-half of the American population oppressed the other half. News headlines treated the movement as a joke. American women, the critics wrote, belonged to the most cherished and indulged class of people in the world—next to American children—harvesting the rich fruits of their men's labor, such as custom kitchens and their very own cars. American wives owned most of the stock and drew on billions of dollars in life insurance and pensions. Detractors snidely suggested that these "strident," white, middle-class mothers were playing anti-establishment games learned from their sons and daughters. Anti-war, anti-male, anti-law-and-order, the wives and children of hard-working American fathers were out to bite the hands that fed them.

In a repeat performance of the first civil rights struggle, white and Black women who had worked side by side with men in the South now claimed that they had been deprived of sexual equality. Male civil rights leaders refused to make common cause with rebellious women. Labor officials showed no sympathy whatsoever for women workers who wanted to wear hard hats. Employers saw women as demanding equal opportunities while still hanging on to the special privileges that protected them from physical exertion and danger. Finally, a phalanx of right-wing supermothers rose up to defend their nests against the growing number of divorcees, family dropouts, and women's libbers. According to the Virginia Slims American Opinion Poll of 1972, the majority of the 3,000 women polled wanted a husband to support them.

When *Harper's Bazaar* editor Natalie Gittelson toured the country interviewing American wives, she noticed that in 1969 hardly anyone had even heard the term "radical feminism," but a year later she "encountered no woman whose thinking about herself in relation to men had not been shaken up or altered by the widening feminist clamor for women's rights." Gittelson's curiosity about the changing sexual mores in America was revealed in a book entitled *The Erotic Life of the American Wife* (1972), which like Pat Loud's story proclaimed the death of the American marriage long before a couple filed for divorce. Here the bored, affluent housewife is as dissatisfied with her experiments in sexual liberation as the restless career wife. Daughters who avoided getting trapped into stagnant marriages are desperate for signs of commitment from the men they love. Those who had chosen total freedom feel exploited by their uninvolved partners and militant wives, "the walking wounded . . . cripples met to mourn their common infirmity—womanhood—and to construct, in spite of it, a platform from which they could function in the world.[12]

Nevertheless, though opponents went to great lengths to deny the validity of the women's movement, statistical evidence alone gave credence to the movement's claim that the old system would no longer work. Between 1968 and 1972, the annual divorce rate had increased by 82 percent. In 1973, a total of 913,000 couples dissolved their marriages, and 1 million followed suit in 1975. As a result, society was faced with a whole new set of social problems. Women deprived of the traditional family benefits— companionship, pensions, insurance plans—had to find new means of surviving financially. Many had to be absorbed into the labor force as long-term, full-time wage earners. Discrimination against women marked every sector of public life, since society was used to considering mothers and wives the only women of status. Black women as always felt the worst of it.

The political activists of the women's movement recognized that the need was more urgent than ever for making public the issues that had been buried in "the privacy of the home." In *Revolution: Tomorrow Is Now* (1973), the National Organization for Women attacked public policies on every front: from inadequate child care to nonexistent maternity leaves, from biases in education to biases in employment; from poorly drawn female models in school textbooks to sexist images of women on television; from male-biased credit ratings to the inequitable distribution of social security benefits. As ever, discrimination in one sector was found to be rooted in another. Since back in 1923, when it had first been proposed, the Equal Rights Amendment (ERA), a straightforward guarantee against discrimination on the basis of sex, had languished. Now its speedy ratification became the joined goal of the women's rights and the women's liberation movements. Although ideologically the two groups differed— women's rights advocates were generally older, middle-class, and committed to working within the political system, while liberationists were more radically feminist with a strong socialist perspective—common concern for the passage of the ERA drew them together.

Once the campaign to ratify the amendment was renewed, a true battle had begun. The same antagonism that had surfaced earlier against women's education and suffrage now characterized the opposition to the Equal Rights Amendment. Fundamentally, the argument raised by opponents to the ERA was this: if women are to be granted equal rights, they must accept equal obligations, but equal obligations will draw them away from the family. The argument was a throwback to the nineteenth-century Beecher model, in which a woman, regardless of her individual talents and qualifications, existed as a valid entity only within the family network. It was there that she earned her keep, her respect, and her rights. Even when childless or career-oriented, women belonged to a species different from men, whose own prescribed role was to provide support for a wife and children. A society that accepted this role division would clearly shape its public policy to favor men over women as actual and potential wage earners. Thus, the Equal Rights Amendment, by ensuring that women and men would be treated as equals on all fronts, including the labor front, challenged the very role divisions that characterized the conventional American family. By virtue of its consistency with the fundamental principle of democracy, the amendment cracked the cornerstone of American society, the family, which was heavily weighted in favor of men.

Housewife and writer Phyllis Schlafly emerged to lead the attack on ex-housewife Betty Friedan and the ERA supporters. If America's 40 million homemakers glutted the labor market, wrote Schlafly, massive unemployment among men would destroy the economy and the moral fiber of the nation. In her countermanifesto, *The Power of the Positive Woman* (1977), she insisted "that man's role as a family provider gives him the incentive to curb his primitive nature . . . deprived of this role, he tends to drop out of the family and revert to the primitive masculine role of hunter and fighter." With Victorian fervor, Schlafly implied that conventional family life was linked irrevocably with God and patriotism, and that the breakdown of traditional roles would lead straight to the collapse of the nation.

The basic arguments Schlafly cited against the ERA were seductively simple: a wife must be supported by her husband, not by the taxpayer; children must be brought up by their mothers, not by institutions; healthy families are able to prosper without government interference; it is up to family members to take care of each other in sickness and old age. Her American dream evoked the founding fathers' wholesome version of the patriarchy, with women performing services at home that kept colonial society functioning. Schlafly seemed to believe that we could all be John and Abigail Adamses, all of us acting on pre-industrial values, blissfully innocent of twentieth-century complexities.

Rather like Abigail Adams herself, Schlafly impressively reflected the features of both a self-made and a man-made woman. She worked her way through college in an ammunitions factory, graduated Phi Beta Kappa, and received a master's degree from Harvard. She worked in a bank until she married Fred Schlafly and assumed the role of the proverbial helpmate for the conservative congressman. She also wrote nine books and raised six children. Beginning in 1974, with her *Phyllis Schlafly Reports*, she emerged as the most outspoken opponent of the women's movement. In October, 1979, *Cosmopolitan*'s editor, Helen Gurley Brown, told *Time* magazine that all the women's magazines together in their joint effort to support the ERA might not be as effective "as Phyllis Schlafly with her rabble-rousing TV appearances."[13] The strength of her campaign rests on a combination of nostalgia for the American dream, warnings designed to frighten her readers, and ridicule meant to discredit supporters and leaders of the movement. The warnings are directed at women who might otherwise turn a sympathetic ear to feminist arguments: a woman who tries to succeed in a male world will fail and will end up alone and abandoned. The ridicule is directed at those who try, charging them with behaving in an unfeminine manner that stamps them as women libbers, malcontents, and misfits out to destroy what they cannot have—a happy family. Giving in to the misdirected women who persist in their demands, Schlafly warns, would mean "sexual suicide" for America.

Schlafly's reference to sexual suicide brings to mind the "racial suicide" that the elite Victorians began to fear as they watched immigrants of all colors and nationalities flood into the nation in the late 1800s. Both concepts are based on the same models of success: the "fittest," who survive natural selection, are those with wealth, property, and family stability. Not surprisingly, the defenders of "total," or "positive," womanhood, the style of living endorsed by Schlafly, invariably belong to the conservative elements of society.

Marabel Morgan's bestseller *The Total Woman* (1973), which created its own national movement, was dedicated to anti-gay activist Anita Bryant. The chapters, widely used for Morgan's "total woman classes," were devoted to winning through sexual manipulation. The book and the movement repeated the Victorian advice that "woman surrenders her life to her husband, reveres and worships him, and is willing to serve him." By doing so "she becomes a priceless jewel, the glory of femininity, his queen."[14]

If Schlafly and Morgan spoke for the most fervent opponents of the women's movement in the seventies, radical feminists such as Susan Brownmiller, who viewed American womanhood from a Marxist perspective, took the most extreme view within the movement itself. As early as 1970, they proclaimed in a "Redstockings Manifesto," "women are an oppressed class. Our oppression is total, affecting every facet of our lives. We are exploited as sex objects, breeders, domestic servants, and cheap labor. We are considered inferior human beings whose only purpose is to enhance men's lives."[15] This view rested on the thinking of Karl Marx and Friedrich Engels, who, although well cared-for married men themselves, identified women as victims of the oppressed class.

The feminist radicals restated Charlotte Gilman's criticism that the family's appetite for consumption sacntioned the exploitation of workers and of women. Since white housewives could belong to both the exploited and the exploiting class, their position in the women's movement was a bone of contention from the start. But increasingly the radicals saw the middle-class housewife as a member of the latter, unless she belonged to the labor force or had racial minority status.

After an initial period of solidarity, each group in the movement began to focus on its own particular concerns, its own loyalties. Lesbians emerged as a separate group, and lesbian separatists as a strong faction within it. Also, the conflict between middle-class professionals and workers and Third World women seemed to preclude the possibility of a solidly unified movement. For example, the political allegiance of most Black women at this time belonged to the Black man's cause. Working women sided with working men, while middle-class women struggled to catch up with the upwardly mobile man's ascent. The World Conference on Women, held in Mexico City in the summer of 1972, seemed to bear out the prediction that in political warfare women would prove more loyal to partisan causes than to sisterhood. At this conference, Cuban women spoke against capitalism, Black women against racism, and Latin and Arab women proudly smiled that they had no childcare problems at all.

The basic principle of new feminism had been Friedan's conviction that all women shared the same problems. In the wake of the 1975 World Conference on Women, this contention appeared to be politically naive. NOW came under increasing attack from the far left as being biased toward white middle-class concerns and couched in white middle-class values. Soon a serious rift became apparent between the poor and Third World women and the spokespeople for the women's movement as a whole. From the perspective of the most exploited woman worker, the Black housekeeper, her "sister"-employer still looked like the same white lady: "She has an office in Boston. She used to do volunteer work, a lot of it; but she said she would work, like men do. My husband thinks she's crazy, and so do I. If I had money, I'd quit this job, and go home and stay home for a thousand years. I'd be with my own kids and not someone else's."[16] How feminist women could stop using other women to do their "dirty" work remained an unanswered question. As more housewives left kitchen and nursery to join the labor force, the more problems they had in finding somebody to do their work at home. In 1950, 8.4 percent of all the employed women had been private household workers. By 1979, the number had dwindled to less than 3 percent. Black domestics by then were older, part-time workers, because younger Blacks with better education found better jobs elsewhere.[17] In contrast to white working-class women, they supported the women's rights movement but they did not find much common cause with white women's needs.

DIVORCE: THE ECONOMIC REALITY

Though the mid-seventies did see a great deal of factioning within the women's movement as specific groups defined themselves, it is also true that by the late 1970s the middle-class divorcee began for the first time to inspire public action on her behalf. After a decade and a half of transition, those women who had been through it were able to begin defining divorce and its repercussions in social and economic, rather than in purely personal terms.

Without her husband, the "missus" found that she had a bit more in common with the maid than before. Upon leaving their husbands, lawyers' wives became legal secretaries, doctors' wives became receptionists, and managers' wives became typists. Divorce served to turn the upward mobility of middle-class marriage into a downward trend for many women. Contrary to the fairy tales invented by Hollywood, the transformation from ordinary wife to ex-wife involved a sudden drop in status and an automatic reduction in living standards.

When the broken home was considered to be primarily a phenomenon related to poverty, it fell into the domain of social workers and welfare agencies. Single mothers were invisible in good families. Today, however, single mothers belong to every PTA, and women without husbands are taken for granted. If the current divorce trend continues, solidly married wives will constitute a minority and girls will no longer expect to be supported solely by husbands. Nevertheless, in 1974, more than 38 million adult women still depended entirely on their husbands' income. When those who did file for divorce learned about the precarious economic situation they faced in doing so, they came in for a rude shock.[18]

Modern marriage may no longer look like a business arrangement, but divorce strips marriage down to its foundation and reveals that even when all is bliss, the power structure of the home is based on money. The partner with the greatest autonomy in the world at large has the greatest authority inside the marriage. If the marriage fails, the dependent partner stands to lose more than the individual with personal resources. Since men are the traditional wage earners, women, at the dissolution of marriage, are the traditional losers.

A wife in a destructive marriage is often more concerned about her emotional than her financial condition. However, in contemplating divorce, she might benefit more from talking to her banker than to her analyst. Just as war brings out the real value of peace, divorce reveals the economic significance of marriage. When the lawyer draws up the separation papers, a wife suddenly finds herself cut off from an income. No outside agency cares how much time and energy she invested in creating and maintaining the household for her family until she demands her share of it. Most husbands fully anticipate sharing their financial resources when they marry, but they, and the law in many states, take it for granted that, in the event of a divorce, what used to be "ours" suddenly becomes his.

The law favors the husband in the division of property even when the wife brought property to the marriage, since he is assumed to have improved on it during the marriage. In some states, the wife loses all but what she has legally kept in her name, even the furniture and the kitchen stove; she is allowed to keep only that property bought in her name exclusively or proven to have been purchased by her money alone. In other states, the property is split in half—often easier said than done when, for example, a couple has been living largely on credit.

Still, existing property is easier to assess than services rendered in the past, especially when those services have never been assessed monetarily. Mary Rogers, in *Women and Money* (1978), warns, "All of a sudden, he will start reminding you that he earned all the money,[19] and that he doesn't have to share any of it with you." Rogers reports that in her professional practice as a financial counselor, she sees far too many women who accept that argument and who do not view themselves as equal partners in the marriage simply because they do not bring home a paycheck.

In 1977, judges finally started to consider a homemaker's services to the household in settling financial disputes accompanying divorces. However, even under this new precedent, the burden falls to the woman to prove her value in economic terms. But, though wage ranges can be determined for almost every other profession one might name, no consensus exists on the monetary value of housework, since it has never been compensated financially. Economists have outguessed each other on the matter, but the basic rate of pay used to compute the value of a homemaker's labor is still largely subjective. According to one study, the average husband aged 35 to 54 spent $7,238 to support his family in 1970, an amount that matched approximately the average annual income at the time. This average worker's wife, on the other hand, could claim that she had contributed at least $4,705 in services, even if she had only been paid the low hourly rates of a dishwasher, cook, or charwoman. If she included her work as interior decorator, nursery school teacher, and caterer, and figured the worth of her work as the standard rates of such professionals, she could claim by the authority of Kenneth Galbraith that her services were worth $13,364 a year. By 1976, Sylvia Porter had raised the homemaker's service fee to $300 a week or $15,600 a year in using the wage rates for 12 different skills including nursing and counseling; and economist Dr. Peter Senn topped this figure on the *Today* show in 1977 with a $21,841 yearly price tag which included $6,000 alone for waitressing.[20]

However, since any husband can present claim that he cannot afford to pay his wife for her services, or that he could hire a private household worker at the minimum wage rate, such cost studies hardly add anything to the market value of the homemaker. Moreover, even the most scrupulous marriage contract will not specify the exact number of hours and the exact type of services which go into the care of an individual home and family.

Other factors contribute as well to the difficulty of standardizing the monetary value of a housewife's contribution. For instance, in terms of hours of labor spent, the husband benefits most from his wife during their early years of parenthood. Older wives consume more than they visibly produce, particularly when health care is added to the cost. However, past contributions and the value of her companionship diminish, of course, in the light of a divorce.

In the early days, when suburbia still looked like paradise and divorce seemed an unlikely catastrophe, a naive housewife considering divorce as an option might have envisioned having an easier time of it. One middle-aged divorcee describes the unrealistic expectations common to middle-class women in those days. She had lived through 25 years of a Victorian marriage in which role division was strictly observed to the extent that the husband "invested" her inheritance in his own business. Only at her divorce proceedings did she discover that her future was no longer financially secure, that she would now have to earn her own keep:

> It was assumed that if a divorce was to occur, the courts and public opinion would see that the woman was financially protected, because part of this unspoken social contract was that in exchange for concentrating her youth and middle years on wifing and mothering, the wife would give up the option to have a career and to learn how to successfully earn money. Gentleness,

kindliness, warmth, and the passive absorption of hostilities and flak that high-pressure jobs produced in husbands are traits that were drummed into us, and were abysmal training for the job market.[21]

In the ideal world, both parents might be expected to contribute half of the expenses and effort necessary for supporting the children and providing them with a home. In reality, however, the court may order the husband to pay anywhere from 10 to 25 percent of his income for child support. The amount decreases for higher incomes, because large allowances are considered unnecessary by hostile fathers who feel that the excess above the required minimum would go to the wife. Recent data have shown that less than half of all the divorced mothers who were entitled to child support collected any money at all after two years, that only 20 percent receive regular support, and that only 8 percent receive alimony.[22]

Alimony was never intended as a pension to reward a wife for her past contributions. Nor, obviously, was it designed as a means of enabling a woman to gain independence. Originally, alimony merely offered a well-to-do husband the freedom to live apart from his wife without losing control over her property and her behavior. Today alimony is rather uncommon. Many wives accept cash or real property settlements in the amount that a lawyer can obtain. The objective of alimony is merely to tide the ex-wife over the period in which she must train or search for a job. Two years is considered generous.

At the turn of the decade 79 percent of all divorced fathers were totally uninvolved in the support of their children. Geographical distance, increasing estrangement, and new commitments to a second family diminish a father's interest in sharing the financial burdens with the mother. Further, as Mary Rogers points out, husbands who wish to evade their court-assessed obligations usually get away with it. Few women are prepared to fight a lengthy and expensive court battle, and few lawyers will assist a woman in such a dispute unless the outcome promises to be very lucrative. Rogers suggests that some women simply cannot afford a separation, and that they should make the transition from dependent homemaker to independent wage earner *before* rather than after initiating a divorce.

The gist of Roger's message is that divorce is an assertive action requiring foresight and planning rather than a passive gesture of defeat. And the purpose of shoring up one's positive energies is not merely to boost the morale: unless the divorcing wife reminds herself constantly that she was an equal partner in the marriage, she will be treated as a parasite or a charity case. Computing what her own and her children's expenses will be is a crucial first step in initiating a divorce, not only to enable her to plan her future, but also for making her financial needs clear to the court. Child care, tuition, mortgage, taxes, and insurance payments all become new quantities to consider after divorce.

Projecting costs is one thing, but meeting them after the divorce is quite another. A wife's share in her husband's social security benefits is at stake if she has been married for less than ten years, and at present the divorced wife can expect only minimal public support. With Aid to Families with Dependent Children (AFDC), the government reluctanly takes over the role of the father-provider for the certified poor. This welfare allowance does not permit the single mother to budget for long-term educational or career goals, but forces her to juggle child care, work, and training opportunities in terms of immediate survival. In its treatment of the poor, the government still punishes those who deviate from the traditional pattern, in which the male is the provider. It is still a long step away from making resources available for the creating of more egalitarian roles within the family.

The cost of raising a child has nearly doubled in the past decade, according to an analysis of data from the U.S. Department of Agriculture made by the Health Insurance Institute. In 1970, it took $1,800 to $2,000 a year to raise a child from birth to the age of 18 (college is therefore not included). Ten years later the cost had risen to a range between $3,400 and $3,800 due to inflation.[23]

The single mother of young children with no or little support from the father inevitably winds up scheduling and budgeting to get through each month. Her mental and physical resources are consumed by the daily challenge of coordinating her triple role as mother, breadwinner, and single adult. A tight budget prevents her from hunting for a good job, her children compete with her work, and her personal needs for growth and companionship interfere with both. Like the immigrant pioneers of a century ago, many single mothers thrive on adversity and grow strong and independent from their struggle. Often, however, such women succumb to a permanent state of apathy. In 1972, 65 percent of the divorced women married again within five years; by 1977, only 25 percent chose that route.[24] Perhaps this is an indication that women are indeed becoming more independent and that the trend to marry for security is less strong nowadays.

Older women who had functioned all their adult lives in a protected place within the center of a family are as vulnerable to poverty as younger mothers. Although childcare is no longer a concern for them, their chances in the job and marriage market are slimmer. Even their eligibility for public assistance diminishes as the children leave the house. Until recently, older divorced women suffered under even more difficult conditions than others in our society who have trouble obtaining employment. Often they were not poor enough to receive welfare, and not old enough to receive old-age benefits, thus essentially falling between the cracks in the system. But in 1977, Senator Birch Bayh from Indiana introduced a displaced homemaker's bill, and the single mother who had already raised her family gained public attention. In the words of the senator:

Women who have been homemakers for a majority of their lives face a myriad of problems when death, divorce or loss of family income forces them back to the labor market. . . . Without marketable skills or training too often these women fall between the cracks of federal programs. She may be ineligible for Social Security benefits because she is too young, or because she is divorced from the wage earner. She is ineligible for federal welfare assistance if she is not physically disabled and her children are past a certain age. And she is unable to apply for unemployment insurance because she has engaged in unpaid labor in the home.[25]

Bayh's bill resulted in funding for 50 displaced-homemaker centers. Later, the bill was incorporated into the Comprehensive Employment and Training Act (CETA) to provide counseling, training, and jobs. Significantly, the public-assistance program for displaced homemakers differed from AFDC in that it focused on women directly instead of on the needs of their children or the deficiencies of their husbands. It also erased the time-honored distinction between divorced and widowed wives, and acknowledged that displaced homemakers, like displaced persons in times of war, are victims of circumstances caused not by themselves, but by social forces beyond their control.

Most significantly, the centers set out to boost the self-confidence of women who call themselves "just housewives." "They don't realize they have strengths," explains Milo Smith, a former displaced homemaker who founded and directed the Oakland (Calif.) Center with Tish Somers.

Many of these women have run volunteer programs, have put in the whole structure of PTA, Girl Scouts, any of the women's types of things, [but] they never related it to the fact that they were good money managers, that they were good administrators, that they were good supervisors, that they were good planners.

Our previous office manager sat here when I was interviewing her to come to work . . . she didn't know how to do anything. She bought old houses, she did the repair work, and did them over herself. She learned how to sell them and make profits on them. She raised four children. She legged her husband's research. She typed his papers till after 35 years she was dumped for the younger woman and came in here, referred by her psychiatrist . . . attempted suicide, she absolutely felt that she could do nothing. Now, that woman was an assertive woman in many ways in that she had gone out and tried to find jobs although she had not worked, [not] actually worked at a paying job, since the war years.[26]

Employers discriminated against both the older person and the ex-house-wife. A homemaker still rates high in public esteem as long as she plays her wife-and-mother act, but as soon as she offers her skills on the labor market, her value plunges, and she has to prove herself doubly worthy of a paycheck. Milo Smith, co-founder of the Oakland Center, was refused the chance to prove herself when she set out to find a job. A brand new degree in social work did nothing for a 50–year-old applicant. That bitter experience made her a political activist who learned to demand her rights from a society that claimed that it owed her nothing, except perhaps a welfare check. Like many an activist before her, she realized that her difficulties were not due to her own "unique failure," but to the economic situation of all women. She perceived that one woman alone can do very little on her own, no matter how hard she works to change herself, unless society changes with her.

The Hope of the Eighties

The housewife seemed to have come of age as a social entity worthy of public concern in the late 1970s. With the continued increase in divorce, the society appeared to have grown uncomfortable with its old habits of devaluing the work of housewives and ignoring the problems of divorced women and single mothers. *The Women's Room* was published in 1977 and Bayh's bill for displaced homemakers was introduced into Congress in that year. Further, a number of significant steps were taken at the National Women's Conference in Houston, in November 1977. First, a homemaker's bill of rights was proposed, which was intended to validate and protect the housewife as a bona fide worker performing services that could be valued monetarily. Also, the conference endorsed legislation that would allow a homemaker to collect social security and disability benefits in her own right and that would enable each spouse to accrue credit based on the family income, regardless of divorce, widowhood, or remarriage.

Eleanor Cutri Smeal, the first NOW president to describe herself as a housewife and the first to receive a salary in that office, announced at the conference that achieving financial recognition for homemaking was a part of a larger program for improving American women's economic condition generally.[27] In 1977, the average annual income of American women—from employment, investment, alimony, and child support—was less than $6,000. For those who worked full-time, year round, the annual income rose to $8,620, compared with the men in that category who earned $14,630. There were 49 percent women versus 73 percent men with full-time jobs in the labor force, and more than a third of the nation's women still had no personal income at all.

With that many women still depending on a breadwinner, a lot would be riding on the strength of the resolve expressed by Smeal. Black women resented the all-white slate of middle-class officers elected by NOW. They belonged to the steadily rising number of women between the ages of 25 and 34 who had not married and among the even stronger contingent of those who were divorced. These wage earners and the fast-growing ranks of married women in the labor force put the traditional values of full-time homemaking (as well as NOW's position) under strain. Those women caught in the transition from one value system to another stood to lose one way or another, since the financial rewards in the labor force still lagged far behind those offered in a marriage to a prosperous man. Whichever road she chose, her future security was not guaranteed. Still, though painful and frequently discouraging, the transformation that many women underwent in the 1970s from dependent housewife to wage earner had been an educational one, and the force of the new feminism as it matured over the seventies resulted in the new confidence and new options for many American women. By the end of the decade—now called the decade of single women—the mainstream culture was reflecting an acknowledgment of women's strength as individuals that would have been unthinkable at the beginning of the 1960s.[28] Whether this acknowledgment was an empty gesture or a sign of permanent social change remained a question to be answered in the eighties. Clearly, however, since the American housewife wanted more power over her own destiny, she would have to make sure that the paycheck in her pocket was her own, and that her credit rating as a worker would not dissolve with her marriage.[29]

NOTES

1. Loud and Johnson, *Pat Loud: A Woman's Story*, pp. 74, 168.

2. Jane De Hart Mathews, "The New Feminism and the Dynamics of Social Change," in Kerber et al., *Women's America*, pp. 397–425, for a survey of the movement.

3. John Kenneth Galbraith, *Economics and the Public Purpose* (Boston: Houghton Mifflin, 1973), pp. 32–33.

4. According to Lopata's profile of the American housewife, the major sources of satisfaction for all housewives was watching the children grow, a happy marriage, ownership of a well-kept home, and enjoying the fruits of their labors with their husbands when the children left home. Loud and Johnson, *Pat Loud: A Woman's Story*, p. 27.

5. Ibid., pp. 189–190.

6. Sue Kaufman, *Diary of a Mad Housewife* (New York: Random House, 1967), p. 117.

7. Sheila Ballantyne, "They Call Me Mummy" (1972), in *Women Working* (New York: Feminist Press, 1979), pp. 176, 183.

8. Madonna Kolbenschlag, *Kiss Sleeping Beauty Good-Bye: Breaking the Spell of Feminine Myths and Models* (New York: Bantam, 1981).

9. Marilyn French, *The Women's Room* (New York: Harcourt/Jove, 1978), p. 290; reprint of Summit Books, 1977; for comparison see Elshtain, *Public Man, Private Woman*, pp. 217–219, where she describes Susan Brownmiller's and Ti-Grace Atkinson's theories of militant feminist separatism.

10. Katherine M. Rogers, *The Troublesome Helpmate* (Seattle: University of Washington Press, 1966), p. 270; Kelley, *Private Woman Public Stage*, chapter 9,

pp. 217–249, "The Crisis of Domesticity: A Crisis of Being," which refers mainly to Catharine Maria Sedgwick.

11. Marge Pierce, "To Be of Use," in *Women Working*, p. 263.

12. Natalie Gittelson, *The Erotic Life of the American Wife* (New York: Delacorte Press, 1972), pp. xi, 236. In addition, Ellen Ross's " 'The Love Crisis': Couples Advice Books of the Late 1970s," in *Women, Sex and Sexuality* (Chicago: University of Chicago Press, 1980), pp. 274–307, offers a good review and bibliography on changing patterns.

13. Phyllis Schlafly, *The Power of the Positive Woman* (New Rochelle: Arlington House, 1977), pp. 95–96.

14. Marabel Morgan, *The Total Woman* (New York: Pocket Books, 1975), pp. 96–97.

15. "Redstockings Manifesto," *New York Times* (March 19, 1970).

16. Robert Coles, *Women of Crisis* (New York: Delacorte, 1978), p. 237.

17. Allyson Sherman Grossman, "Women in Domestic Work: Yesterday and Today," *Monthly Labor Review* (Aug., 1980), pp. 17–21.

18. Of the 30 million who were employed, their median earnings were $6,335 compared with $11,186 for men (Jane R. Chapman, *Economic Independence for Women* [Beverly Hills, Calif.: Sage Publications, 1976], *Sage Yearbooks in Women's Policy Studies* vol. 1, p. 12).

19. Mary Rogers and Nancy Joyce, *Women and Money* (New York: Avon Books, 1979), p. 126.

20. Ann G. Scott, "The Value of Housework: For Love or Money," *Ms.* (July, 1972), pp. 56–59; John Kenneth Galbraith, *Economics and the Public Purpose*, pp. 56–59. Galbraith called the housewife a cryptoservant "available, democratically, to almost the entire male population." If it were not for this service, all forms of household consumption would be limited by the time required to manage such consumption—to select, transport, prepare, maintain, clean, service, store, protect, and otherwise perform the tasks that are associated with the consumption of goods. Galbraith readily attached a $13,364 price tag to these services and, echoing Charlotte Gilman, he claimed that the family was no longer a facilitating instrument for increased consumption, that women were therefore entitled to professional child care, flexible working patterns, better jobs and better education. See also Janet Zollinger Giele, *Women and the Future: Changing Sex Roles in Modern America* (New York: The Free Press, 1979), pp. 11–12. According to economist Carol Fethke and lawyer Nancy Hauserman, the work of homemakers is devalued because it generates no income: "Society tends to assume that the lack of information on the value of homemakers' work indicates a lack of any economic value at all. For this reason, homemaking has been called the 'invisible occupation,' " "Homemaking: The Invisible Occupation" (*Journal of Home Economics* [Summer, 1979], pp. 20–23); and Caroline Bird, *The Two-Paycheck Family*, p. 96.

21. Interview with author, March, 1980.

22. Giele, *Women and the Future*, p. 225; Glazer, *Woman in a Man-Made World*, p. 294.

23. "Child-Rearing Costs Double," *Berkeley Gazette*, April 12, 1980.

24. Giele, *Women and the Future*, p. 151.

25. Birch Bay, "The Displaced Homemaker"and following articles by different authors "Occupation: Homemaker," *Journal of Home Economics* (November,

1977), pp. 8–25. See also *Journal of Home Economics* (Summer, 1979); entire issue devoted to Displaced Homemakers.

26. Interview with Milo Smith, Displaced Homemakers' Center, Mills College, Oakland, conducted by Laurel Cook, 1980.

27. "And NOW, the President," profile of Eleanor Cutri Smeal, *Redbook Magazine* (August, 1977), pp. 83–84.

> It makes me angry that some people have blamed housewives for voting against ERA.
> In the seven years I've been a member of NOW I've seen that very often it is the
> housewives who are most active, who do the day-in, day-out work of the movement.
> They want to have better opportunities for themselves and for their daughters.

For Black reaction, see Giddings, *When and Where I Enter*, pp. 340–348.

28. "1970s—a Decade of Single Women," *San Francisco Chronicle* (March 20, 1980), p. 5.

29. For a more detailed survey of the economic and political situation of the homemaker see Rae Andre, *Homemakers: The Forgotten Workers* (Chicago: Univ. of Chicago Press, 1981), chapter 9, "The Displaced Homemaker," appendix 1, "National Platforms for Homemakers' Rights."

8

The New Pioneers: Family Life in the 1980s

We must now move toward the creation of open systems.
— Margaret Mead, *Culture and Commitment*, 1978

Contrary to predictions, housewives did not become extinct in the late 1970s, nor did the nuclear family turn to dust and blow away. The true hallmark of the period, as it has been and will be for all of history, was change, and the changes that began surfacing then are being felt even more strongly at this writing, in the first decade of the 1980s. But which of these changes have true significance for the way we will live at home from now on?

Nationwide, the crucial factor that changed the fabric of American family life was work. Since 1950, the number of married women in the labor force more than doubled; the number of families maintained by women, however, nearly tripled. On the one hand, these labor statistics of the 1980s reflected a new reality where the American dream was no longer supported by a male breadwinner and a female homemaker, both on a full-time schedule within their separate domains.[1] On the other hand, they did not really soften the sharp contrast between economically advantaged and disadvantaged families. Yet although an employed mother managed to increase her family's buying power, she decreased her involvement in the kind of activities that had traditionally set the homemaker apart from the working woman. The great question of the 1980s still begs for an answer: Who is responsible for home care and for family care besides the housewife? The sexual revolution of the 1970s opened the way for exploring alternative solutions to traditional household problems, but as long as the nation's major institutions refused to recognize the need for accommodating a diverse population, the adjustments to each new wave of change had to be made by each individual homemaker and her family. Thus, while the traditional image of the white, middle-class nuclear family was projected around the country as the emblem of the United States, only 15 percent of all American families matched the conventional model, in which the father earned the wages and the mother, dependent on her husband for support, remained at home to care for her children and husband.[2] Meanwhile a whole spectrum of wage-earning housewives and working mothers was to be found in American households across the nation, ranging from supplementary pin-money earners to primary breadwinners supporting entire families. Further, the American consciousness was gradually, if grudgingly, admitting that families might reflect any number of variations on the old two-parent, two-child theme. Working mothers, nonworking fathers, absent mothers, absent fathers, widows, widowers, remarried parents, unmarried parents, childless couples, step-parents, foster parents, stepchildren, foster children, immigrant families, cross-cultural families, communal families, collective communities—all these elements, though none were new, were now acknowledged to be components of real families, if only because sheer strength of numbers forced them into the public eye.

It is among these millions who do not fit the old mold that we find the new pioneers of the 1980s. Instead of fixing our eyes on role models that worked under conditions in the past bearing little resemblance to our modern change-oriented lives, we must observe with respect every attempt at adaptation arising from every corner of society, no matter how unnoticed or unheeded that corner has been up to now. It is from the very pockets of society that have been ignored that the new pioneers are emerging.

To understand the directions in which the new pioneers will take us we must admit that the greatest strength of a society lies in diversity, not conformity. In the fifties, once the mass media, and particularly television, had seized the public imagination, the society seemed bent on denying the multiplicity that had always characterized American culture. Instead, we chose the blandest possible minority—the white, unbroken, affluent, middle-class family—to represent the whole population. We dressed everyone in their Sunday best, scrubbed and brushed them until every hair was in place, and, with a heavy-handedness typical of our style of developing myths, ignored the hidden expectations, secret resentments, and impossible demands that abounded within the typical nuclear family. How much personal unhappiness has resulted from our refusal to value qualities that do not conform to the norm? How many of us who were raised on the "rightness" of this image yearn for something in our own lives that never existed in reality?

Margaret Mead, the pathbreaking anthropologist, flatly rejected the tendency to yearn for the return of a mythical past. In evaluating the American family in *Culture and Commitment* (1978) she wrote, "It is the adults who still believe that there is a safe and socially approved road to a kind of life they themselves have not experienced who react with the greatest anger and bitterness to discover that what they had hoped for no longer exists for their children." According to Mead, truly successful pioneers rely on their earlier learning, but manage at the same time to transform their behavior to meet the needs of a new environment. She concluded that "we must now move toward the creation of open systems that focus on the future—and so on the children, those whose capacities are least known and whose choices must be left open."[3]

By now, scholars from all disciplines have reevaluated the past in light of our ethnic diversity and found that Americans share a rich heritage of survival skills which have helped them to cope with economic uncertainty, discrimination, and disruption. Therefore the most qualified guides into an uncertain future are those pioneers who not only survived when the support system they had counted on collapsed, but managed to create a new structure that served them better. A typical homemaker for most of her life, Milo Smith faced the traditional fate of the widow whose husband's death left her without a provider—old age in poverty. But she refused to accept that destiny without exploring other alternatives.

Portrait of a New Pioneer

"I did it from the seat of my pants," says Milo Smith about her transformation from displaced homemaker to pioneer activist in the Jobs for Older Women movement:

Everything was so new to me about being a public figure. I had been a quiet person, a quiet person behind my husband. Because you see I deferred to all of his quiet way of life, so that I never really thought that I would ever come out and be the big mouth that I have become. That poor man is like the whirling dervish in his grave, I'm sure.

My husband was the autocrat of the breakfast table. He made all of the major decisions. He handled all of the money. I did not. Even when I worked, I handed him my pay. I felt it was my role.

My husband died at 51. I didn't think I was the biggest dummy in the world, but I had no idea that all widows didn't get Social Security. I found out that the earliest I could get any kind of Social Security would be at age 60. I was only 47. And, then, taking minimal Social Security, you're stuck with that the rest of your life. You are locked into the downward spiral to poverty. Then, the inequities in the pension system, my husband had paid into a pension system for almost 30 years. I assumed that I would get that income. But, the fine print said that he had to have been old enough to be retired and collecting the pension before there was [sic] any survivors' benefits. I got nothing from the pension. Not one dime. And, I will never get one dime. That was our money paid in and, yet, the system at that time allowed that kind of thing to happen. Since I had to work I wanted to go into something where I really would feel useful and where I could earn a decent living and totally support myself. I decided to go back to school. I graduated from Berkeley in Social Work and I figured I was on my way. I wasn't that gung ho about doing it and I was bored lots of the time, because I had lived through half of what I had to take at school. I grew up in New York with all the minority groups, all the ethnic organizations, and all that. Anyway, I figured, where do you go now to get the job since you have this new piece of paper and everybody is going to want this wonderfully experienced woman who has come out with a new piece of paper? I went to the employment development department and they told me plain that at 50 I was unemployable . . . a woman of 50. That, that new piece of paper meant nothing because I had no recent work experience.

That's when the anger began. I began to feel all the inequities in the system. I began to feel a victim of the system. That man in that employment development department office made me so angry. He just absolutely told me I was unemployable and to go to the welfare office, and I wasn't eligible for welfare. I felt—how dare this man tell me that my life was wiped out? I went out the very next day and got a job. That was my interesting job in the mortuary. The thing is I could have gotten that job without ever having gone through school. I moved into the mortuary and I did evertything. Everything I had ever done before fit into that job. I did their bookkeeping and billing. I had a beauty shop at one time, so I could do any kind of cosmetic stuff that was necessary. I counseled the bereaved with my new social work degree. I had been an autopsy assistant in the Army during WWII, so I was used to being around dead bodies, so it was not this terrifying thing. My actual work hours did not start until 4:00 in the afternoon, so I volunteered every day in aging programs until I got the credibility for working in my field. That took two and one-half years of volunteer work. . . . So you see, I've used every approach—schooling, volunteerism, background, "packaging," pulling together everything, but I didn't know what I was doing. But I did it.

From all that stuff with Jobs for Older Women we finally brought a class action suit against the Union. That was based on my Rosie the Riveter days, before I was married. In talking to the woman who was running the younger women's program, I said to her, "Well, we're the old Rosie the Riveters and Winnie the Welders." She was so young she didn't even know we had done that.[4]

Pioneers of Poverty

Nancy Lee Hall dedicated her book *A True Story of a Single Mother* (1984) "to all the brave single mothers of the world. Their courage is great, for they are scorned by established society, underpaid, overworked, victimized by bureaucratic institutions, and left with few alternatives. They receive no medals. They just keep struggling." Her autobiographical account tells of her painful transformation from abandoned homemaker with six children, three of whom still needed financial support, to working woman and author. Her drive for dignity eventually wins out over her demanding fight for child support from her husband and for financial aid from welfare. Her last telephone call to the social worker resulted from the edict that she do away with the family dog. She informs him that she wants to be taken off welfare immediately. He explains to her that she cannot afford to let her children go hungry, whereupon she replies:

> "Look, you. I have exactly five cents in my purse, and I still want you to drop me. Drop me and forget I exist! Your stupid welfare is killing me! Your money isn't enough to live on and yet you call it fraud if I turn someplace else for help. What about the children's father? He's the fraud! You're so afraid I'm going to cheat you, you want me to move my family to the slums and give up everything we've got—including our pet dog. Save your money! And don't call me again! I'd rather starve!"
>
> "I hope you won't regret this, Nancy. We're just trying to help you."
>
> "I'll keep my dignity, thanks, Goodbye!"
>
> Don't tell me about welfare mothers, I thought. Society saw me and the children as losers, not Karl, who had abandoned us. For every dollar they gave us, they took away our independence and pride. If the social worker had known I was taking money from Tim, [her son] I would have gone to jail. Yet I never would have survived on welfare without Tim's help.
>
> A day later, I found a job drafting.. Maybe because I was angry and aggressive, I had to borrow money from friends because I wouldn't be paid for two weeks, but I was on my way again.[5]

Essentially the displaced homemaker is a product of the male-provider system: fathers would take care of their children; husbands would take care of their wives. This system did not work for all people. In 1983, 6.8 million white and 2.8 million black women maintained families, largely because one out of every two marriages ended in divorce or because the single mother had never been married. The latter seems to have become an increasing option among those couples where the man is not expected to play a significant role as provider. Underemployment and unemployment have had such pervasive effects on Black families that a whole alternative pattern of home and work, male and female, parent and child relationships has emerged from the need to survive social inequities. Nowadays, there are more Black teenage single mothers than white. Because they drop out of school, they have less education and their chances for well-paid employment remain considerably lower. The fact that this trend continues in spite of the efforts of Black educators and sociologists seems to indicate that young Black mothers rely on a different value system. Motherhood certainly has an important part in it.[6] But contrary to the mainstream cultural enforcement of female dependence on male support, Black women repeat the lesson they learned over the past two hundred years: the man you depend on today may not be yours tomorrow. And the children you bear will be yours to raise. Today more and more young white women are learning this set of facts for life in poverty, because they too may have no provider for their children other than the welfare worker.

As Carol Stack shows in her survey of Black family life in urban poverty, the women described in *All Our Kin* (1974) have had little reason to believe in mainstream values. Instead, the residents of The Flats relied on "strategies that the poor have evolved to cope with poverty," such as sharing their resources to benefit the members of the larger kinship network. Eventually they would have to depend on that network. For example, Carol Stack describes Julia Ambrose and Ruby Banks, who, trusting the outside system at first, married men they believed to be good providers and moved with them out of The Flats. After her husband was laid off his job, Julia was forced to apply for welfare benefits for her children. Ruby Banks returned to The Flats without her husband, wihin a year of her marriage, embarrassed, disappointed, and depressed. Her pride was injured. She acquired a bitter resentment toward men and toward the harsh conditions of poverty. After the separation, Ruby's husband moved into his older sister's home in a neighboring town. His spirit and optimism toward family life also had been severely weakened. It is therefore not surprising that most Black women who grow up in poverty form relationships with men, children, and friends that are very different from those formed by women seeking to maintain nuclear families. Claudia Williams offers one woman's acceptance of the possibility for friendship from the father of her children without expecting him to be a parent full-time:

> Some days he be coming over at night saying "I'll see to the babies and you can lay down and rest, honey," treating me real nice. Then maybe I won't even see him for two or three months. There's no sense nagging Raymond; I just treat him as some kind of friend even if he is the father of my babies.[7]

Claudia was making the best of a bad situation, but she also qualifies as a true pioneer of modern family life, because she is able to maintain a friendship with the father of her children even though he failed to live up to middle-class expectations of a father's responsibilities. The problem of overcoming rage and disappointment in order to salvage some kind of support, even if it is fragile and marginal, is one that has to be confronted by more and more middle-class women who share Claudia's dilemma, but not her self-reliance.

Are these the new role models for white single mothers who beside economic hardship must overcome the fear and loneliness? Unlike Claudia Williams, Jacqueline Marie, a white single mother, had no kin to take her in, but a newly founded single-parent housing project offered her a home. Here she describes her feelings in her journal:

> First night here—feel dejected, lonely, faced with making home in another old place—needs work, paint, cleaning, lights—have slight cramps, bleeding, fatigue, tension, stomach is upset—Caitlin crying—no friends here—she

doesn't like own room, didn't want to move—I understand—I hope we gain—
women here seem depressed—moving is hard for single parents—ultimately
we're all alone.

I am forced   once again
to make a home
for me   my child   my cat
Out of dingy cobwebbed corners
four-walled bareness
too little light   space   privacy
too much dirt   grayness
too many boxes
of treasures   packed away
to open
on a new day.

One week later, having done a great deal toward making a real home,
Jacquelyn Marie continues:

Feeling much better—apartment almost the way I want it—do something
with kitchen—paint? Painted Caitlin's room, furniture—clean, pleasant,
bright—have to still have lights—did some cleaning—hanging my pictures,
plants, dolls, new India print bedspread and curtain—more space.
    Women here into many things, interesting—we will work together, I hope.[8]

So far the rewards for women's pioneering efforts have mostly been
personal. Ridge Road House, the single-parent housing project that Jacquelyn Marie moved into, collapsed due to lack of funding and official
support. During its five years, the community developed innovative methods in sharing limited resources; parents exchanged childcare, household
labors, and repairs. They gardened and shopped cooperatively and met
regularly for mutual support in finding jobs, scholarships, and public assistance, but also in getting from one day to the next with dignity. For a
short period professional childcare was available to the 11 young families
at Ridge Road House. But when the monies from a church grant ran out,
the women and children who lived there could not pay the rent that single
individuals without children were able to pay in this university neighborhood.
    Pioneering ventures in low-income families are famous for failing for
economic reasons. In fact, most programs—involving childcare, housing,
job training, or flexible working hours—that might help working women
take care of themselves and their families are ignored or attacked by funding agencies. This financial neglect reflects a more general indifference in
the private and the public sectors, both of which profit from keeping wives
dependent on their husbands and husbands dependent on their employers.
    Childcare is the chief concern among most families in which the mother

works or in male single-parent families in which the father works. For the workers in such families, success on the job largely depends on the quality and affordability of the childcare available. Obviously, a worried parent concerned about a child's well-being during the day will not prove to be the most effective worker. And career women's promotions almost always slow down when they have children, as Fabe and Conan have pointed out in *Up against the Clock: Career Women Speak on the Choice to Have Children* (1979). In fact, the more lucrative and ego-building the career, the more stringently it requires that the family home run smoothly. According to tradition success on the job demands the *whole* man or woman. Part of that tradition is the correspondence of upper-management principles with upper-class family principles. This neat dovetailing in which the two sets of values reinforce each other punishes once more the victims— mother and child—for not conforming to the standard male-provider pattern.

As if to prove the point, statistics show that marriage stability seems to decrease with a woman's financial independence. Two possible explanations account for this finding. Either women earning a good living are apt to walk out of a marriage that no longer suits their needs, or their greater work commitment interferes with their marital relationship to the degree of making it impossible.[9] It comes as no surprise that Naomi Sims, author of *All About Success for the Black Woman* (1982), advises her readers to depend on their own rather than their husbands' careers, or if necessary to stay single. She says why:

> The more we strive for success, the more money we make, the more prestigious our jobs become, the less likely we are to find a suitable mate. Black women and Black men have been fighting with each other for generations, overtly and covertly, because so many Black women have had to be both breadwinners and double-duty parents. If it is not the fault of the Black man that he is "behind" in the struggle for success, it is certainly not our fault that we must continue that struggle. It is a question of economic survival: forty-one percent of all Black families in this country have only one head, a Black woman; and her income is $8,500—precisely half the average income for white families with only one head.[. . .]Black men demand us to make sacrifices in our careers that they would have no intention of making themselves.[10]

The Double-Life Wife

For achievement-oriented women everywhere today, conflicts between work and family are inevitable. But in white families who do not share the economic history of the Black family, the wife usually yields her career to the husband's in order to protect the children—and the marriage—from undue stress. Despite the drastic increase in those mothers of young children who are married and employed, husbands continue to be the primary breadwinners. And wives continue to place family responsibilities before job responsibilities—in all but Black families. An opinion poll conducted by the *Los Angeles Times* in August, 1984, revealed that half the respondents of both sexes still believed in separating job and family priorities by gender. Sixty percent of the women listed the family as the most important thing in their lives. Only 8 percent of the women called their jobs most important—even though 31 percent supported their families financially and 24 percent worked for extra income.[11] That same year the magazine *Ms.* (June, 1984) ran a feature on two-career couples who twisted their personal lifestyles around to meet pressing job demands. The author showed commuter couples who lived together only on a part-time basis, and maintained separate residences close to their jobs. She also described women who refused to follow their husbands to a new location unless they could find equal employment. This article, as well as the new series of advice books reviewed in it, came up with the same conclusion as the growing professional literature on the subject:[12] Even in these (one presumes) financially advantageous arrangements, the woman who makes the decisions and adjustments where new roles are being created still walks the high wire between job and household duties, and not always with the applause from her employer or her husband.

The resistance to change from within the family has been due partly to ignorance as to how roles and family responsibilities might be shared. Fathers lag far behind mothers in actively adapting when the woman alters the old family patterns by going to work. Recent studies on shared household responsibilities reveal that housework even for children is still divided along the old male-female lines. The husband repairs the roof while the wife cooks the food. He fixes the car while she cleans the house. He selects the insurance while she selects the groceries. She dresses the children; he takes them to the ballpark. The boys mow the lawn; the girls wash the dishes. Although most men feel that they should share in domestic responsibilities, few actually perform more than sporadic household chores, and many pay babysitters rather than perform childcare duties. They are reluctant to make the trade-off because they do not seem to get the same satisfaction from housekeeping and child rearing that both men and women derive from wage earning, and they still retain the privilege of choosing how and how much to participate on the home front.

This cultural imbalance is based on the historical distribution of power among those who have money and property. They have always had the right of choice. As feminist historians have clearly shown, wives gain prestige when they earn money, even if they make only half of what their male counterparts earn, but men stand to lose the respect of their peers if their income declines. For "normal" men, not working means being unemployed, and being unemployed implies that something is wrong. Further, when a wife brings home a larger paycheck than her husband, his self-esteem often declines seriously. While the working wife gains acceptance, the *husband* of a working wife often still judges himself—and is judged by his peers—according to the standards of a time when only the wives of incompetent or incapacitated men went to work.[13]

As noted earlier, unemployed immigrant men did not spend much time in the home. The same was and is still true for unemployed Black men. In the minds of those who are already vulnerable to negative reactions regarding their masculinity and social status, doing "women's work" only adds to the degradation of unemployment. As William R. Beer explains in *Househusbands: Men and Housework in American Families* (1983):

> A study of men who do housework, then, is not a study of men who do unpaid work around the house, because there are millions of men in America who do a very great deal of such work. It is a study of men who do what is conventionally defined as women's work. Men who do housework are crossing one of the deepest and longest standing barriers in human society.[14]

Philip Blumstein and Pepper Schwartz investigated the power of money, work, and sex in a book entitled *American Couples* (1983). They compared unmarried men and women living together, married men and women, and also lesbian couples and gay male couples in their same population. The authors came to the startling conclusion that in all but lesbian relationships, money determines the power structure which influences the decision-making processes from major acquisitions to minor household duties. The person with the largest income has also the greatest freedom of choice. For husbands or male partners in either homosexual or heterosexual relationships this means no housework if they are the primary breadwinners.[15] Lesbian couples, however, do not seem to care about money as much as about child rearing. Although sharing childcare was frequently an attractive reason for living together—lesbian communal households became very popular in the 1970s—issues of individual preferences for certain methods preferred by one mother over those practiced by another caused a large amount of friction and even breakups. It was also one of the most difficult aspects in cooperative childcare in Jacqueline Marie's single-parent community.

It appears that nothing so straightforward as fair division of labor can erode the longstanding patterns of work and power within the home. Where self-images are at stake, an exhausted, overstressed superwoman is apparently more tenable in most households than a male partner who feels threatened in his masculinity. The most courageous pioneers, therefore, are the househusbands—those men who reverse the old patriarchal power structure in order to accommodate the new mother providers.

The New Pioneer Father

There *are* fathers at the domestic frontier who are beginning to assume major domestic roles. What induces these men to overcome possible ridicule and scorn from their peers? What would it take for society as a whole to recognize them as pioneers, instead of lambasting them as misfits? Some househusbands already are at odds with social norms—homosexuals, for instance, who have been denied custody of their children. Men with disabilities are often viewed as falling outside the traditional masculine world. Quite often, though, where family roles do change, extreme financial pressure is the motivation. Necessity compelled women to seek outside employment long before it became acceptable, and necessity now ties men to their homes, because neither kin nor paid help are available to many young couples with low income.

My brother-in-law Jonathan is a good example of one whose special circumstances encouraged a total disregard of social norms. Jonathan was born deaf. He and his wife, Dorothy, who is also deaf, have three hearing children. The oldest child has a learning disability as well as a physical handicap. When he was employed, Jonathan worked as a linotype operator, but even then he worked mostly night shifts so he could do the shopping with his wife (she does not drive) and share in the childcare. When his newspaper laid off the linotype operators, he applied for other jobs, but had difficulty finding work—partly because of his deafness, partly because linotype operation is nearly obsolete. His wife was able to find a part-time job, and he received his unemployment compensation, so he took over most of the housekeeping and the "mothering." He is an excellent cook and bakery chef, a fast cleaner, an economical shopper, a constant family chauffeur, but most of all he is a patient father. His handicapped son needs special exercises and stimulation every day, and Jonathan works with him on a schedule. He also does volunteer work for the deaf in his church and deals with the children's teachers. His wife enjoys her job and takes care of financial aspects of household and family. Dorothy and Jonathan have had to reverse the traditional roles, but like true pioneers they have taken control of their lives creatively, innovatively.

Younger couples often bring a roommate-type attitude to their marriages. They do often start as roommates and set up housekeeping together before signing the marriage contract, dividing home care by mutual agreement. When the first baby arrives, however, even in non-traditional marriages, the women usually find themselves putting in considerably more than 50 percent of the hours.[16] It appears that we pattern our family behavior after our own childhood experiences, so that the slow evolution from traditional to non-traditional living is not surprising. Studies indicate that couples who come from two-income families or who grew up with single parents are more open to mixing male and female roles.

Though the labor is divided more fairly in these pioneering efforts, it is by no means diminished. Housework and child rearing still exact the enormous amount of energy they always did. One couple I know sent me a schedule for a typical weekday in their equal-time marriage. The woman is a free lance editor and writer, the man manages a print shop in a nine-to-five job and has a budding free-lance photography business. Their son, three years old, has been in some form of part-time child care since he was two months old:[17]

5:00 a.m.	Phil [husband] gets up; eats breakfast; makes Jackie's [son] lunch for school. Drives to work (where his darkroom is) to develop negatives and make prints until his workday in the print shop starts.
7:00 a.m.	Jackie and Diane [wife] get up, eat breakfast. Diane straightens house. Diane makes business calls for the day while Jackie plays in yard.
8:30	Diane and Jackie do errands in town, go to park, go to library. Phil begins workday as a printer.
11:30	Diane bicycles Jackie to school, returns home, starts workday at noon.
5:00	Diane starts dinner.
5:30	Phil picks up Jackie, goes to market.
6:00	Family dinner.
7:00	Phil does the dishes; has play time with Jackie. Diane resumes her workday.
8:30	Phil puts Jackie to bed; usually falls asleep with him accidentally.
9:30	Diane ends her workday, opens a novel, and collapses in a heap.
Saturdays	Phil has Jackie; Diane works in library.
Sundays	Diane has Jackie; Phil takes pictures and works in darkroom.

Phil and Diane have to ask each other out to lunch and make dates with each other for weekend evenings in order to spend time alone together. Often a romantic dinner has the effect of putting them both to sleep. But they feel pleased that by sharing the housework and childcare each puts in some high-quality time with their son while still managing to work full-time. They ascribe their ability to maintain their schedule to pure necessity. Neither earns enough to support the family alone. Thus, inflation and the increasing cost of living have been important influences on their style of family life.

Divorce is another major shaper of new family patterns. Traditionally, the mother retains custody of an infant in a divorce, but another couple I know reversed the trend. Their baby was born after the wife had established her career and after they had been married for ten years. But the marriage deteriorated to the point where the child seemed to be a wedge rather than a bond, and they got divorced soon after the birth. Still, once the couple had sorted out their initial resentments, they were able to separate their problems with each other from their relationships with their child. When the boy was three months old, they agreed that he would spend half the week with each parent. The mother, a lawyer, finds the arrangement convenient for her work pattern, and the father, a writer and teacher, has had no trouble shifting his job commitments to fit his schedule as a father. In fact, he enjoys this active role as father to the extent of wanting a second child, but not a second wife. When I asked how he knew what to do with a baby (the boy is now five), he proudly said, "I gave advice to his mother actually; I took care of my youngest sister from the day she was born, because my mother was busy with the four other kids." To the question, "Who was your role model?" he answered spontaneously, "My mother, of course. She was wonderful with us kids. I do everything the way I remember her doing it—the discipline, the games, tucking him in at night, everything."[18]

On the edge of society live those children whose parents have rejected heterosexual roles. Growing up with two mothers or two fathers according to *Whose Child Cries: Children of Gay Parents Talk about Their Lives* (1983) plunges sons and daughters into deeper controversies at an earlier age than children of heterosexuals. The five families interviewed by Joe Gantz expose not only the rigid attitudes of the so-called normal community toward the social pariah, but also the confusion that all modern parents share when they ask themselves: Do I want to bring up my child to fit my world or theirs? Black parents are asking the same question about the white world, as do Hispanics and Asians. Earlier immigrants took it for granted that upward mobility meant Americanization, as soon and as thorough as possible. But what if your color or your sexuality puts you automatically into a class of your own? What if you disapprove of the so-called normal world and want to protect your child from its values? The children themselves seem to hurt mostly from the rejection their parents suffer—the silent or outspoken disapproval of teachers, fellow students, and neighbors. They learn to defend themselves by defending their parents or to deny their own identity by hiding from exposing the truth. In addition, they undergo the stress of living through the aftermath of divorce, intensified by bitter custody battles. They worry a great deal as to whether something is wrong with the gay parent they love or with whom they want to be friends. Most of all, they fear that something is wrong with themselves. Joe Gantz draws a sad, but hopeful, portrait of these young pioneers who grow up by learning to accept and to love those who are different from themselves. Thirteen-year-old Selina watches her father's lover cook and clean. He is the only mother she has ever known. She is not sure if he can serve as a role model for her, she confesses, but there are plenty of mothers to pick from among her friends, and this way she can have her choice. Her father, Dan, explains,

> We're just two people trying to raise a child. We're trying to give her a halfway decent start in life, despite the handicaps that we present for her. I think as she gets older and becomes more secure there will be less tension. She won't be so reluctant to speak for fear she'll let the cat out of the bag. ... We're a close-knit family, I would say. ... We argue and we fight, but we still care a great deal about each other. ... What we do is, we try to protect each other as much as we can.[19]

Is this not what all parents are trying to do, regardless of their racial or social background? By looking at those who frankly espouse non-standard roles at home, we may begin to wonder to what degree we are ready to accept surrogate nurturers for our children. Perhaps we can also guess why men are so reluctant to play the homemaker role, and why we as parents are hesitant to train our children for a future that we find difficult to understand, because we ourselves feel more secure in the past, even if we do not quite approve of it.

The New Working Mother: Superwoman or Nervous Wreck

In this book, we have traced the progression of women entering the work force: first utterly poor family women, next more independent young single women, and then single mothers, thrust into the labor market by necessity. Finally, with the spiralling costs of America's consumer industry, families have started regarding two incomes as a necessity rather than a luxury. As a result, there has been a constant influx of married women into the labor force.

As women came to be viewed as workers, remnants of the old images fell by the wayside or were transformed. The most notable transformation has involved the old stereotype of "the lady." The middle-class, super-mother mold was being shattered. No longer satisfied with displaying a husband's wealth, many ladies took up regular employment, not necessarily for pay but for prestige and influence and, most significantly, to acquire potentially marketable skills.

With the interest that the rich were showing, work itself suddenly acquired a new glamor for the mass media. It had taken 80 years, but the associations between work and poverty and degradation were finally breaking down. Working mothers appeared on television and in women's magazines as worthy of attention and even as gutsy, entertaining heroines. New hair styles, new fashions, entirely new styles in personality were being sold to the public as part of the new working women's "culture." New magazines inspired readers to see themselves as glamorous professionals during the day and as loving mothers, gourmet cooks, and sexy playmates at night.

Affluent mothers with careers overshadowed the more humdrum, domestic side of the double-work life as well as the unresolved woman's issue of quality childcare for all that needed it. The same ideology that blinded the displaced homemakers into believing their futures were financially secure has blinded the new generation of working girls who believe that they can launch into a lucrative career and also take care of a baby or two. Myths such as the one of the Great American Housewife in the 1880s and The Black Superwoman in the 1980s avoid the enormous complexities involved with the job of integrating family and work in an economy rooted in a couple's two separate lives, each geared to contribute to the success of the other.

The interdependence of our private and our political destiny is a major aspect of family life we find difficult to comprehend. If men in early America picked helpmates for wives and wives chose providers, they were at least aware of an economic reality that was closely connected to their personal lives. As modern couples focus almost exclusively on sexual and personal relationships, they are often unprepared for both the financial and individual commitment required to long-term parenthood.

With more than one million children a year currently involved in divorce, a substantial number of youngsters will also have to get used to step-parents and their respective children at an age when questions of identity, territorial defense against intruders, parental authority, and peer pressure add enormous stress to family relationships under any circumstances. Professional counselors are becoming increasingly involved with homes and schools, but they are frequently divided among themselves in regard to family policies, individual rights, and child development theories. In addition, as more and more women function as providers, they too are drawn into the competitive environment of the marketplace, where traditionally human emotions have been stifled. In what environment, she must ask herself, will I spend most of my life? For which environment am I raising my children? How can she fight a constant battle on two frontiers—one to overcome those economic boundaries which have kept women in the bondage of low pay and low self-esteem, the other to overcome sexual prejudices in home and family responsibilities? Neither can be won alone. Both need the cooperation of the entire community.

Childcare remains the most urgent requirement on the working mother's agenda. Although Title XX Social Services Program spent $2.9 billion on daycare in 1979, the United States ranks far behind France, Sweden, Hungary, and Germany in all mother-child services, including the provision of family benefits in health, housing, and insurance. At present, only the rich can afford high-quality childcare while mothers are at work. The same is true, by the way, at the other end of the age spectrum: only the rich can afford quality nursing care for their aging parents. Individual families who do not have considerable buying power must either accept low-cost services over whose quality they have no control, or they must provide their own. In most cases, this means that mothers of young children or daughters of old parents have to curtail or even postpone their participation in a balanced double life.

So far the issue of childcare has remained a "woman's issue" because the only organizations that have recognized its positive significance have been women's and children's advocacy groups. Such concerned groups range from local self-help centers to national organizations, all lacking funding and political influence for large-scale reforms. In this respect conditions have not really changed since the settlement movement took on urban reforms at the turn of the century. Both the government and the business sector, which stand to gain in women worker competency by attending to the issue, have evinced a distinct lack of concern for parents without partners. A few corporations—for instance, a handful in the computer industry—have recognized that accommodating parental needs is good business.[20]

Anthropologists, economists, and feminist sociologists are changing public opinion on preconceived notions about the family, but all of their efforts combined have not been able to change the government's official attitude toward the family, let alone convince the government to establish a separate family policy. During the Carter administration Walter Mondale admitted that we now have a family policy by default—a series of unrelated, makeshift programs that help citizens to cope temporarily with job and family crises but that do not get them truly out of trouble.

Now even crisis intervention has disappeared. In the fifth year of the Reagan administration, budget cuts threaten some of the most effective programs of the 1970s. Many, such as Headstart, had been designed to help children with enrichment programs, to bridge the educational gap between advantaged and disadvantaged families. And it seems unlikely that a more balanced view of family needs will prevail over President Reagan's so-called "save America, pro-family" policy, which credits only the nuclear top-earner families with respectability.

Perhaps a less conservative stance about the family has become popular among the true majority of double-wage earners. And although the single, female head of household is rarely counted among affluent Americans, her interests and those of the married working mother are no longer as divided as in the past. Both women carry the dual responsibilities of job and children, and both want high-quality childcare. The spectrum of female wage earners now ranges from the promotion-oriented, child-free single woman to the family-oriented working mother—and the well-healed career woman is still the trend setter. Perhaps as sex discrimination and motherhood united women of different races and classes in the past, so job and family stress owing to the lack of support from the dominant male political power structure will strengthen future female allegiances.

From her new vantage point in the marketplace, the housewife cannot help but see the truth: that the home reflects economic conditions in the nation as a whole, not merely her housekeeping skills or, worse, her failures as a wife. In her pioneering passage from home into the labor force, the housewife has joined with other women and men in ways that were once impossible. The time has come for her to teach her children again at home, both daughters and sons—and her husband too, if he is willing to learn—that labor for pay can be integrated with labor for love. But in a society defined through buying power she can no longer afford labor for love without labor for pay.

NOTES

1. "Families at Work: The Job and the Pay," *Monthly Labor Review*, vol. 106, no. 12 (December, 1983), pp. 16–22, gives important statistics; the entire issue is devoted to married couples' employment and women's labor participation in 1983 by age, race, etc.

2. *Monthly Labor Review* (April, 1979).

3. Margaret Mead, *Culture and Commitment* (Garden City, N.Y.: Anchor/ Doubleday, 1978), pp. 86–87.

4. Interview with Milo Smith at Mills College, Oakland, conducted spring, 1979, by Judy Vassos for *Midlifery*, edited by Laurel Cook.

The following remarks were sent to the author by Milo Smith on April 16, 1985:

> It was about seven years of searching and bungling before I *earned* my first dollar—how many women in mid-year can expend that kind of time or even support themselves in the process?
>
> This was the basic concept behind the older women's movement—to provide a safe, comfortable place where women in mid-life could go and procure the info [sic] they might need—a one-step support center—where they would receive the help needed from their "peers." The staff at the D.H.C. was recruited in the main from the client group. We had the faith and understanding that these women had learned something over a life-time.
>
> The "Rosie the Riveter" segment — this related to age discrimination in the trades. The young women who were interested in "non-traditional" work as a means of preparing for better paying jobs—moving out of the female segregated, low paying areas—were restricted from using the apprenticeship system. At that time (prior to the class action suit) there was an upper age limit of thirty-one years—for all applicants—male or female.
>
> The "pension" issue—this was a "biggie" for many women—fraught with inequities. Only this past year under the federal Women's Economic Equity Act has anything been done. . . .
>
> Also, I feel it is significant to note that the Oakland Center for Displaced Homemakers was the first in the Country—set up and designed by the victims themselves—based on their own perceptions of their needs. This was not a solution arrived at by any power that be who recognized a problem and set out to solve it. The struggle still goes on but we have seen wonderful changes coming about in the past ten years that hopefully will help the women coming after us.

5. Nancy Lee Hall, *A True Story of a Single Mother* (Boston: South End Press, 1984).

6. Chodorow, *The Reproduction of Mothering*, pp. 35–36, refers to ghetto Blacks in Stack's *All Our Kin* as a society where women "reconstitute" one another as mothers, inferring that mothering is highly valued. This could mean that girls need to become mothers in order to be recognized.

7. Carol Stack, *All Our Kin: Strategies for Survival in a Black Community* (New York: Harper, 1974), p. 126.

8. Unpublished diary written by Jacqueline Marie in Berkeley, Calif., September, 1974.

9. Philip Blumstein et al., *American Couples: Money, Work, Sex* (New York: W. Morrow, 1983), p. 309. E. D. Macklin et al., *Contemporary Families and Alternative Lifestyles* (Beverly Hills, Calif.: Sage Publications, 1983, pp. 116–179), reviews findings on role conflict and work overload as reasons for marital stress.

10. Naomi Sims, *All about Success for the Black Woman* (New York: Doubleday, 1982), pp. 183–184.

11. "Working Women Polled—Family Top Priority," *San Francisco Chronicle* (Sept. 10, 1984), front page.

12. Husbands and wives tend to underestimate their spouses' contributions and overestimate their own. Greatest agreement was reported in the stereotype jobs at home. Past studies often reported only the perspective of one spouse and reflected poorly on frequency of husband's performance (Sarah Fenstermaker Berk, *Women and Household Labor* [Beverly Hills: Sage, 1980], *Sage Yearbook in Women's Policy Studies*, vol. 51, p. 221).

A *McCall's* opinion poll in 1977 revealed that husbands of working wives were slightly—but not strikingly—more inclined to help around the house, and working wives were somewhat more apt to rate their husbands poorly in sharing domestic chores. Forty-four percent said they did not do a fair share of housework, as against 38 percent of at-home wives. Of all working women, only 12 percent had paid help (*McCall's*, February, 1977, p. 198).

A survey by advertising firm Cunningham and Walsh reported that in 1980, "70 percent of husbands cook, 56 percent do grocery shopping, 47 percent vacuum, and 41 percent wash the dishes" ("Man's Work Is Never Done," *Family Weekly*, September 21, 1980, p. 42).

For a detailed research report on role division and household chores see Beverly and Otis D. Duncan, *Sex Typing and Social Roles* (New York: Academic Press, 1978); and Ann Oakley, *The Sociology of Housework* (New York: Pantheon/Random House, 1974), pp. 135–165. Oakley's study is based on interviews with British housewives who reflect a more marked class consciousness. Middle-class women reported more help from husbands than working-class women. This discrepancy was not very relevant for American families according to Sarah Berk's findings. Oakley and Berk agree, however, on the rarity of egalitarian job distribution and on the housewife's enduring role as main houseworker and child rearer. Jane C. Hook, *Becoming a Two-Job Family* (New York: Praeger, 1983), reports on follow-up results of interviews about role transference.

13. A typical male response:

I make enough money to support my family. Maybe not enough for two weeks at that beach she dragged us to on my vacation last year or for the second [vacation] she said she needed for her job, but we eat okay, don't we? There was no reason for her to go back to work. Her place is at home. It was good enough for my mother, it should be good enough for her.

Jane Adams, "Does Working Wreck Some Marriages?" *McCall's Working Mother* (September, 1979), p. 49.

Susan Kennedy confirms that working-class men were consistently least favorable to the idea of married women's working and that their wives shared that view until the 1970s when better jobs and the desire for a higher living standard changed women's attitudes. Increasingly working-class women also participate in community and labor politics, shedding the image of the house-bound blue-collar wife of the fifties and sixties (Kennedy, *If All We Did Was to Weep at Home*, pp. 230–240). For a survey of attitudes see Weiner, *From Working Girl to Working Mother*, pp. 99–143.

14. William R. Beer, *Househusbands: Men and Housework in American Families* (New York: Praeger, 1983), p. xii.

15. Blumstein, *American Couples*, pp. 53–93, "Income and Power: A Struggle for Control." "Both heterosexual and homosexual men feel that a successful partner should not have to do housework" (p. 151).

16. Caroline Bird, *The Two-Paycheck Marriage*, p. 270; *Redbook Magazine (July/ August, 1978)*, p. 98.

17. *Submitted privately to author.*

18. *Private conversation with author.*

19. Joe Gantz, *Whose Child Cries: Children of Gay Parents Talk About Their Lives* (Rolling Hills, Cal.: Jalmar Press, 1983), pp. 36–37.

20. Valora Washington and Ura Jean Oyemade, "Employer-Sponsored Child Care: A Movement or a Mirage?" *Journal of Home Economics* vol. 76, no. 4 (Winter 1984), pp. 11–15. Significantly this issue is devoted to families and work focusing on the employed mother. For a summary of childcare policies, 1920–1960, see Weiner, *From Working Girl to Working Mother*, pp. 133–140. Mildred Hamilton, "Everywhere you look, it's a family affair," San Francisco *Examiner & Chronicle* (October 20, 1985), S–1, reports new enthusiasm for starting families by baby boomers supported by consumer market research. Mary Ryan warns against new mystique that draws attention away from women's problems with childcare. Although Ryan credits San Francisco's new law that requires developers of high-rise office buildings to provide space or funding for childcare centers, sociology professor Arlie Hochschild found only 6 or 7 companies out of 100 that catered to family needs. Her book, *The Second Shift* (New York: Random House, 1986), is based on her six-year study of two-income families.

Bibliographical Essay

A history of the housewife has to encompass four main areas of research. Each treats the housewife in a specific context and with a particular methodology: (1) from a sociological point of view, as a member of her family and community; (2) from a political point of view, as a participant in the American political system and free-market economy; (3) from a psychological point of view, as an individual shaped by early influences during childhood and subject to emotional pressures during adulthood. Each category can be subdivided by professional theories about such characteristics as class, gender, education, work and family patterns, and individual behavior. (4) And finally we find her own point of view in autobiographies, diaries, letters, oral histories, and interviews. My focus is directed toward long-term historical trends on the one hand and toward individual, highly personal perceptions on the other. This bibliographical essay, then, is intended as a supplement. Instead of repeating each title mentioned in the footnotes, I will only comment on some essential works that have contributed to my own interpretation of the past and on some additional texts which can help to broaden and deepen the reader's own research.

1. THE HOUSEWIFE IN FAMILY SOCIOLOGY

Ronald L. Howard, *A Social History of American Family Sociology, 1865–1940* (Westport, Conn.: Greenwood Press, 1981), introduces the reader to conceptions and attitudes about the family, especially the differences between early social workers and reformers, on the one hand, and sociologists on the other. Social workers and reformers were out to save the family from destructive elements— industrialization, urbanization, poverty, divorce, etc.—while sociologists perceived the family as strong rather than weak, although subject to evolutionary process and adaptable to change. For examples of social case studies which reflect the professional attitudes toward working mothers between 1911 and 1925, see: Margaret Frances Byington, *Homestead: The Households of a Mill Town* (New York:

Charities Publications Committee, 1910; Arno Reprint, 1969); O. G. Cartwright, *The Middle West Side: Mothers Who Must Earn* (New York: Russell Sage Foundation, 1914); and Gwendolyn S. Hughes, *Mothers in Industry: Wage-Earning by Mothers in Philadelphia* (New York: New Republic, 1925).

In *The Employed Mother in America* (Chicago: Rand McNally, 1963), Ivan Nye and Lois W. Hoffman show the progress toward demographic casework and offer a critical review of the literature for and against mothers' employment. They already include the current trend of adding other disciplines to the sociological perspective, and they report divergent opinions of economists (pro), sociologists (divided), and psychologists and child-development experts concerned with protecting mothers from overwork and stress and children from neglect. With the increase of younger mothers in the labor force, the volume of case histories has grown proportionally and so has the socioeconomic information about marital status, class, education, and race of all working mothers. Interviewers in the last decades have paid more attention to the distribution of housework and to the effect of personal income on marital and family power. While earlier studies were concentrated on the lower working class, modern surveys include the middle class and suburbia, as well as ethnic and racial minorities, in their considerations of the diverse working population. To single out so-called typical dual wage earners thus becomes almost impossible beyond the statistic level. The following list of titles is only a sample of the increasing volume of literature devoted to paid and unpaid work in the family.

For my own purpose Helen Z. Lopata's *Occupation Housewife* (New York: Oxford University Press, 1971) furnished the most interesting details about the aspirations of lower-middle-class housewives bent on upward mobility. Chaya S. Piotrkowski, *Work and the Family System: A Naturalistic Study of Working-Class and Lower-Middle-Class Families* (New York: Free Press, 1979), illustrates the complexities of interaction between the father as primary breadwinner and the family. The interviews are selective but detailed and provide a revealing follow-up to my own chapters on the domestic Saint and on Supermother. Recent studies such as that by Margaret R. Davis, *Families in a Working World: The Impact of Organizations on Domestic Life* (New York: Praeger, 1982), and by Jane C. Hood, *Becoming a Two-Job Family* (New York: Praeger, 1983), investigate the conflict experienced by wage-earning housewives who must satisfy the expectations of two formally separate roles. Gains in marital bargaining power are weighed against the mental stress which results from guilt about neglected nurturing and recreational activities. William H. Beer's optimistic evaluation of role reversals in *Househusbands: Men and Housework in American Families* (New York: Praeger, 1983) is not borne out in the literature devoted to this popular topic.

With disturbing regularity the results of major surveys such as *Two Paychecks* (Beverly Hills, Calif.: Sage Publications, 1982), edited by Joan Aldous, report little change in arrangements for childcare and housekeeping. They remain the responsibilities of women. Research as to why this is so reaches into both past and present circumstances. Ruth Schwartz Cowan's *More Work for Mother: The Ironies of Household Technology from the Open Hearth to the Microwave* (New York: Basic Books, 1983) offers some plausible answers as well as excellent sources on labor-saving technologies and role reversals in housework. Rae Andre in *Homemakers: The Forgotten Workers* (Chicago: University of Chicago Press, 1981) and Sarah F.

Berk in *Women and Household Labor* (Beverly Hills, Calif.: Sage Publications, 1980) investigate the present status of homemakers in terms of hours, dollar value, social security, and government policy. They establish a *work*-oriented methodology for sociologists which departs from the *role*-oriented research of family historians. Michael Geerken and Walter R. Gove provide a brief explanation of role-oriented research in family behavior. They investigate the roles in work and housework played by husbands and wives—*At Home and At Work* (Beverly Hills, Calif.: Sage Publications, 1983). They differ considerably in family theory and research practice from Berk and Andre because they look at the nuclear family as separate from the socioeconomic world at large. Summaries of interdisciplinary research findings about women's work in the family and in the marketplace are represented in Helen Z. Lopata et al., "Families and Jobs," in *Research in the Interweave of Social Roles*, vol. 3 (Greenwich, Conn.: JAI, 1983). The authors evaluate both positive and negative reactions from scholars who perceive a trend toward neglect of the family, and low quality in education of children and care for seniors, because the withdrawal of middle-class mothers from the family is not balanced by adequate personal and institutional substitutes. Here Michelene R. Malson reports on "Black Families and Childrearing Support Networks" which rely strongly on grandparents, friends, and neighbors. The nature of women's employment in relationship to stress at home is also examined. Once again, the conclusions are mixed. The discrepancy between dual-earner families in the comfortable middle class who can afford quality childcare and single wage-earning mothers who remain on the lower end of the poverty line brings an increasing awareness of politics into the American working family. *Women in the Workplace: Effects on Families* (Norwood, N.J.: Arblex Publishing, 1984), edited by Kathryn M. Borman et al., is an example of the collected contributions from a wide-ranging circle of interdisciplinary research which confronts family problems with public policy issues. Nowadays much research ends with a recommendation for a revision of government policies calling for equal support of wage-earning mothers and fathers. However, Sarah Gideonse's introduction to this volume shows a pragmatic orientation which has often been lacking in sociological scholarship since the profession turned from the reformist school of thought toward scientific detachment.

Scientific detachment seems difficult to achieve, however, when personal and political values constantly interfere with the professional judgments of experts who consult private families and public agencies on health, education, and welfare. The debate continues between those experts who reflect an ideological bias toward "intact" families, compassing white middle-class moral and economic values, and those who defend pluralistic family patterns. In each case the role of women in the family is pivotal in regard to traditionally gender-related functions. Virginia Tufte and Barbara Myerhoff, eds., *Changing Images of the Family* (New Haven, Conn.: Yale University Press, 1979), furnished important insights for my own evaluation of family values outside the middle class, as well as a clear definition of family-oriented research. Here Barbara Laslett's essay on "The Significance of Family Membership" and Solomon and Mendes' essay on "Black Families: A Social Welfare Perspective" stimulated my own thinking toward accepting the family as a safety-net which stretches to various shapes and sizes, depending on the economic needs and cultural background of its membership. This volume also confirmed my views about the effect of idealized images which create guilt in the subcultures whose members cannot match the prescribed social norm. The 1981 Groves Conference on Marriage and the Family was devoted to the plurality of America's families and the individualistic pursuit of happiness. Eleanor D. Macklin and Roger H. Rubin edited the conference papers under the title of *Contemporary Families and Alternative Lifestyles* (Beverly Hills, Calif.: Sage Publications, 1983), where the emerging family constellations of the 1970s are addressed by professionals in child and family development, by sociologists, and by therapists and educators. The book acknowledges—besides the traditional American family—unmarried couples, single parents, and gay and lesbian partnerships. It also recognizes that individuals move from family to single or group living at different periods in their lives. Pluralism has gained respectability, says the conclusion, but "the vast majority of Americans marry, remain married, bear and rear children, and are primarily provided for by male breadwinners."

2. THE HOUSEWIFE IN POLITICS

Feminist scholarship has contributed the major research on the politicization of housework by studying the housewife as an integral part of labor economics. A collection of essays entitled *Rethinking the Family: Some Feminist Questions* (New York: Longman, 1982), edited by Barrie Thorne and Marilyn Yalom, provided me with the most concise statement about the family from the feminist perspective. The contributors emphasize the political rather than the *natural* or personal context of the family and of women's position in it. They belong to various disciplines besides sociology: anthropology, history, psychology, psychiatry, philosophy, economics, and law. But all of them question the assumption that one type of biological nuclear family determines for all others what is *normal* according to gender-typed job definitions. In their political rather than personal interpretation of family behavior, feminists look for social rather than individual solutions to problems. Especially important for my own evaluation of conflicting images about home and motherhood was Nancy Chodorow's essay "The Fantasy of the Perfect Mother" and Clair Brown's examination of the relationship between housework and market economy. The introduction by Barrie Thorne, "Feminist Rethinking of the Family: An Overview," provides a concise description of the feminist point of view. For a spirited explanation of the feminist perception of gender and housework see "Beyond the Backlash: A Feminist Critique of Ivan Illich's Theory of Gender," *Feminist Issues*, vol. 3, no. 1 (Spring, 1983). Nona Glazer's "Paid and Unpaid Work: Contradictions in American Women's Lives Today" in Borman et al., *Women in the Workplace*, pp. 169–208, reflects the more radical stance of Marxist feminists, who interpret the division of labor by gender in terms of capitalist exploitation of women through the patriarchal structure of the family. This concept is also explained by Natalie J. Sokoloff in *Between Money and Love: The Dialects of Women's Home and Market Work* (New York: Praeger, 1980), which includes a historical review of Marxist feminism. For a critique of this theory and an explanation of the difference between radical and liberal feminism from a philosophical perspective, see Jean B. Elshtain, *Public Man, Private Woman: Women in Social and Political Thought* (Princeton, N.J.: Princeton University Press, 1981). Political scientists Joyce Gelb and Marian Lief Palley's *Women and Public Policies* (Princeton, N.J.: Princeton University Press, 1982) has a useful introduction, "Feminism and the

American Political System," and in chapter 5 deals with the implications of "Title IX: The Politics of Sex Discrimination."

Among the numerous histories of American women which I consulted, I wish to call attention to a few titles in particular. Mary P. Ryan, *Womanhood in America: From Colonial Times to the Present* (New York: F. Watts, 1983) emphasizes the political over the personal interpretation of history as reflected by such historians as Carl Degler, *At Odds: Women and the Family in America from the Revolution to the Present* (New York: Oxford University Press, 1980). Feminist historians have taken issue with Degler's interpretation that the companionate marriage proved a gain in woman's actual control over her own and her family's life. I am indebted to Degler's extensive bibliography and broad historical analyses of personal relationships between husbands and wives, mothers and children. But as a supplement to my own research I recommend Linda Kerber and Jane D. Mathews's collection of historical documents and analyses, *Women's America: Refocusing the Past* (New York: Oxford University Press, 1982). Its precise definitions of feminist theories and family ideologies, set within the economic context of specific periods in history—each with a solid bibliography—make this the ideal textbook to accompany my more personal focus on domestic history. Because I did not deal with domestic servants except in the context of personal statements from individual housewives, I suggest Faye E. Dudden's history, *Serving Women: Household Service in Nineteenth-Century America* (Middletown, Conn.: Wesleyan University Press, 1983), for further reading. Paula Giddings, *When and Where I Enter: The Impact of Black Women on Race and Sex in America* (New York: W. Morrow, 1984), presents a provocative feminist analysis of Black history with emphasis on the long-standing struggle against racism and sexism in the development of female leadership both in the civil rights movement and in the marketplace. Although I have restricted to my notes references to studies of particular time periods, I would like to include one work of this type in this section—Suzanne Lebsock's *The Free Woman of Petersburg* (New York: Norton, 1984)—because it offers an excellent historical amalgam of demographic and social documentation with a lucid explanation of statistical evidence in the context of other primary and secondary sources on Black women in the nineteenth century. Her annotated bibliography is also a critical review of the literature. Her research into household and work patterns adds many insights to both Black and women's history which could only come from public records such as deeds of property, work and marriage contracts, and wills. I would recommend this work not merely for its interesting data, but also for a model of future historical research based on public evidence as to women's private lives.

Demographic records are an important source of information on household membership, employment patterns, and family income. Statistics are too often quoted out of context in popular literature, and certain age groups and minorities are rarely mentioned anywhere except in census reports. The Women's Bureau of the U.S. Department of Labor regularly publishes statistics on wage-earning women by race, marital status, etc. See, for instance, Elizabeth Waldman et al., "Working Mothers in the 1970s: A Look at the Statistics," *Monthly Labor Review* (October 1979), pp. 39–49--and, by the same author, "Labor Force Statistics from a Family Perspective," *Monthly Labor Review* (December 1983), pp. 16–20. The entire issue is devoted to "Families At Work: The Jobs and the Pay" and includes much information on women's wages, childcare, etc. Census reports on cities and counties go back to Colonial times. For a summary consult U.S. Bureau of the Census, *Historical Statistics of the United States, Colonial Times to 1970*, Bicentennial ed. (Washington, D.C., 1975).

3. THE HOUSEWIFE IN PSYCHOLOGY

Professional and popular case histories of the housewife fill volumes of journals and magazines each year. Psychological perceptions like sociological perceptions of the housewife are mainly focused on her relationships to husband, children, and parents, but psychologists lock her conflicts almost totally within her own frame of mind. Psychologists see the private and not the public conflicts, individual and *not* cultural problems. In addition to my references in the notes to Chapters III and VI, I wish to mention two books. Barbara Ehrenreich and Deirdre English's important history, *For Her Own Good: 150 Years of the Experts' Advice to Women* (Garden City, N.Y.: Anchor Press, 1979), supplements my own work with factual and bibliographical detail. Nancy Chodorow's *The Reproduction of Mothering: Psychoanalysis and the Sociology of Gender* (Berkeley, Calif.: University of California Press, 1978), especially chapter 3, "Psychoanalysis and Sociological Inquiry," explains the relationship between the two methods of research and chapter 11, "The Sexual Sociology of Adult Life," addresses the familial division of labor and the ideology of gender.

4. THE HOUSEWIFE IN HER OWN WORDS

The autobiographical accounts of housewives from the distant and recent past form an important element of my book. References to Abigail Adams, Harriet Beecher, Mary Church Terrell, Pat Loud, etc., are given at the end of each chapter. But again I wish to point to a few works which make valuable new contributions to biographical research on the housewife. Kathryn Kish Sklar's biography *Catherine Beecher: A Study in American Domesticity* (New Haven, Conn.: Yale University Press, 1973,) convinced me that the housewife had a history and inspired me to trace the Beechers' influence into present times. Joy Day Buel and Richard Day Buel's reconstruction of the life of Mary Fish from her own and her family's papers in *The Way of Duty: A Woman and Her Family in Revolutionary America* (New York: W.W. Norton, 1984) presents a rich documentation of domestic life. The authors link actual quotes with their narrative accounts, and they stay close to the original manuscript while adding necessary explanations and historical information. Purists may prefer a manuscript in its entirety, but for my own purpose the reading was easier in this format. A similar document was created by Claudia L. Bushman with *"A Good Poor Man's Wife": Being a Chronicle of Harriet Hanson Robinson and Her Family in Nineteenth-Century New England* (Hanover, N.H.: University Press of New England, 1981), where quotations from the manuscript are integrated in a text augmented with historical narrative, notes, and bibliography. It is true that housewives who documented their daily activities are the exception rather than the rule, but nevertheless, their testimony offers a glimpse of ordinary family worries and housekeeping chores. In the quest for biographical evidence of Black women's domestic lives, *We Are Your Sisters* (New York: W. W. Norton,

1984), edited by Dorothy Sterling, provided me with necessary source material. It is a collection of interviews and writings from slavery to the 1880s.

Collective biographies of ordinary women are now becoming increasingly popular with the emergence of oral history as a research tool. Interviews of women in family and work settings are also part of investigative journalism resulting in articles and books such as Gail Sheehy's bestseller *Passages: Predictable Crises of Adult Life* (New York: Dutton, 1976). Philip Blumstein and Pepper Schwartz's interviews in *American Couples: Money, Work, Sex* (New York: W. Morris, 1983) reflect the preoccupations of the 1980s in an interesting juxtaposition of married, unmarried, heterosexual, and homosexual patterns.

But even with massive compilations of statistical and narrative accounts of women's private and public lives, there are many unfilled gaps, especially about those who are not part of the American dream lifestyle, who are poorer, older, different, disabled, and who are never asked what kind of life they would choose for themselves.

Index

About the Author

ANNEGRET S. OGDEN is Associate Librarian in the Bancroft Library at the University of California, Berkeley. She has written extensively for *The Californians* and *Bancroftiana*.